Blonde Heat

Blonde Heat

The Sizzling Screen Career
of Marilyn Monroe

RICHARD BUSKIN

BILLBOARD BOOKS
an imprint of Watson-Guptill Publications
New York

"I am trying to prove to myself that I am a person. Then maybe I'll convince myself that I am an actress."

MARILYN MONROE

This book is dedicated to Marilyn the actress.

Senior Acquisitions Editor: Bob Nirkind
Associate Editor: Elizabeth Wright
Production Manager: Hector Campbell
Cover and interior design: Jay Anning

Copyright © 2001 by Richard Buskin

First published in 2001 by Billboard Books, an imprint of Watson-Guptill Publications a division of BPI Communications, Inc. 770 Broadway, New York, NY 10003
www.watsonguptill.com

Library of Congress Cataloging-in-Publication Data
Library of Congress Card number: 2001093248

ISBN: 0-8230-8414-0

Photo credits. Richard Buskin Collection: pages 36, 63, 65, 214. Cinema Collectors: pages 43, 44-45, 48, 77, 102, 103, 108, 216, 217, 220. Corbis: page 21. George Erengis Collection: page 141. Photofest: pages 14-15, 19, 26, 27, 31, 32, 34, 37, 39, 46-47, 50, 52, 54, 56, 57, 58, 60, 67, 69, 70, 72, 75, 78, 81, 82, 83, 86, 88-89, 92, 93, 94, 97, 98, 100, 105, 107, 109, 112-113, 115, 117, 118. 120, 121, 122, 124, 127, 130, 133, 134, 136a & 136b, 138, 142, 144, 147, 148, 149, 150, 151, 152, 153, 154, 155, 156, 157, 158, 159, 160, 164, 166, 167, 168b, 170, 172-3, 174, 176, 177, 178, 181, 182, 183, 184, 186, 188, 189, 191, 196, 198, 201, 202, 205, 208, 210, 213, 218, 222, 225, 226, 227, 228, 231, 232, 235, 237, 238, 241, 242, 247, 248, 250, 254. Greg Schreiner Collection: pages 2-3, 252. William Travilla: page 168 (upper left). 20th Century Fox: pages 243, 246. George Zeno Collection: pages 1, 12, 23, 40-41, 53, 84, 129, 193, 195, 197, 206, 236, 244.

Manufactured in Italy

First printing, 2001

1 2 3 4 5 6 7 8 9 / 08 07 06 05 04 03 02 01

Acknowledgements

This book was researched and written over the course of several years, and I am indebted to the numerous people who generously provided me with their time, assistance and information. Marilyn had already been dead for more than three decades when I started this project back in 1993, and, being that the films from the early stages of her career utilized cast and crew members who were mostly older than she, it was very fortunate that a great many of them were not only still alive, but also willing and able to be interviewed about events that had sometimes taken place close to a half-century before. My only regret is that a number of them did not live to see this publication.

For their interviews I would like to thank Richard Allan, Gene Allen, Steve Allen, Daphne Anderson, Keith Andes, James Blakely, Ellie Bowers, Rand Brooks, Jack Cardiff, Macdonald Carey, George Chakiris, Tony Curtis, Alex D'Arcy, George Erengis, Colleen Townsend Evans, Tom Ewell, Eileen Heckart, Celeste Holme, Jean Peters Hough, Jack Lemmon, Mary Loos, Jeffrey Lynn, Judy MacHarg, Philip and Aurora Mitchell, Evelyn Moriarty, Ron Nyman, Donald O'Connor, Tommy Rettig, Ginger Rogers, Stanley Rubin, Jane Russell, Bill Sarris, Max Showalter, Allen 'Whitey' Snyder, Gregory L. Walker, Eli Wallach, David Wayne, Billy Wilder, Michael Woulfe and Paul Wurtzel.

For their assistance with research or helping to arrange the aforementioned interviews I would also like to thank Walter Bernstein, Rick Carl, David Cohen, Kirk Crivello, Ernest Cunningham, Susan Doll, Arlene Donovan, Shawn Griggs, Irene Hayman, Roman Hryniszak, Bob Iuliucci, Michelle Justice, David Lanaghan, Boyd Magers, Connie McCauley, Dick McInnes, Flick McKinney, Jeff Mintz, Effie Novi, Vanessa Reyes, Henry Schipper, Mona Syring, Corrina Topoquesa and Allen J. Wiener, as well as the staff of the Agency Department at the American Screen Actors Guild, Alan Adler at the Twentieth Century Fox archives, Paul Camp and Brigitte J. Kueppers in the Arts-Special Collections Department of the UCLA Research Library, the staff in the Archives of Performing Arts at the University of Southern California, the staff at British Actors Equity, the staff at the British Film Institute Library, the staff at the Margaret Herrick Library at the Academy of Motion Picture Arts and Sciences Center for Motion Picture Study, Carmen Fanzone at the American Federation of Musicians, Paul Kerr at October Films, Val Linberg at Washington State University's Edward R. Murrow School of Communications, and Tim Williams at *TV Guide*.

And lastly, for their support and interest in this project, special mentions go to my agent Linda Konner; Bob Nirkind and Elizabeth Wright at Billboard Books; Patrick Miller, who provided great assistance not only with regard to locating some of the photos, but also ascertaining quite a few of the film facts; the members of the Marilyn Remembered fan club in Los Angeles; and the President and co-founder of that fan club, Greg Schreiner, a great friend whose belief in this book was as unwavering as his love for Marilyn, and whose tremendous ongoing assistance helped make it all possible.

Contents

Acknowledgements   4

A Guide to This Book   7

Fade-In: Marilyn the Actress   9

Bit-Roles and Broken Dreams: 1946-1950   13

Screen Test #1–Twentieth Century-Fox Photographic Test   20

Scudda Hoo! Scudda Hay!   22

Dangerous Years   25

Extra–The Rumored Appearances/The Appearance That Never Was   28

Ladies of the Chorus   30

Screen Test #2–*Born Yesterday*   35

The Inanimate Performance–*Riders of the Whistling Pines*   36

Love Happy   37

A Ticket to Tomahawk   42

The Asphalt Jungle   48

The Fireball   53

All About Eve   56

Screen Test #3–*Cold Shoulder*   63

The Television Advertisement–Royal Triton Gasoline   65

Right Cross   66

Home Town Story   68

The Fox Playmate: 1951-1952   73

As Young As You Feel   76

Love Nest   80

Screen Test #4–*Let's Make It Legal*   84

Let's Make It Legal   85

Screen Test #5–*Wait 'Til the Sun Shines, Nellie*   90

Screen Test #6–*Night Without Sleep*   91

The Repeat Performance–*Okinawa*   92

Clash By Night   93

Don't Bother to Knock   100

We're Not Married   106

Monkey Business   111

O. Henry's Full House   116

Niagara   120

*After You Get What You Want
You Don't Want It: 1953–1954*   *131*

Gentlemen Prefer Blondes   136

The Guest Appearance–*The Jack Benny Show*   146

How to Marry a Millionaire   148

River of No Return   156

There's No Business Like Show Business   166

The Seven Year Itch   176

Running Wild, Mighty Bold: 1955–1962   *187*

The TV Interview–*Person to Person*   193

Bus Stop   195

The Prince and the Showgirl   204

Some Like It Hot   212

Let's Make Love   222

The Misfits   230

The Unfinished Project–*Something's Got to Give*   240

Fade-Out: Immortal Images   *255*

Index   256

A Guide to this Book

In focusing on Marilyn's complete screen career, this book concerns itself with the studio-produced films and screen tests that helped shape that career, as well as the handful of official TV appearances that she made during the course of it. Accordingly, the book does not attempt to provide details about every last piece of celluloid that recorded her image: home movies, newsreels, the 8-mm silent color Blue Book Agency footage of "Norma Jean Dougherty" modeling a swimsuit and summer dress in 1945, or even the wardrobe and costume tests that used to be routinely shot as part of a feature film's pre-production.

The screen tests that were used to audition newcomers or judge someone's suitability for a particular role are a different story. Six appear within these pages; it is quite possible that Marilyn appeared in more, but these are the only ones that are supported by concrete evidence or the recollections of seemingly reliable sources. On the other hand, while every attempt has been made to supply the budgets for all of her movies, in some cases this was not possible, and the studios were not willing to impart such information.

Most notable in this regard was the attitude of Twentieth Century-Fox, after a written request had been forwarded for the attention of company owner Rupert Murdoch. "If it has been our policy up until now not to give out this information, then we will abide by this policy," came the reply from his office, implying that no one is quite sure just what the policy actually is, but that it's easier—and certainly less risky—to simply say no. In some respects, little has changed since Marilyn's day.

RATINGS KEY

The movies are rated as follows:

★
Stinker

★½
Stinker with Some Saving Graces

★★
Poor

★★½
Fair

★★★
Pretty Good

★★★½
Good

★★★★
Very Good

★★★★½
Excellent

★★★★★
A Bona-Fide Classic

All of the film and TV productions in this book are listed in the order in which Marilyn worked on them, which does not necessarily coincide with the order in which they were released. As for those release dates, while original TV airings can quite simply be accessed from contemporary issues of *TV Guide,* initial film screenings are an altogether more complex issue. This is because movies are released on different dates in different markets, which in the United States amounts to individual cities. Sometimes they might debut in New York before Los Angeles or vice versa, and they might also be tested out in certain smaller markets before even reaching the big cities. The fact that these dates can be days, weeks, or even months apart accounts for release dates can vary wildly from one movie-related book to another.

Indeed, depending upon the source, an early Marilyn movie such as *Dangerous Years* was released in either 1947 or 1948, while *Love Happy* was in 1949 or 1950. However, for the purposes of this book, only one source is being utilized, that from which the Academy of Motion Picture Arts and Sciences derives its information when adjudicating eligibility for the Academy Awards—the original release date of each film in Los Angeles County, as collated by the Margaret Herrick Library at the Academy of Motion Picture Arts and Sciences Center for Motion Picture Study.

With regard to cast and crew details, the names of credited people have been reproduced as they appear on the screen rather than as they appeared in the often inaccurate promotional material that accompanied a film's release or rerelease. Likewise, the plot synopses have been compiled by viewing each of the movies and television shows, rather than relying on the aforementioned publicity information.

"THE SLEEPING PRINCE"
LOP 301

001 01

DIRECTOR
LAURENCE OLIVIER

CAMERAMAN
JACK CARDIFF

INT: NIGHT

DATE 7/8/56

Fade-In:
Marilyn the Actress

BEYOND HER SELF-CONTRIVED IMAGE as a sex symbol and her posthumous status as a twentieth-century icon, Marilyn Monroe was an actress who created immortal moments of celluloid magic. The scheming siren in *Niagara*, the wide-eyed gold digger in *Gentlemen Prefer Blondes,* The Girl upstairs in *The Seven Year Itch,* the bedraggled entertainer in *Bus Stop*, the ukulele-playing singer in *Some Like It Hot*—these are just some of the movie roles that Marilyn made her own, and that provided her with the means to deliver a line, strike a look, render a song, or turn in a performance that is indelibly etched in the pop culture psyche and in the annals of film history.

Marilyn worked hard at what she did, training under several top drama coaches, including Lee Strasberg at the renowned Actors Studio in New York, who acknowledged her as one of the two greatest talents he had ever been associated with. The other was Marlon Brando. However, to those who were on a film set with Marilyn Monroe, her talent was often less tangible than enigmatic. After all, how could someone who consistently missed her marks, fluffed her lines, failed to match takes, and displayed no discernible technique produce such incredible results?

Time after time, in interview upon interview for this book, Marilyn's former colleagues —independently, and without being led by a particular line of questioning—echoed the recollection of Max Showalter, who appeared with her in *Niagara* and *Bus Stop*:

> A lot of what anybody taught her was absolutely gone once she got before the camera, because there she was, trying to remember the lines and trying to do it right. Once she got into the scene she became so involved with everything that hitting the marks meant nothing to her at all. Well, I was totally shocked when I saw the finished product. I had no idea she was going to be that good. It was a remarkable thing. Having studied technique and worked with a lot of good actors in New York, it was just amazing. It was almost as if God said, "Marilyn, I am with you and I will see you through," and there she was, shining like an angel, no matter what happened.

"She wasn't an actress, she was a genius," said Jack Cardiff, who was the cinematographer on *The Prince and the Showgirl*. "You know, if you try to compare Charlie Chaplin with Laurence Olivier, of course Laurence Olivier was a great actor, but Charlie was a

> *"Most of us maybe use eighty or eighty five percent of our talents in a hot take, but I think Marilyn came close to using a hundred percent in the takes that were printed. She could use what she had more fully than anybody I have ever worked with."*
>
> JACK LEMMON

Scene One, Take One—Elsie arrives at the Carpathian embassy. Before filming was through, there would be numerous scenes and countless takes.

genius. I mean, he wasn't an actor at all really, but he had this genius for comedy, and to a minor degree I think the same could be said for Marilyn. She had something that came out. I mean, physically she looked lovely. She looked like a child and paradoxically she was terribly sexy. She had the thing that I suppose all men think about: a girl who wants protecting, plus the obvious sex appeal."

"No matter what her lack of technique was, every shot of her—as long as she didn't back out of her light—was a treasure," asserted David Wayne, who appeared in more films with Marilyn than any other actor. "She just could not be badly photographed. It was impossible."

True enough, yet the genius that Jack Cardiff alluded to, described by director Billy Wilder as "the kind of quality which God either does or doesn't give you," brings us to Jack Lemmon's spot-on analysis of what separated Marilyn Monroe from her peers: the natural ability to give practically everything she had when she got it right. For this she needed the film medium, with its capacity for short takes, multiple takes, and close-ups.

"What she had was more than personality," said Don Murray, who appeared alongside Marilyn in *Bus Stop*. "That's what makes stars, whereas an excellent screen actress is someone who can be very honest and very real and full of emotion in very, very short spurts. That's all that is required. Based on what I saw, I think Marilyn was aware of the process, but I don't think she was aware of the results. In other words, I don't think she knew when she was achieving what she was setting out to do. I don't think she was aware of that at all, and so that's where she needed both her coach and the director to reassure her, 'Yeah, that was good. That was the one.'"

Murray recalled, "During the making of *Bus Stop*, everyone who worked on it—especially those of us with stage experience, like Eileen Heckart, Hope Lange, Betty Field, and myself—were constantly saying, 'My God, how are they going to cut it together to get a performance?' Then, when the first preview took place, we were all stunned. We couldn't believe how good Marilyn was. That's when all of us stage people came to realize that the screen medium is a totally different animal. Consistency didn't seem to mean a damn thing, especially when you were a star and they had the patience to do a lot of takes and cut together the best pieces. I therefore think that Marilyn Monroe was a superb screen actress, but I couldn't see her making it on stage unless she underwent a total transformation."

Max Showalter agreed: "If you're the typical pro, you go in and the first take is like opening night. You may be able to do better on the second and third takes, but beyond that, if you have to go 15 or 20 takes, you begin to lose your energy, because you have given so much. All of a sudden your whole energy level is dropping down and down and down, but it never did with Marilyn. She could go on take after take after take after take!"

That she certainly could. And she could also arrive on the set late, very late, doing everything possible to delay the moment when she had to leave her dressing room and go before the cameras. However, aside from some isolated incidents later on, when personal troubles and a drug dependency began to overwhelm her, Marilyn was never intentionally mean to her co-workers, and the chronic tardiness of which she was guilty throughout her career was not the result of prima donna behavior. It was, rather, a symptom of her deeply-rooted insecurity and her fear of failure.

"Marilyn had a phobia of appearing in front of people," said Donald O'Connor, who costarred with her in *There's No Business Like Show Business*. "So, if God forbid strangers walked on the set, it would be very difficult. She'd get through it, but she'd start to perspire. A lot of people misunderstood that, but I used to wait around for her because I knew what was going on. It was very painful for her. She loved to work and she wanted to get in there, but to do it was sickening for her. Rex Harrison suffered from that phobia and Deanna Durbin suffered from it. That's the main reason she quit motion pictures."

In July of 1962, talking to Richard Meryman of *Life* magazine for what would be her last ever interview, Marilyn put things into her own perspective: "I don't want to be late, but I usually am, much to my regret. Often, I'm late because I'm preparing a scene, maybe preparing too much sometimes. But I've always felt that even in the slightest scene the people ought to get their money's worth. And this is an obligation of mine, to give them the best. When they go to see me and look up at the screen, they don't know I was late. And by that time, the studio has forgotten all about it and is making money. Oh, well."

Between 1947 and 1961, Marilyn Monroe appeared in melodramas, crime dramas, comedies, westerns, and musicals, directed by such Hollywood legends as Billy Wilder, John Huston, George Cukor, Joseph L. Mankiewicz, Joshua Logan, Jean Negulesco, Otto Preminger, Howard Hawks, and Fritz Lang. At the same time she also appeared alongside stars ranging from Sir Laurence Olivier, Clark Gable, Bette Davis, Barbara Stanwyck, Charles Laughton, George Sanders, Joseph Cotten, Richard Widmark, Robert Mitchum, Eli Wallach, and Montgomery Clift to Cary Grant, Jack Lemmon, Tony Curtis, Jane Russell, Ginger Rogers, Mickey Rooney, Betty Grable, Ethel Merman, Donald O'Connor, Groucho Marx, and Lauren Bacall.

These were many of the biggest names of the time, yet Marilyn not only held her own in their company, but in certain notable instances totally outshone them. "Marilyn could be marvelously funny and very moving at the same time," George Cukor once said. "This is a very rare thing . . . She was pretty, but much more than that, her face moved beautifully, which is very important for an actress. A lot of them have lovely faces which don't move with beauty . . . She was truly unique."

A select group of actors can be wonderful in a bad film, others are invariably lousy in a good one. Marilyn was somewhere in between, her performances often matching the standard of material. Completely natural, vulnerable, endearing, and affecting at her best, compared to affected, awkward, and overly mannered at her worst, she would rise to the heights of a great movie and sometimes sink to the depths of a bad one. Nevertheless, as George Cukor noted, she was always totally watchable: "Besides her natural endowments and thespian gifts, Marilyn had that unique quality that makes a great star: the quality of excitement she generated. Something happened when she came on the screen, even in a long shot where she merely walked across a scene at the farthest distance from the camera. Your eyes couldn't help focusing on her. Just that walk across the screen generated excitement when it was Marilyn."

During her lifetime, the films in which Marilyn appeared generated hundreds of millions of dollars, yet compared to other less famous celebrities of her generation, she didn't earn all that much in return. Still, as Don Murray observed, this was never her chief concern. "I once told her, 'You know, you're the biggest star and you ought to be making more money,' and she said, 'I don't care about being a star and I don't care about money.' I said, 'Well, what do you want?' and she said, 'I just want to be wonderful.' That was great. It was very true, and she got her wish."

Since her death at the age of 36 in 1962, there has been a massive body of work dealing with the most intricate details of Marilyn Monroe's private life, yet there has never been a single volume providing comprehensive, in-depth information about the main subject for which she should be acknowledged and remembered most—her illustrious and wide-ranging screen career. I hope that this book will, at long last, give Marilyn Monroe the recognition she so richly deserves for her unique talents and her unwavering dedication to her work.

RICHARD BUSKIN, *Chicago, 2001*

Bit Roles and Broken Dreams: 1946–1950

BORN AND RAISED in the City of Angels, her mother a one-time film cutter at RKO Studios, Norma Jeane Dougherty was a Hollywood native whose first steps into the world of movies were taken on Wednesday, July 17, 1946, just over six weeks after her 20th birthday. On that day, in Ben Lyon's office at the Twentieth Century-Fox studios on Pico Boulevard, she read a few lines from the script of the 1944 wartime melodrama, *Winged Victory*, and set in motion a career that would span 16 years, encompass numerous highs and lows, and make Marilyn Monroe a worldwide legend.

Separated from Jim Dougherty, the merchant marine whom she had married in June of 1942 (and would divorce in September of 1946), the former Norma Jeane Baker had enjoyed an increasingly successful modeling career for the past 18 months. She had appeared on more than 30 magazine covers, been filmed in swimsuits and summer clothes, and even changed her hair color from light brown to a golden blonde. On the roster of the Blue Book Agency, she had displayed a natural talent for making love to the still camera, yet it was the movie camera in front of which she really aspired to perform.

To that end, Blue Book Agency owner Emmeline Snively had contacted Helen Ainsworth, manager of the West Coast office of the National Concert Artists Corporation, and on March 11, 1946, Norma Jeane had signed a contract with Ainsworth's talent agency. Thereafter, it was Ainsworth who had arranged the meeting with Ben Lyon, the star of stage, screen, and radio who was now a head talent scout for Twentieth Century-Fox.

As a result of her reading some of actress Judy Holliday's lines from *Winged Victory*, Norma Jeane earned the chance to film a photographic test a couple of days later. Studio chief Darryl F. Zanuck wasn't exactly bowled over when he viewed the silent color footage, but heeding the advice of Lyon and cameraman Leon Shamroy, he agreed to offer Norma Jeane Dougherty a low-risk, six-month, $75-per-week contract.

As brokered by Helen Ainsworth's colleague, Harry Lipton, and countersigned by Norma Jeane's guardian, Grace McKee Goddard, the Fox contract commenced on August 26, 1946. At the same time, according to Ben Lyon's later recollection, he and wife Bebe Daniels set about finding a new name to replace the distinctly awkward-sounding Dougherty. Norma Jeane opted for Monroe, her mother's maiden name, and

"Funny business, a woman's career. The things you drop on your way up the ladder so you can move faster. You forget you'll need them again when you go back to being a woman."

MARGO CHANNING IN *ALL ABOUT EVE*

Mingling with cast and crew on the set of her first film, Scudda Hoo! Scudda Hay! *in 1947, Marilyn (center) sits above leading lady June Haver and below fellow starlet Colleen Townsend (top-right).*

Lyon agreed that it was suitably easy to pronounce, but neither Norma Jeane Monroe, Norma Monroe, nor Jean Monroe exactly rolled off the tongue. Then Lyon thought of his blonde-haired, blue-eyed former fiancée, the late actress Marilyn Miller. How about Marilyn Monroe?

Norma Jeane wasn't convinced. But, in the face of Lyon's persistence, and his other suggestion of "Carol Lind," she finally consented. Still, she was never really comfortable being called Marilyn—she wouldn't legally change her name to Marilyn Monroe until March 12, 1956—and this was evident to Jean Peters when the two of them first met in acting classes on the Fox lot soon after signing their short-term contracts.

Peters recalled in 1994,

At that time I knew her as Norma Jeane . . . She wanted to come up with a name, and I was arguing with her that she should call herself Meredith something. I always liked the name Meredith, but she didn't go for that. Ben Lyon came up with Marilyn Monroe while I was in Mexico for six months shooting *Captain from Castile*, but when we were in class together she was Norma Jeane. Helena Sorell and Craig Noel were the acting coaches and Marilyn was terrific. We used to have a class of maybe 12 or 14 people who were all under contract for anywhere from $50 to $150 a week. None of us had great wardrobes, and so almost every day she used to wear this wonderful outfit with a baby blue angora sweater, a silver conch, a tight white straight skirt and white French pumps . . . Adorable. She was a dedicated want-to-be-actress/movie star, whereas for a lot of us it was strictly a lark and the studio was almost an extension of a college campus. Darryl Zanuck used to call it the Country Club, and it was. It was fun. We were young, we liked each other, and there was a lot of camaraderie.

Frankly, I was happier doing the classes than I was making films. I didn't have what Marilyn had, which was this fantastic drive and the ability to really, really work on things. I can no longer visualize what the other kids were doing in acting class with Helena Sorell, but I can see Marilyn doing her bit. She was doing a thing about a girl hanging clothes on a line on a windy day, and there was a fellow—a farmhand or somebody—so she was trying to keep her skirt down, which was like a forerunner of what happened in *The Seven Year Itch*. She was good, and you wanted to watch her.

Maybe, although Zanuck wasn't yet eager to watch her on the big screen. While producing the award-winning *Gentleman's Agreement* in late 1946, the studio boss was also overseeing the scripts, budgets, casting, editing, and promotion of every other Fox film, and either he didn't have immediate use for the untried acting services of Marilyn Monroe, or else she earned her steady paycheck as an uncredited extra on any number of movies that were in production around the lot. Nevertheless, according to Colleen Townsend Evans, who worked with Marilyn on what was the first film project for both of them, there were no assignments as an extra after she herself signed with Fox at the start of 1947.

Townsend, (who went on to land larger roles later), said when I interviewed her in

Sitting pretty with the man who championed her cause and helped launch her film career—53-year-old super-agent Johnny Hyde fell madly in love with Marilyn following their meeting at a party in late 1948, and during the last two years of his life he used all of his power and influence to acquire roles and a long-term studio contract for the struggling actress who was 31 years his junior.

1994, "The studio never used me for any crowd scenes. The only tiny part I had at Fox at that time—and I imagine it would have been the same for Marilyn—was in *Scudda Hoo! Scudda Hay!*"

Indeed, according to a largely fictitious studio biography of Marilyn that was issued by publicist Harry Brand on December 30, 1946, the "eighteen-year-old" who was "being ballyhooed as sort of a junior Lana Turner . . . has no picture assignments; she's down for six months of intensive grooming before she faces a camera, with dramatic lessons, dancing lessons and voice training."

Marilyn turned up regularly at the studio to attend classes, study makeup and costuming, and pose for publicity photos, and shortly after Fox picked up the six-month option on her contract in February of 1947, she was finally cast in her first movie, the aforementioned *Scudda Hoo! Scudda Hay!* Ben Lyon, meanwhile, was keen to ensure that his discovery justified his belief in her, although, as screenwriter Mary Loos was able to observe, it was not always easy to get Marilyn to play by the rules.

Loos recalled, "When we were eating lunch at the studio, the writers sat at a table together and we would watch all of the action going on . . . Well, in the early days Ben Lyon was always trying to get Marilyn to behave properly, but she used to wear these fuzzy pink sweaters without any underpinning. On one occasion she was sitting at the table wearing one of these things and looking rather fetching, and Ben got annoyed. He went up to her and said, 'Marilyn, I tell you all the time, there are some very important people in this commissary. Why don't you dress better?' Then he walked off, at which point she turned to us and said, 'I guess Ben doesn't like pink.'"

In May of 1947, Marilyn was assigned another tiny part in the film *Dangerous Years,* but that was it as far as the credited roles were concerned. That August, Fox didn't renew her contract and she was out of a job. Nevertheless, she did continue to attend informal classes at the Actors' Lab on L.A.'s West Side, where seasoned New York stage actors such as Morris Carnovsky and his wife Phoebe Brand presented plays and tutored students on specific scenes. Marilyn also played a supporting role in a student production of the comedy *Glamor Preferred* at the Bliss-Hayden Miniature Theater in Beverly Hills, and as 1947 turned into 1948, she started making friends in high places.

The first and possibly most influential of these was Joseph Schenck, the 69-year-old executive producer at Twentieth Century-Fox, whose lecherous eyes zoned in on Marilyn at one of his Saturday night poker parties, and whose advances she felt obliged to accommodate. In return for satisfying the old mogul she would be introduced to other people of influence, and a few years later he would be a powerful ally when she returned to the Fox fold. What's more, she wouldn't be afraid to let people know this.

It was thanks to Joe Schenck that, in February of 1948, Marilyn was invited to the office of Harry Cohn, the head of Columbia Pictures. The result was a six-month, $125-per-week contract commencing on March 9. Cohn saw to it that Marilyn's hairline was permanently heightened via electrolysis, that her hair itself was dyed a much lighter blonde, and that she was assigned to vocal coach Fred Karger and drama coach Natasha Lytess. In June, Lytess secured Marilyn an audition for one of the lead roles in a low-budget musical titled *Ladies of the Chorus,* and by early July she had been hired for this movie, which took ten days to shoot.

"One day when we broke for lunch, I saw her at a drive-in eating place," recalled Judy MacHarg, who was an uncredited dancer in the movie. "I was in my car, she was alongside me in a snappy convertible, and so I said, 'How is it that such a pretty young girl would be having lunch all by herself?' She said, 'Oh, I don't mind, it's alright.' I said, 'Well, I'm sure you have dates who take you out,' and she said, 'Oh yes, I go out with George Jessel and Joe Schenck.' At the time I thought, 'How could she possibly want to be with those old timers? Poor child! That's no fun!' But now, knowing how ambitious she was, I can see what she was doing."

Nevertheless, in spite of her ambition, Marilyn didn't submit herself to Harry Cohn's questionable charms, and when her six-month contract was up she was again without a job. Not that her time at Columbia had been completely wasted—far from it, for while 32-year-old vocal coach Fred Karger improved Marilyn's singing, paid to have her slightly protruding front teeth fixed, fueled her interest in fine literature, won her love, and quickly broke her heart, the studio's head drama coach had a much more lengthy and far-ranging influence on her career. A German-born student of legendary director Max Reinhardt, Natasha Lytess would be Marilyn's personal tutor over the course of six years and 22 movies, up to and including *The Seven Year Itch.*

According to Lytess, when the two of them first met, "Marilyn was inhibited and cramped, and she could not say a word freely. Her habit of barely moving her lips when she spoke was unnatural." Well, the coach soon put a stop to that. As a result of her daily instruction in breathing and diction, Marilyn learned to move her lips and enunciate more clearly, although to such an extent that, while she assumed the habit of intermittently lowering her top lip as if trying to cover her front teeth, her voice took on a low, breathy quality, and each word was distinct from that which preceded and followed it. These would all be facets of the trademark MM persona, and ones that people impersonate to this day. However, while they would work to her advantage when she was portraying comically dumb characters such as Lorelei Lee in *Gentlemen Prefer Blondes* (1953), they would look and sound ridiculous when Marilyn was allowed to overemphasize the affectations for a more serious role, such as that of Kay Weston in *River of No Return* (1954).

Eventually, Marilyn's next drama coach, Paula Strasberg, had to painstakingly modify those exaggerated facial and vocal mannerisms. But, back in 1948, Marilyn turned to Natasha Lytess for professional advice and moral support, while friends such as actor John Carroll and his wife Lucille Ryman, director of MGM's talent department, provided her with much-needed financial assistance. The last few months of that year passed fairly uneventfully, but then at a party thrown by either Joe Schenck or producer Sam Spiegel (accounts vary), Marilyn made the pivotal connection of her career. 53-year-old Johnny Hyde was executive vice-president of the all-powerful William Morris Agency, and when he encountered the voluptuous, unemployed actress who was 31 years his junior, it was lust at first sight, quickly followed by a bad case of unrequited love.

Soon after the party, Johnny and Marilyn became sexually involved, and within a few months he had left his family and moved with his mistress into a rented house in Beverly Hills. Johnny was obsessed with Marilyn and constantly asked her to marry him, and although she looked upon him more as a father than as a husband, the little man with the big contacts persisted in doing all that he could to advance her career. Buying out Marilyn's contract from agent Harry Lipton, Johnny arranged for her to have cosmetic surgery to soften the line of her chin and remove a slight bump from the tip of her nose, and he also started to call in favors from many of his business associates.

The first to respond was producer Lester Cowan, who, with Groucho Marx, selected Marilyn in early 1949 for a scene-stealing walk-on in the Marx Brothers' final movie, *Love Happy.* Thereafter, while her agent-boyfriend was having little success drumming up further assignments for her, she attended more classes at the Actors' Lab, studied the works of Sigmund Freud, Marcel Proust, and Thomas Wolfe, earned $50 from photographer Tom Kelley when posing for her famous nude calendar shots, and went on a promotional tour for *Love Happy,* during which she was dubbed "The Mmmm Girl."

In August, Johnny Hyde got Marilyn an audition at her old studio, Fox, where she was signed for another bit part in the musical comedy-western *A Ticket to Tomahawk*, before landing her first significant role in a landmark movie. This was John Huston's *The Asphalt Jungle*, yet how she actually managed this feat is still open to conjecture.

In his 1980 autobiography, *An Open Book*, Huston asserted that "Marilyn didn't get the part because of Johnny Hyde. She got it because she was damned good." However, this recollection has to contend with the claim that Marilyn's benefactor, Lucille Ryman, made Huston an offer he couldn't refuse: either cast Marilyn Monroe in *The Asphalt Jungle* or Ryman would sell Huston's horses to recoup the $18,000 he owed her for stabling them at the ranch she and John Carroll owned.

Marilyn's unsubtle attempts to be sexy during her audition—"over-emphasizing her figure at every point," according to producer Arthur Hornblow, Jr.—apparently almost made her lose the part to harder-edged Lola Albright. (One report had Huston reaching inside MM's sweater, pulling padding out of her bra, and quipping, "You've got the part, Marilyn.") But then Lucille Ryman stepped in, informing Huston that Marilyn would cost them considerably less than the $1500 per week Albright was used to receiving. Huston's response was to test a number of other starlets before Ryman finally "persuaded" him to give Johnny Hyde's ingénue another chance.

Of her second audition, for which she spent three days and nights rehearsing with Natasha Lytess, Marilyn herself would later recall: "When I first read for him I was so scared I shook. I'd studied my lines all night, but when I came in to read I just couldn't relax. He asked me to sit down but there were only straight-backed chairs all around the room, so I asked him if I could sit on the floor—just to get comfortable. But I was still nervous, so I asked if I could take off my shoes. 'Anything, anything,' he said. Then I read for him—and I was sure I was awful—but before I had a chance to say anything he kind of smiled and said I had the part, all right. Then he said I'd probably turn into a very good actress, which is really what I wanted to be."

Despite Lucille Ryman's alleged pressure, Johnny Hyde's undeniable influence, and Lola Albright's "unavailability," it is doubtful that in 1949, having already directed such superior films as *The Maltese Falcon, The Treasure of the Sierra Madre* and *Key Largo*, John Huston would have cast someone he didn't truly want in one of his movies. *The Asphalt Jungle* is now considered one of Huston's finest films, and Marilyn certainly repaid his and everyone else's faith in her by holding her own amid a uniformly excellent cast. Thereafter, with the aid of not only Johnny Hyde, but also publicist Rupert Allan and drama coach Natasha Lytess—who left Columbia Pictures to dedicate herself to Marilyn's career—the work assignments began to flow more frequently.

In 1950, Marilyn augmented her one and only TV commercial with appearances in no fewer than four movies: *The Fireball, All About Eve, Right Cross*, and *Home Town Story*. The last two, like *The Asphalt Jungle*, were released by MGM, yet neither Johnny Hyde nor Lucille Ryman was able to convince head of production Dore Schary that Marilyn's performances should be rewarded with a long-term contract. Darryl Zanuck at Twentieth Century-Fox, on the other hand, was impressed by the rushes he saw of Marilyn in *All About Eve*, and after the requisite overtures from her relentless yet physically ailing agent, the Fox boss agreed to give Marilyn another screen test, this time for a movie titled *Cold Shoulder*, slated to costar Victor Mature and Richard Conte. The studio ultimately aborted the project, but by October of 1950 Zanuck assigned Marilyn a role in *Will You Love Me in December?*, a screen adaption of the Paddy Chayefsky comedy *The Great American Hoax*, (eventually retitled *As Young As You Feel*).

On December 16, 1950, with a full Fox contract for Marilyn finally in the works, Johnny Hyde departed with his secretary for a rest in Palm Springs. Two days later he was dead, having finally succumbed to the heart condition that had plagued him since before he met Marilyn. As Johnny himself had told her, Marilyn's financial security would have been her payoff for acceding to his proposals of marriage. She was never able to regard him in those terms, however.

"He not only knew me, he knew Norma Jeane too," she would later say. "He knew all the pain and all the desperate things in me. When he put his arms around me and said he loved me, I knew it was true. Nobody had ever loved me like that. I wished with all my heart that I could love him back."

The mentor and the ingénue—German-born drama coach Natasha Lytess entered Marilyn's life in 1948 and exerted a powerful influence on her over the course of six years and 22 movies.

Screen Test #1

Arranged by Ben Lyon, directed by Walter Lang, and shot by Leon Shamroy, this silent color test was filmed on the set of the Betty Grable/Dan Dailey movie *Mother Wore Tights* (directed by Lang and released in 1947).

Fox's head of wardrobe, Charles LeMaire, outfitted Norma Jeane. Florence Bush probably styled her hair, and at around 5:30 A.M. the solitary cast member and small crew assembled for the shoot. Allan "Whitey" Snyder—who had gained his nickname as a young Californian, courtesy of his sun-bleached blonde hair—took care of Norma Jeane's makeup that day, and in October of 1994 he was still able to recall their initial conversation:

> I said, "Have you ever been photographed before in a motion picture?" and she said, "No, but I know what I want," so I said, "Okay." I wasn't going to argue with her. She was just another gal, and we used to deal with so many of them. I therefore did her hair and makeup the way she wanted it, she went onto the test stage and the cinematographer, Leon Shamroy—one of the top Technicolor photographers, who I did many, many pictures with before and after—looked at her and said, "What the hell is that out there?" I said, "It's another kid who wants to be in pictures," and he said, "Well, the makeup's awful." Now, most people would let you hang there, but no, Marilyn stepped up and said, "What's wrong? This is the way I wanted it." Shamroy said, "Why don't you take her back to the makeup department and wash that crap off?" So we did, of course, and she got a stock contract.

Intended solely as a means by which studio boss Darryl Zanuck could assess the newcomer's looks and screen presence, the photographic test featured her walking back and forth across the set, sitting on a high stool, lighting a cigarette, putting it out, and finally walking towards a stage window.

Marilyn recalled 16 years later that, "For some strange reason, instead of being nervous and scared, I just tried very hard, because I knew Mr. Lyon and Mr. Shamroy were taking an awful chance . . . If it didn't work out well, they might get in trouble."

In 1951, multiple Oscar-winner Leon Shamroy told *Collier*'s magazine: "When I first watched her, I thought, 'This girl will be another Harlow,' and I still do. Her natural beauty plus her inferiority complex gave her a look of mystery . . . I got a cold chill. This girl had something I hadn't seen since silent pictures. She had a kind of fantastic beauty like Gloria Swanson . . . and she got sex on a piece of film like Jean Harlow. Every frame of the test radiated sex. She didn't need a soundtrack—she was creating effects visually. She was showing us she could sell emotions in pictures."

That is, after Norma Jeane's makeup had been redone as per Shamroy's request. For his part, Whitey Snyder would eventually serve as Marilyn's personal and professional makeup artist, and the two would become close friends. "She was wonderful," Whitey recalled shortly before his death. "She was so great, she was so different. After we'd been working together for a while we'd do her makeup in about twenty minutes to half an hour at the most. You know, it was just a routine—boom, boom, boom. You do what you've got to do, and she knew what we had to do and that was it. Outside of some of the very early films, I did every picture that Marilyn ever did. Some guys, like George Masters, were always trying to muscle in there, but he never did her makeup, he never even got close to her. I read articles about what he did with her at still sittings and things like that, but I was there and he sure as hell wasn't. He never did a picture with her."

Walter Lang and Leon Shamroy, meanwhile, would work with Marilyn on one more occasion, when they teamed up for the 1954 movie *There's No Business Like Show Business*.

SCREEN TEST #1

Twentieth Century-Fox, July 19, 1946, Color

The Fox camera identifies the location, and Marilyn's appearance identifies the time period as 1946–1947. However, that cameraman doesn't look like Leon Shamroy, and the park bench and background foliage depict an outdoor scene rather than one in which MM would sit on a high stool, smoke a cigarette, and walk towards a stage window. Popular claims that this and other shots of her in the dropped-waist bodice and tiered tulle skirt are from her first screen test therefore have to be questioned. The set *could* have been adapted from one that appears about an hour and 15 minutes into Mother Wore Tights, *but it's equally likely that this depicts Marilyn filming a small and ultimately unused part in another movie.*

Scudda Hoo! Scudda Hay!

SCUDDA HOO! SCUDDA HAY!

★★½

A Twentieth Century-Fox Release
Produced by Walter Morosco
Directed by F. Hugh Herbert
Screenplay by F. Hugh Herbert
From a novel by George Agnew Chamberlain
Cinematography by Ernest Palmer
Sound by Eugene Grossman and Roger Heman
Art Direction by Lyle Wheeler and Albert Hogsett
Music by Cyril Mockridge
Costume Design by Bonnie Cashin
Edited by Harmon Jones
Released: April 26, 1948
Running Time: 98 minutes
Technicolor

CAST

Rad McGill	June Haver
Snug Dominy	Lon McCallister
Tony Maule	Walter Brennan
Judith Dominy	Anne Revere
Bean McGill	Natalie Wood
Stretch Dominy	Robert Karnes
Milt Dominy	Henry Hull
Roarer McGill	Tom Tully

Uncredited:

Ches	Les MacGregor
Mrs. McGill	Geraldine Wall
Sheriff Bursom	Ken Christy
Judge Stillwell	Tom Moore
Jim	Matt McHugh
Barber	Charles Wagenheim
Dugan	Herbert Heywood
Ted	Edward Gargan
Elmer	Guy Beach
Malone	G. Pat Collins
Jeff	Charles Woolf
Stable Hand	Eugene Jackson
Girl Friend	Colleen Townsend
Girl Friend	Marilyn Monroe

The Plot

Snug is unhappy living on the farm with his mean-spirited stepmother Judith and surly stepbrother Stretch. When his father goes off to sea, bequeathing all of his possessions to his natural son in the event of his own death, Snug takes on work as a farmhand for irascible Roarer McGill and, under contract to pay $5 a week for one year, buys two mules from him.

The mules, Moonbeam and Crowder, start working well for Snug, but life is made difficult by nasty Stretch, who is not only making advances to Snug's sweetheart, Rad, but also attempting to have him fired from his job and thus unable to keep up the payments on the mules. The stepbrothers eventually come to blows, and Rad pledges her love for Snug, who then gets himself fired so that he and his donkeys can work together with nice old Tony Maule. However, when Tony drinks away their joint income and Snug is unable to make his weekly $5 payment to Roarer, it looks as though the mules will be repossessed, until Rad steps in and hands over her own $5 to her greedy father.

News comes that Snug's Pa has died at sea, meaning that the son has now inherited the family farm. Stretch gets caught trying to cripple the mules, and, disgraced and defeated, he and his mother leave the farm for good, to be replaced there by Snug and Rad . . . as well as the two mules, of course.

Behind-the-Scenes Facts & Opinions

What a fuss! Never has so much importance been attached to a couple of donkeys. Attractively filmed in Technicolor to capture the outdoor scenery, *Scudda Hoo! Scudda Hay!* is a pleasant enough picture about "country folk"—or at least Hollywood's idea of them—that never really amounts to very much. The lead performances could all be described as fairly charming if slightly tame; most notable among these is nine-year-old Natalie Wood's portrayal of Rad's mischievous kid sister Bean, (her seventh screen appearance).

For years there has been a debate about whether or not Marilyn actually appears in this movie, possibly triggered by her own assertion during her 1955 *Person to Person* TV interview with Edward R. Murrow that she uttered just one word, "Hello," and that it was later cut. She was, however, wrong, because around 58 minutes into the film Marilyn can be fleetingly seen walking down some church steps and saying, "Hi, Rad," to which June Haver responds, "Oh, hi Betty." Blink and you'll miss it. Furthermore, as confirmed by the March 12, 1948, "dialogue and continuity script taken from the screen," the scene was also in the film as originally released.

Considering that she never appears again, such a brief glimpse of the Betty character makes little sense in context with the rest of the picture. However, this was not the original intention, for the February 19, 1947 shooting script confirms that another slightly longer scene featuring Marilyn was definitely shot, only to be edited out just prior to the film's release.

This took place at the lake, preceding the segment in the released version in which Snug spies Stretch and Rad approaching the creek together in a boat. Stretch is sunning himself on the dock when a boat approaches containing Betty and June (Colleen Townsend), described as "a couple of pretty bobby-soxers":

Betty (gayly): Hi, Stretch.

Stretch (drawling): Hi, Betty—Hi, June.

June (coyly): Is it all right with you if we swim off your dock?

With one bare foot, Stretch shoves the nose of the boat out into the stream again.

Stretch (grinning): No—it ain't.

Betty: Ah, Stretch—why not?

Stretch: You're too young. Come back in a couple of years' time.

Giggling, the two kids pull out of the shot.

Those "pretty bobby-soxers" Betty and June row their boat in front of the camera . . . and straight onto the cutting-room floor.

Unfortunately for both kids, they were also pulled out of the film. All that survives is a long-distance background shot of two girls rowing; neither of their faces is visible, but, rest assured, they belong to Colleen and Marilyn.

Colleen Townsend retired from the screen in the early 1950s after marrying Presbyterian minister Louis Evans. Tracked down to their residence near San Francisco in 1994, she commented: "It wasn't much of a part either for Marilyn or for me, was it? . . . I never really knew her very well—you know, we didn't socialize together—but I remember her best from the classes that we attended together at the Actors' Lab, and I just have very, very fond memories of her. . . . Basically, at her heart, she was a very sweet person, a very loving person."

Jean Peters originally tested for the part of Rad, and on the strength of that audition she was assigned by Fox to make her screen debut starring opposite Tyrone Power in *Captain From Castile*. Unlike Marilyn, Jean got her big break right at the start of her career. Yet, as she told me in 1994, she still would have liked to land that role in *Scudda Hoo! Scudda Hay!*: "I loved that part, because it was a farm girl, there were mules in it . . . Instead I ended up playing a Spanish gypsy."

The June 5, 1947 shooting script refers to the film as *Summer Lightning*, but while this name was subsequently used in the U.K., the original title was retained in the U.S. As for the meaning of *Scudda Hoo! Scudda Hay!*—well, if the movie is to be believed, this is not, as the advertisements professed, "a cry that stirs young hearts to love," but simply the donkey-language equivalent of "giddyup."

The Critics' Views

"Made for people who like good shots of honestly sweaty farm activity with sentimental tears dripping as heavily as the perspiration. The drips are honest and sincere in both directions."

New York World-Telegram

"Having exploited the equine, canine and deer fields rather exhaustively, the screen has turned to a couple of mules for its latest tribute to our four-footed friends. . . . Whatever might have been done to endear the mule to the American public has been accomplished, but your correspondent likes Lassie better."

Herald Tribune

Public Reaction

Costing $1,685,000 to film, *Scudda Hoo! Scudda Hay!* grossed $2 million during its first run. Today, it enjoys only very occasional screenings on TV and is notable chiefly among Marilyn fans for being the first motion picture that she worked on, even though it was in fact released after her second movie, *Dangerous Years*.

Dangerous Years

The Plot

Schoolteacher Jeff Carter spends his spare time running a social club for teenage boys in Middleton, USA. His efforts there are undermined, however, by the arrival of Danny Jones, a hotshot troublemaker who begins to involve other youths such as Willy, Doris, Leo, and Tammy in his petty criminal activities. When Jeff learns of the gang's planned raid on a perfume warehouse he intercepts the robbery, but as the kids flee Danny shoots and kills the kindly schoolmaster.

Danny is arrested and charged with the murder, and during the trial it is revealed that he was raised in the same orphanage as Connie, the daughter of the man who is now prosecuting him, district attorney Edgar Burns. Connie was born after her parents' separation, and the DA himself only learned of her existence when contacted years later by a nurse at the orphanage. That same nurse now shows up at the courthouse and tells Danny that she had lied to Burns out of sympathy for Connie, who was sick and in need of better surroundings. In truth, the DA's child is actually Danny himself!

Danny is duly found guilty of murder and sentenced to life imprisonment. Yet, harboring no grudges over his punishment, he manfully decides to keep the truth about his birth from both Connie and the DA.

Behind-the-Scenes Facts & Opinions

An obscure early entry in the cycle of juvenile delinquency flicks that would become all the rage during the next decade, *Dangerous Years* was typical of the low-budget 'B' movie fare produced by Sol M. Wurtzel. Indeed, the veteran producer turned out so many bargain-basement movies over the years that it was not uncommon to hear insiders quip that Fox's product was "going from bad to Wurtzel!" This film helps illustrate why.

A teen exploitation vehicle that supposedly demonstrates how, during "the dangerous years of our adolescence," decent kids can be led astray due to peer pressure and negligent parents, this Arthur Pierson-directed picture is full of cardboard characters and wooden acting. Furthermore, thanks to Arnold Belgard's hackneyed story and screenplay, there are some highly dubious coincidences. However, most laughable of all—and, it has to be said, one of the very few good reasons for viewing this film—is a courtroom scene in which the DA takes "harassing the witness" to new heights. Cross-examining the girlfriend of the accused killer, Mr. Burns is so aggressive towards the poor child—screaming at her, slamming his fist, and leaning close enough to ensure that she almost falls backwards behind the witness stand—that one is actually left in seerious doubt as to who is the true threat to society.

Dangerous Years was filmed in August of 1947, just days before Twentieth Century-Fox dropped the option on Marilyn's contract. Nevertheless, aside from presenting her with another, slightly larger speaking role, the movie also provided her first big-screen close-up. As Evie, a waitress at The Gopher Hole, "that jukebox hangout on Highway Hill," Marilyn spends most of her limited on-screen time either deflecting the approaches of the upstart gang members or eyeing up some of the local male talent

---

DANGEROUS YEARS

★

A Twentieth Century-Fox Release
Produced by Sol M. Wurtzel
Directed by Arthur Pierson
Story and Screenplay by Arnold Belgard
Cinematography by Benjamin H. Kline
Sound Supervision by Max M. Hutchinson
Art Direction by Walter Koessler
Music by Rudy Schrager
Edited by William Claxton and Frank Baldridge
Released: January 16, 1948
Running Time: 59 minutes
Black & White

CAST

Danny Jones	William Halop
Willy Miller	Scotty Beckett
Edgar Burns	Richard Gaines
Doris Martin	Ann E. Todd
Weston	Jerome Cowan
Connie Burns	Anabel Shaw
Leo Emerson	Darryl Hickman
Gene Spooner	Dickie Moore
Phil Kenny	Harry Harvey, Jr.
Tammy McDonald	Gil Stratton, Jr.
Judge Raymond	Harry Shannon
Jeff Carter	Donald Curtis
August Miller	Joseph Vitale
Evie	Marilyn Monroe
Miss Templeton	Nana Bryant
Adamson	Tom Kennedy

Uncredited:

Reporter	Mimi Doyle
Alec	Lee Shumway
Woman	Claire Whitney

While the young'uns can't help making a play for her, Evie only has eyes for handsome schoolteacher Jeff Carter.

herself. When Gene, a fresh-faced punk, greets her with a simple "Hi, Evie," her demeaning response is "Hi, small change." "Hey, wait!" stammers Gene. "I've got money tonight! Am I going to see you tonight?" "If I'm not too tired," is the surly reply. Clearly, Evie has a preference for the more worldly type.

Although filmed after *Scudda Hoo! Scudda Hay!*, *Dangerous Years* was the first of Marilyn Monroe's screen appearances to be released to movie theaters. In any event, neither one was likely to attract the attention of Hollywood talent scouts, and neither one did.

Scotty Beckett, meanwhile, was about to endure problems in his private life similar to those experienced by his on-screen troubled teen character, Willy Miller. A former child star whose career was on the wane by the time he appeared in *Dangerous Years,* Beckett would soon be involved in numerous bouts with the law, including arrests for drunken driving, carrying a concealed weapon, illegal possession of narcotics, and assault. Although he eventually became a car salesman, Beckett ended up killing himself with sleeping pills in Hollywood at the age of 38.

The Critics' Views

"Director Arthur Pierson has seized upon a good script, has handled it with delicacy, has side-stepped numerous pitfalls of over-sentimentality, and has aroused and maintained interest throughout. The happy result is a high-grade budgeter."

HOLLYWOOD REPORTER

"This yarn is strictly fiction. It might have some resemblance to real life, but the dividing lines of fact and fabrication are too obvious. . . . Film is minor scale stuff that limps along. It contributes little to the sphere of dramatic entertainment."

Marilyn navigates her way past Darryl Hickman and Scotty Beckett in "that jukebox hangout on Highway Hill."

Ladies of the Chorus

LADIES OF THE CHORUS

★★

A Columbia Pictures Release
Produced by Harry A. Romm
Directed by Phil Karlson
Screenplay by Harry Sauber and Joseph Carole
From a story by Harry Sauber
Cinematography by Frank Redman
Art Direction by Robert Peterson
Musical by Mischa Bakaleinikoff
Choreography by Jack Boyle
Edited by Richard Fantl
Released: December 2, 1948
Running Time: 61 minutes
Black & White

CAST

May Martin	Adele Jergens
Peggy Martin	Marilyn Monroe
Randy Carroll	Rand Brooks
Mrs. Carroll	Nana Bryant
Billy Mackay	Eddie Garr
Salisbury	Steven Geray
Alan Wakeley	Bill Edwards
Bubbles LaRue	Marjorie Hoshelle
Joe	Frank Scannell
Ripple	Dave Barry
Ripple, Jr.	Myron Healey
Peter Winthrop	Robert Clarke
Flower Shop Girl	Gladys Blake
Doctor	Emmett Vogan

Uncredited:

Mr. Craig	Paul E. Burns
Usher	Donald Kerr
Old Lady at Party	Almira Sessions
May's Fan	Al Thompson
Chorus Girl	Judith Woodbury
(Bit Part)	Dorothy Tuttle

MM'S SONGS

"Every Baby Needs a Da-Da-Daddy" by Allan Roberts and Lester Lee

"Anyone Can Tell I Love You" by Allan Roberts and Lester Lee

Marilyn's front teeth were straightened and her hairline permanently heightened via electrolysis before she started filming Ladies of the Chorus.

The Plot

Among the chorus line dancers in a burlesque show are Peggy Martin and her overly protective mother, May. When headliner Bubbles LaRue quits the production following a backstage spat with these two, May is asked to take her place. Instead, she pushes her daughter into the starring role and Peggy becomes an instant hit with the patrons, one of whom is a wealthy young man named Randy Carroll. Immediately smitten, Randy anonymously inundates Peggy with orchids. When she discovers that he is the sender, they go out on a date, Randy asks her to marry him, and Peggy accepts —pending her mother's consent.

As it happens, May approves of Randy, yet she is concerned that his mother will object to his wedding a burlesque queen. This is because, many years before, May's marriage to Peggy's father was annulled when his socialite family learned the truth about her professional activities. Therefore, May wants Randy to tell his mother all about Peggy before going any further. Randy agrees but fails to do so, and this becomes clear to the dancing duo when they pay a visit to Mrs. Carroll's lavish home in Cleveland. Unaware of Peggy's background, Mrs. Carroll throws an engagement party for the young couple, but when one of the entertainers recognizes the new fiancée and unwittingly reveals that she is a burlesque queen, the upper-crust guests are outraged. Mrs. Carroll, on the other hand, accepts May and Peggy for who they are, and she demonstrates this to all concerned by performing a musical ditty that she supposedly learned in her own days on the stage. In fact, this is just a ruse to placate the guests, but it also results in two happy couples: Peggy and Randy, and May and her longtime suitor Billy Mackay.

Behind-the Scenes Facts & Opinions

Shot in just ten days, *Ladies of the Chorus* provided Marilyn Monroe with a number of firsts: her first film part of any significance, which also happened to be her first costarring role; her first celluloid opportunity to sing and dance; her first big-screen kiss; and her first press reviews. (That of Tibor Krekes in *The Motion Picture Herald* is generally credited as the first.) Beyond that, however, it was just another of the bargain-basement musicals that studios churned out as support features during the 1930s and 1940s, and as such it didn't exactly launch her career.

On March 10, 1948, the day after signing a standard six-month contract with Columbia Pictures, Marilyn had been introduced to the studio's head drama coach, Natasha Lytess, and voice coach Fred Karger, each of whose efforts paid off on-screen. For though Marilyn's dancing could be described as somewhat stiff-jointed during her initial rendition of "Anyone Can See I Love You," her acting and singing in *Chorus* are undoubtedly more accomplished.

"Amazingly, this young lady wasn't very comfortable with her body, although I saw that more in the film than at rehearsal," recalled Judy MacHarg (then going by her maiden name, Woodbury)—one of the movie's uncredited ladies of the chorus. "It was just a B-movie, but for her it was an important part and so she rehearsed and

rehearsed and rehearsed, all alone with the choreographer. Phil Karlson, the director, was a sweet man. He was very patient, very nice. After all, on a B-movie they didn't fool around. You were expected to turn up and do it."

A decade before enjoying the privilege of giving Marilyn her inaugural on-screen kiss, Rand Brooks had portrayed Scarlett O'Hara's first husband in *Gone With the Wind.* Now, as the romantic lead in a routine programmer, he found himself wooing yet another fledgling star, although there was no way that he could have known this at the time.

"Marilyn was awfully sweet and I think she did a good job," Brooks told me just under half a century later. "She always turned up on time, she worked hard, she knew her lines, and her singing was more than adequate. However, she hadn't had much film training, so I'd move her back and tell her where the light was, because things like hitting your marks can be disturbing to young actors and actresses. By that time I'd had quite a lot of experience making movies, but I wasn't about to upstage Marilyn. My agent had told me, 'Don't make any passes at her,' and about a week into filming he said, 'I hope you're not doing anything foolish.' Well, who would make a pass at her? She was just a young, naive little girl. Adele Jergens, who was playing her mother—now *there's* a woman!

"I personally wanted to inject the film with some humor and play my role for laughs. I mean, a leading man who is afraid to tell his mother that he's going out with a chorus girl is not, to my way of thinking, a very strong character, but Phil Karlson said, 'Oh, this is serious! Your mother could be upset if you marry a showgirl!'"

As for that showgirl, some of the MM facial affectations are already evident in *Ladies of the Chorus*—although her trademark lowering of the upper lip is nowhere to be seen—and, thanks in part to Fred Karger paying to have her slightly protruding front teeth fixed, Marilyn looks very attractive. Nevertheless, studio boss Harry Cohn wasn't too impressed.

"What did you put that fat pig in the picture for?" Cohn reportedly shouted at his executive assistant Jonie Taps after seeing some rushes. "What are you doing, fucking her?" This was standard patter for a man of whom Hollywood gossip columnist Hedda Hopper once said, "You had to stand in line to hate him." As a result of Cohn's assertion that "The girl can't act," Marilyn's option wasn't picked up when her contract elapsed, and within a few years happy Harry would be licking his wounds.

Marilyn herself later asserted that the real reason she was dismissed from Columbia was because she rejected Cohn's sexual advances and an invitation to rendezvous aboard his yacht. Whatever the truth may be, when *Ladies of the Chorus* was released that October, Marilyn was singled out for some favorable press reviews (although her name was misspelled as "Merilyn" by the critic for the *Independent Film Journal*). Garbed in a long coat and dark glasses, she went to see the film at the Carmel Theater on Santa Monica Boulevard, but nobody recognized her.

Performing "Every Baby Needs A Da-Da-Daddy," Marilyn is flanked by (fourth from left) Judy Woodbury and (fourth from right) Adele Jergens.

The look of love—by the smile on her face you can tell that Marilyn is gearing up for her first screen kiss from Rand Brooks.

"I kept driving past the theater with my name on the marquee," she would later recall. "Was I excited. I wished they were using 'Norma Jeane' so that all the kids at the home and schools who never noticed me could see it."

And if those kids didn't see it, then they would get a second chance to catch a glimpse of Marilyn's *Chorus* performance when a segment was inserted into Columbia's 1952 World War II movie, *Okinawa*. As for *Ladies of the Chorus*, when it was reissued following Marilyn's rise to stardom, the opening credits were amended so that her name appeared above the title.

The Critics' Views

"Enough musical numbers are inserted, topped with nifty warbling of Marilyn Monroe. . . . Miss Monroe presents a nice personality in her portrayal of the burly singer."

VARIETY

"Marilyn Monroe is cute and properly naive."

HOLLYWOOD REPORTER

"One of the bright spots is Miss Monroe's singing. She is pretty and, with her pleasing voice and style, she shows promise."

MOTION PICTURE HERALD

Screen Test #2: Born Yesterday

Columbia Pictures
1948
Black & White

Although no celluloid, photographic, or documented evidence has yet come to light, Marilyn reportedly tested for the role of Billy Dawn in *Born Yesterday* during the time when she was under contract to Columbia.

Written by Garson Kanin and set in Washington D.C., *Born Yesterday* is a classic comedy about a tycoon junk dealer who hires a bookish reporter to introduce some culture into the life of his uneducated girlfriend. Actress Judy Holliday was a smash when portraying this prototypical dumb blonde in the hit 1946 Broadway production of Kanin's play, and she would subsequently scoop an Oscar for her reprisal of the role in the 1950 film version, directed by George Cukor and costarring Broderick Crawford and William Holden.

In his 1971 book *Tracy and Hepburn,* Kanin claimed that Marilyn Monroe filmed a test as Billy Dawn, and that "Those who saw it thought it was excellent. But Harry Cohn, the head of the studio, did not trouble to take the six steps from his desk to the projection room to look at her."

Given Judy Holliday's aforementioned stage success, it probably would have taken a rising or established Hollywood star to snatch the film role from her grasp. Such would be the case a few years later when, despite Carol Channing's widely acclaimed origination of the part on Broadway, she would lose out to Marilyn Monroe for the movie portrayal of Lorelei Lee in *Gentlemen Prefer Blondes*. In 1948, however, Marilyn was not a star in any sense of the word, and neither was she ready to take on the role of Billy Dawn that Judy Holliday played to perfection. Harry Cohn may have erred in his decision to decline the option on Marilyn's contract, but, as the filmed results were to prove, he knew what he was doing when casting the leads for *Born Yesterday.*

The Inanimate Performance: Riders of the Whistling Pines

In spite of her snub by Columbia, Marilyn did manage to fit in one other screen appearance during her brief stint at the Gower Street studio. The modern-day Gene Autry wester, *Riders of the Whistling Pines* revolves around a gang of outlaws destroying timberland and framing do-gooder Gene on a cattle-poisoning charge while setting him up for murder.

Amid all the action, Marilyn portrays the late wife of a crop-dusting pilot . . . . Well, at least her publicity photo does. The pilot's wife died when he was overseas during World War II; since then, he has carried her with him everywhere. Several times during the black-and-white movie we see Marilyn's face full-frame (filling the screen), including the scene where the widower asks Gene to sing one of his favorite songs for his dead wife, and Autry duly obliges by serenading the photo with "Hair of Gold."

Towards the end of the film, the picture is placed prominently on the grieving man's aircraft control panel. Unfortunately, this is its last appearance, for after receiving a salute from its owner, it goes down with him and the plane.

**RIDERS OF THE
WHISTLING PINES**

A Columbia Pictures Release
Produced by Armand Schaefer
Directed by John English
Written by Jack Townley
Photographed by William Bradford
Art Direction by Harold H. MacArthur
Music by Mischa Bakaleinikoff
Edited by Aaron Stell
Released: March 15, 1949
Running Time: 70 minutes
Black & White

While Gene Autry sings "Hair of Gold," a Columbia publicity shot of Marilyn appears on the screen.

Love Happy

The Plot

Shifty private eye Sam Grunion recounts how for the past 11 years he has been trying to track down a million dollars' worth of missing Romanoff diamonds. The story begins when the jewels are smuggled into the U.S. inside one of the sardine cans delivered to a food store. Madame Egelichi is the mastermind behind this operation, yet her plans are thrown into disarray when the all-important can with a black cross on the lid is among a number that are pilfered by Harpo, a crafty kleptomaniac who is trying to support a struggling—and starving—acting troupe that is rehearsing for a musical revue titled *Love Happy*.

Various attempts are made by Egelichi to locate the elusive sardine container, but it is Harpo who sees a cat eating from it outside the theater and quickly pockets the valuables. An Egelichi associate then discovers the empty can with the tell-tale mark on the lid, and the chase is on. When the show's leading lady, Maggie Phillips, is upset over a falling-out with her costar boyfriend, Harpo gives her the diamond necklace as a birthday gift. Said boyfriend subsequently assures Maggie that the necklace is worthless, and so she dumps it on top of the theater piano, which in turn leads it into the hands of Chico while he is performing during the show's opening night. Madame Egelichi spots this from her box seat and dispatches her henchmen to recoup the jewelry, but they are diverted by Harpo when

LOVE HAPPY

★★

A United Artists Release
A Mary Pickford Presentation of a Lester Cowan Production
Directed by David Miller
Screenplay by Frank Tashlin and Mac Benoff
Based on a story by Harpo Marx
Cinematography by William C. Mellor
Art Direction by Gabriel Scognamillo
Music by Ann Ronnell
Choreography by Billy Daniel
Costume Design by Grace Houston and Norma
Edited by Basil Wrangell and Al Joseph
Released: March 8, 1950
Running Time: 81 minutes
Black & White

CAST

Harpo	Harpo Marx
Faustino	Chico Marx
Detective Sam Grunion	Groucho Marx
Madama Egelichi	Ilona Massey
Maggie Phillips	Vera-Ellen
Bunny Dolan	Marion Hutton
Alphonse Zoto	Raymond Burr
Throckmorton	Melville Cooper
Mike Johnson	Paul Valentine
Mr. Lyons	Leon Belasco
Mackinaw	Eric Blore
Hannibal Zoto	Bruce Gordon
Grunion's Client	Marilyn Monroe

Uncredited:

Young Woman	Lois Hall
Cop	Edward Gargan
Actor	Colin Keith-Johnston

Modeling the strapless gown for a 38-second appearance that merited an "Introducing Marilyn Monroe" credit in the opening titles. This was actually her fourth film.

he flashes some fake jewels that he lifted from the costume of a chorus girl.

The chase leads to the roof of the theater, where matters are confused when Chico enters the fray and the real diamonds end up back in Harpo's hands. Sam Grunion and Madame Egelichi both arrive on the scene, and when the detective ends up with the jewels, the heistress suddenly takes a fancy to him. Harpo still has one more trick up his sleeve, however—he slyly retrieves the necklace from Grunion's coat pocket and disappears into the night with what he thinks is the fake jewelry. As for Sam Grunion; he subsequently marries the thwarted but glamorous Ms. Egelichi.

▶▶ *"Mr. Grunion, I want you to help me."*
"I have a little sand left. What seems to be the trouble?"

Behind-the-Scenes Facts & Opinions

The Marx Brothers' thirteenth and final film appearance as a team, *Love Happy* is also one of their weakest efforts. Full of cheap sets, tacky costumes, and shoddy editing, it bears all the hallmarks of a Poverty Row production. Furthermore, at no time do the three brothers appear together on-screen. Groucho was paid just $35,000—half his normal fee—to intermittently serve as the on-screen narrator, then crop up in one brief scene with Harpo towards the end, and in another with Chico in which their separate camera shots are simply edited together. Nevertheless, the following obviously contrived Groucho segment, inserted about an hour into *Love Happy,* that amply justifies the movie's inclusion in this book.

As Sam Grunion is about to leave for the theater to retrieve the missing jewels, there is a knock at his office door and in walks Marilyn, stunning in a strapless gown. "Is there anything I can do for you?" asks the leering detective, before turning to the camera and admitting, "What a ridiculous statement."
MM: Mr. Grunion, I want you to help me.
Grunion: I have a little sand left. What seems to be the trouble?
MM: Some men are following me.
Grunion: Really? I can't understand why. . .

Marilyn is quickly hustled out of the office, and she departs with the first cinematic swaying of her soon-to-be-famous derrière. Total on-screen time: 38 seconds, yet those seconds merited the ingénue an "Introducing Marilyn Monroe" credit in the opening titles (even though this was her fourth film).

Marilyn would later recall about her audition for the role, "There were three girls there and Groucho had us each walk away from him . . . I was the only one he asked to do it twice. Then he whispered in my ear, 'You have the prettiest ass in the business.' I'm sure he meant it in the nicest way." At the age of 58, Groucho Marx still had a keen eye for fresh young talent.

"No acting, just sex again," was Marilyn's appraisal of her *Love Happy* performance. "I had to wiggle across a room. I practiced jiggling my backside for a week. Groucho loved it."

There is some ambiguity about who actually set up Marilyn's audition with producer Lester Cowan; her first agent Harry Lipton, Hollywood agent Louis Shurr, agent/lover Johnny Hyde, her friend, actor John Carroll, or, broke and out of work, Marilyn herself. Either way, Cowan deferred to Groucho's judgment as to who should be selected for the role, and after all three hopefuls tried to satisfy his request for "a young lady who can walk by me in such a manner as to arouse my elderly libido and cause smoke to issue from my ears," Groucho decided that Marilyn was "Mae West, Theda Bara and Bo Peep rolled into one."

According to Marxian biographer Richard Anobile, Groucho would later say, "Boy,

did I want to fuck her. She wore this dress with bare tits. . . . She was goddam beautiful. I may have tried to lay her once, but I didn't get anywhere with her. . . . She was the most beautiful girl I ever saw in my life."

Marilyn was paid $500 for her screen appearance, $300 to pose for promotional photos, and $100 per week to partake in a national publicity tour. For this she was given a wardrobe allowance which, on the advice of Johnny Hyde and acting coach Natasha Lytess, she invested in wool suits, sweaters, high-necked blouses, and a jacket. However, after suffering through the summer heat of Chicago and New York, she bought some more lightweight clothing and continued on to Detroit, Cleveland, and Milwaukee before quitting the tour in Rockford, Illinois, and returning to Los Angeles.

Billed by the press as the "Mmmm Girl" and "Woo Woo Girl," Marilyn gained some decent exposure from the *Love Happy* publicity junket, but the film itself was a bust. Initially conceived to help Chico pay off some of his gambling debts, it was based on a story by Harpo and largely carried by him on-screen. After all, the blonde-wigged mime didn't have to spout any of the half-baked jokes written by Ben Hecht (who wisely remained uncredited), Mac Benoff, and Frank Tashlin in order to get his laughs—even sub-par Marx Brothers has its magical moments, and in *Love Happy* many of these relate to the shenanigans of Harpo's mischievous but lovable sensitive-idiot character, as well as Chico's interpretation of his mute sidekick's offbeat sign language.

Billed as a "New Musical Girlesque," this slapstick farce ran out of financing while it was being filmed in early 1949, and so the producers had to resort to the then highly unusual practice of on-screen product endorsement. As a result, in the scene towards the end of the movie where Egelichi's henchmen chase Harpo around the roof of the theater, there are giant illuminated signs for Baby Ruth candy, GE lamps, Fisk, Wheaties, Mobil Oil, Bulova watches, and Kool cigarettes.

Despite this resourcefulness, the film wasn't released for nearly a year while the decision was being made about whether it would be distributed by Eagle-Lion or United Artists. Ultimately, the film's reviews were mixed and its box office performance was disappointing.

The Critics' Views

"The 'story' is flimsy even for a Marxian extravaganza. . . . Ilona Massey, as a Russian vamp who has gone through eight weddings and three murders to gain possession of the diamonds, provides optic appeal, along with Marilyn Monroe and various leggy chorines."

Los Angeles Times

"The Marx Brothers return to the screen in *Love Happy,* a zany comedy with music that may appeal to their faithful fans, but has little entertainment value to offer the average filmgoer."

Hollywood Reporter

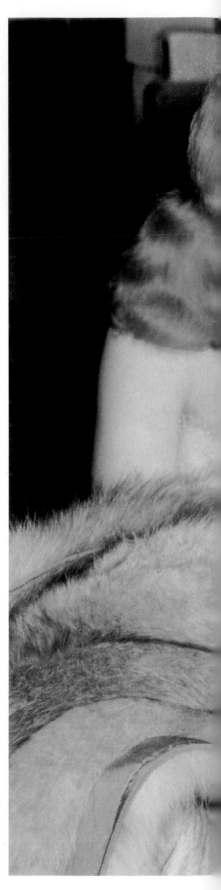

During a break on the set, Groucho delivers some of his smoothest lines to a lady whom he perceives as "Mae West, Theda Bara and Bo Peep rolled into one."

A Ticket to Tomahawk

A TICKET TO TOMAHAWK

★★★

A Twentieth Century-Fox Release
Produced by Robert Bassler
Directed by Richard Sale
Screenplay by Mary Loos and Richard Sale
Cinematography by Harry Jackson
Sound by W.D. Flick and Harry M. Leonard
Art Direction by Lyle Wheeler and
George W. Davis
Music by Cyril Mockridge
Costume Design by René Hubert
Edited by Harmon Jones
Released: April 21, 1950
Running Time: 90 minutes
Technicolor

CAST

Johnny Behind-the-Deuces	Dan Dailey
Kit Dodge, Jr.	Anne Baxter
Dakota	Rory Calhoun
Terence Sweeney	Walter Brennan
Chuckity	Charles Kemper
Madame Adelaide	Connie Gilchrist
Sad Eyes	Arthur Hunnicutt
Dodge	Will Wright
Pawnee	Chief Yowlachie
Dawson	Mauritz Hugo
Crooked Knife	Chief Thundercloud
Long Time	Victor Sen Yung
Mayor	Raymond Greenleaf
Charley	Harry Carter
Velvet Fingers	Harry Seymour
Annie	Marion Marshall
Ruby	Joyce McKenzie
Clara	Marilyn Monroe
Julie	Barbara Smith
Fargo	Jack Elam

Uncredited:

(Bit Part)	Edward Clark
(Bit Part)	Paul Harvey
(Bit Part)	Charles Stevens

MM'S SONG

"Oh, What a Forward Young Man You Are"
by Ken Darby and John Read, performed
with Marion Marshall, Joyce McKenzie,
Barbara Smith and Dan Dailey

The Plot

It is September of 1876 and Johnny Jameson, a slick traveling salesman of sundry items, including subscriptions for the *Saturday Evening Post,* is the only paying passenger aboard Engine Number One, the *Emma Sweeney,* as it makes its maiden voyage along the new Tomahawk and Western Railroad that runs through the Colorado Rockics. Dawson, the evil owner of a rival stagecoach line, employs members of the Overland Gang to disrupt the competition by launching a boulder onto the tracks, and Johnny—known as Johnny Behind-the-Deuces courtesy of the pack of trick cards that he peddles—unknowingly hitches a ride via horse with two of the gang members into the nearby town of Epitaph.

There, convinced that trains are of great importance to local and national prosperity, elderly Marshall Dodge deputizes his young and feisty granddaughter, Kit Dodge, Jr., to ensure the *Emma Sweeney's* safe passage to Tomahawk. Dawson, meanwhile, dispatches his men to cause trouble by dynamiting the train and inciting local Arapaho Indians to sabotage the railroad. To that end, his chief henchman, Dakota, along with other Overland Gang members, infiltrates Kit's posse . A charter decrees that the Tomahawk and Western Railroad will forfeit its license if the train doesn't safely transport at least one passenger to Tomahawk by September 5, and further hindering matters is the fact that there is no track for 40 miles between Epitaph and Dead Horse Point because the rails were lost in a storm on their way from England.

The only passengers are Johnny, one other man, and a showgirl troupe. Suspecting him to be a member of the Overland Gang, Kit orders Johnny to assist the locomotive's journey, and this he duly does, helping her to thwart Dawson and his cronies, and in the process winning Kit's affections. What's more, he also negotiates peace with the Arapaho Indians, enlists their help, and, when the train breaks down just a few feet short of Tomahawk, he convinces the mayor to extend the town limits. The railroad has fulfilled its charter, and Johnny subsequently marries Kit and takes a job on the *Emma Sweeney.*

Behind-the-Scenes Facts & Opinions

Featuring eye-catching locations, colorful period costumes, and good on-screen chemistry between Dan Dailey and Anne Baxter, *A Ticket to Tomahawk* is a charming comedy-western that provides solid lightweight entertainment.

Efficiently directed by Richard Sale, who also cowrote the screenplay with his then-wife Mary Loos, *Tomahawk* had a large cast and crew setting up camp in Durango, California, during August and September of 1949.

"Durango is more of a fancy ski resort these days, but back then it was a pretty rough location," recalled Loos, (the niece of *Gentlemen Prefer Blondes'* writer Anita Loos), when I interviewed her in 1994. "The little narrow-gauge railroad that we

filmed traveled between there and a town named Silverton, and at that particular time the train only ran twice a week. Well, we got to rent it and use it all the time, and so we'd chug back and forth in that wild country, and we filmed the closing scene in Silverton. A lot of the local ladies had been there during the gold rush, and I remember when a little girl looked at Marilyn and started imitating her, somebody pointed to the kid and said, 'Look at her. She's just like her mother: a hooker!'"

Marilyn appears four times in the movie, either just looking pretty in the bright yellow dress that was designed especially for her or indulging in group dialogue. However, her most notable scene is that in which she sings and dances with Dan Dailey and her fellow showgirls. Portrayed by Marion Marshall, Joyce Mackenzie, and Barbara Smith, these ladies—together with Connie Gilchrist, who plays their boss, Madame Adelaide—are the subject of a script in-joke during the aforementioned final segment

Performing "Oh, What A Forward Young Man You Are" with fellow showgirls, Marion Marshall, Joyce McKenzie and Barbara Smith.

filmed in Silverton. As he gets set to depart on the train, Johnny bids farewell to his wife and five small daughters: "Bye, Connie, Barbara, Marion, Marilyn, and Joyce. Goodbye!"

As it happens, in the original script of February 11, 1949, there are six showgirls including Eloise and Gladys, all of whom are "homely as mud fences." Describing the girls "in various stages of deshabille" while inside their tent—sporting camisoles, ruffled bloomers, robes, and old-fashioned nightgowns—this same script notes: "These are thoroughly decorous clothes. We want the femininity of the period shown, not a display of flesh."

Nevertheless, studio chief Darryl F. Zanuck knew where to draw the line. He asserted during a script conference on May 5, 1949, "Madame should have only four girls, and they should all be beauties. Select stock girls for this." Eloise and Gladys were quickly eliminated before Marilyn took the advice of agent/lover Johnny Hyde and, once again thanks to casting director Ben Lyon, landed the largely decorative role of Clara.

"Johnny Hyde was very important to her," Mary Loos recalled. "She would get on the phone long-distance and talk and talk and talk to him. Otherwise she was fairly withdrawn when we were in Durango, and she was also reluctant to get up early. Even then I think she was fatigued with life. She caught a cold on location and she wanted to take all of this penicillin. A local doctor warned her, 'I don't know if you should have that much,' but she said, 'It won't bother me.' Well, she got a rash, and she got a rash in a very embarrassing place, but that didn't stop her from telling people to 'Look at this rash I've got!' They were kind of astounded."

Still, during her five weeks on location, Marilyn also took the opportunity to display her charms in a more crowd-pleasing way, according to Loos:

> We were trying to raise money for the local hospital, and so Twentieth Century-Fox assembled a baseball team to play the home team. Locally this was a pretty big event. The bleachers were full of people from that part of Colorado, and Marilyn was asked to take part, so she worked out a gag where she was up at bat, and as she started running to first base her blue jeans fell down to reveal her black lace undies. Well, you should have heard the bleachers. They went wild.

A Ticket to Tomahawk would be released in April of 1950, by which time, thanks to Johnny Hyde's inavaluable efforts on her behalf, Marilyn would have already completed filming her first notable role in a really terrific movie.

The Critics' Views

"Here is a surprise Western package that should set up the audience with amazement and then knock them happily over with its smart handling. Said handling is in the best tradition of spoofing the form but it also becomes as rugged and bloodthirsty, with all the necessary action, as they ever did come."

FILM DAILY

"Writers Mary Loos and Richard Sale hoke up the standard ingredients of the oater epic, using both burlesque and clever satire to keep treatment light and chuckles cascading. Also, they provide plenty of good action and thrills, and Sale's direction whips it along."

DAILY VARIETY

The Asphalt Jungle

The Plot

Seasoned criminal Dix Handley is released from police custody after a witness fails to identify him as the perpetrator of a stickup the previous night. Commissioner Hardy castigates Lt. Ditrich for failing to link Dix to a recent spate of armed robberies, as well as for not trailing Doc Riedenschneider, a dangerous villain who has just been released from prison. Ditrich is warned that his job is on the line, while Doc sets about executing his plan for a million-dollar jewel heist.

While shady bookmaker Cobby will fund the escapade—paying $25,000 to safe-cracker Louis Ciavelli, $10,000 to driver Gus Minissi, and $15,000 to "hooligan" Dix Handley—respected society lawyer Alonzo D. Emmerich agrees to put up $500,000 to fence the stolen goods and thus avert police suspicion. Lt. Ditrich is also on Cobby's payroll, but what nobody knows is that Emmerich is broke and is planning to double-cross his partner. Only Doc is suspicious of Emmerich, and he entrusts Dix with the job of making sure that the lawyer pays up when he is supplied with the jewels.

The robbery itself goes according to plan, until reverberations from the vault-opening blast set off alarms all over the neighborhood. Police cars are everywhere, and when a night watchman crosses paths with the robbers, Dix punches him, the watchman drops

Despite the fact that she never encounters either of them in the film, this publicity still shows Marilyn trying to subtly entice Sterling Hayden away from Jean Hagen.

his gun, which then goes off, and a bullet lodges itself in Louis' stomach. Avoiding the police, Gus drives Louis home while Doc and Dix deliver the jewels to Emmerich and his heavy, Bob Brannom. Emmerich now admits that he doesn't have the necessary funds at hand, and he fails to convince Doc to hide the hot property with him while he raises the cash. Brannom pulls out a gun and orders Doc to hand over the jewels. Dix pulls out his gun and kills Brannom and is wounded in the process.

Trying to salvage a bad situation, Doc spares Emmerich's life so that the lawyer can negotiate with the insurers of the jewelry, agreeing to secretly return them in exhange for 25% of their appraised value. Emmerich is also left to dispose of Brannom's body, but when the police later fish it out of a river, they see a possible link between the murder and the jewel heist, and they question Emmerich. The lawyer states that he was with his mistress, Angela Phinlay, when the robbery took place, and as soon as the police leave, he phones Angela and tells her to confirm his alibi.

Doc appears to be the police force's only suspect. However, after the treachorous Lt. Ditrich forces Cobby to squeal on his colleagues, the cops visit Emmerich at the riverside cottage where he keeps Ms. Phinlay, and they intimidate the frightened young woman into admitting that she lied about being with "Uncle Lon" on the night of the robbery. Emmerich then shoots himself, Louis and Dix die of their wounds, and Gus, Cobby, Doc. and Lt. Ditrich all end up behind bars.

Behind-the-Scenes Facts & Opinions

A classic film noir, boasting gritty dialogue, realistic settings, atmospheric cinematography, and authentic characterizations, *The Asphalt Jungle* established the blueprint for all caper/heist movies. As such, it has been frequently imitated but rarely equaled. It has even been remade three times: as *The Badlanders,* a 1958 Western starring Alan Ladd and Ernest Borgnine; as *Cairo,* a 1963 British potboiler starring George Sanders; and as *Cool Breeze,* a 1972 update starring Thalmus Rasulala, in which the diamond-robbery spoils are to be used to set up a black people's bank.

Few of the main characters in *The Asphalt Jungle* emerge with much integrity, but all are highly believable. Both the law enforcer and the legal advocate are utterly corrupt, and the criminal collaborators are simply victims of their own weaknesses: Dix Handley wants to return to the farm of his youth, yet he commits armed robbery to help fund his gambling habit; Alonzo D. Emmerich, who asserts that "crime is only a left-handed form of human endeavor," is undone by an over-lavish lifestyle and a half-witted mistress; and Doc Riedenschneider allows his preoccupation with young women to distract him from evading arrest. (In fact, even Commissioner Hardy displays shortcomings in his hour of glory; towards the end of the film, while fatally wounded Dix Handley is still on the run, the commissioner holds a press conference and crows that "Three men are in jail, three men are dead—one by his own hand—one man's a fugitive. . . ." Unfortunately for Hardy, he can't add. At that point, four men are in jail and two are dead.)

The movie's setting, a major Chicago-like city in the Midwest, is, for a good reason, never specified. According to John Huston's personal files, producer Arthur Hornblow, Jr., studio boss Dore Schary and he all wanted to use the name of an actual city, but a number of the real-life police commissioners of those cities objected. Similarly, several of the character's names had to be changed in the Huston-Maddow script in order to avoid litigation, and as if all of that weren't enough, the filmmakers then had to contend with the censors.

THE ASPHALT JUNGLE

★★★★½

A Metro Goldwyn-Mayer Release
Produced by Arthur Hornblow, Jr.
Directed by John Huston
Screenplay by Ben Maddow and John Huston
From a novel by W.R. Burnett
Cinematography by Harold Rosson
Sound by Douglas Shearer and Robert B. Lee
Art Direction by Cedric Gibbons and Randall Duell
Music by Miklos Rozsa
Edited by George Boemler
Released: June 20, 1950
Running Time: 112 minutes
Black & White

CAST

Dix Handley	Sterling Hayden
Alonzo D. Emmerich	Louis Calhern
Doll Conovan	Jean Hagen
Gus Minissi	James Whitmore
Doc Erwin Riedenschneider	Sam Jaffe
Police Commissioner Hardy	John McIntire
Cobby	Marc Lawrence
Lt. Ditrich	Barry Kelley
Louis Ciavelli	Anthony Caruso
Maria Ciavelli	Teresa Celli
Angela Phinlay	Marilyn Monroe
Timmons	William Davis
May Emmerich	Dorothy Tree
Bob Brannom	Brad Dexter
Dr. Swanson	John Maxwell
Janocek	James Seay
James X. Connery	Thomas Browne Henry
Andrews	Don Haggerty
Jeannie	Helene Stanley
Franz Schurz	Henry Rowland
Tallboy	Raymond Roe

Uncredited:

Driver	Benny Burt
Night Clerk	Frank Cady
Woman	Jean Carter
Policeman	John Cliff
William Doldy	Henry Corden
Red	Charles Courtney
Policeman	Ralph Dunn
Policeman	Pat Flaherty
Maxwell	Alex Gerry
Policeman	Sol Gorss
Truck Driver	Fred Graham
Vivian	Eloise Hardt
Evans	David Hydes
Reporter	Fred Marlow
Karl Anton Smith	Strother Martin
Girl	Patricia Miller
Secretary	Howard Mitchell
Eddie Donato	Alberto Morin
Girl	Kerry O'Day
Jack, Police Clerk	Tim Ryan
Policeman	Jack Shea
Reporter	Joseph Darr Smith
Policeman	Ray Teal
Girl	Leah Wakefield
Suspect	William Washington
Woman	Constance Weiler
Woman	Judith Wood
Man	Wilson Woo

To start with, they were informed that if, as originally intended, safecracker Louis Ciavelli were shown in bed with his wife Maria, the entire scene would be deleted by the British Censorship Board. Furthermore, it had to be made clear that Dix's friend, Doll Conovan, was not a prostitute, but that she worked in a clip joint. When she stays the night with Dix, the censors declared that any inference of sex in that scene, even if "presented in an attractive manner," would be unacceptable. The result was that Dix simply provides Doll with a place to stay. On the other hand, the initial scene in which Emmerich is at his lover Angela's home was approved with the proviso that he not follow her into the bedroom when she retires for the night. No detailed action showing how the jewelry store safe was opened was allowed, and terms such as "lousy," "loused-up" and "drug addict" were deemed unfit and had to be replaced.

In the original script, Emmerich's mistress—described in W.R. Burnett's novel as "voluptuously made"—was named Angela Finlay. John Huston opted to have her known simply as Angela, yet she was referred to by her full name twice during filming, and by the time production closed on December 28, 1949, it was too late to dub in a new name. A couple of days later, Huston issued instructions that she should appear in the cast list as Angela Phinlay.

Performing in the role, amid standout performances by the likes of Sterling Hayden, Louis Calhern, and, most notably, Sam Jaffe as the stoic criminal mastermind Doc Riedenschneider, Marilyn acquits herself admirably. She is alternately seductive, innocent, calculating, and vulnerable as the sugar daddy's plaything, and during filming she was instinctively aware that her limited on-screen time would be an attention grabber. "I don't know what I did," she told drama coach Natasha Lytess upon completing her final scene in a couple of takes, "but I do know it felt wonderful."

In time, Marilyn would come to regard this as one of her finest dramatic performances, yet it wasn't a case of all work and no play on the *Asphalt Jungle* set. According to a June 18, 1950 report in the *San Francisco Chronicle* (which twice made references to Marilyn "Munroe"), John Huston made sure that his new discovery would catch Louis Calhern's eye while filming a scene in which Emmerich walks into his study and finds Angela clad in "gorgeous attire." The cameras rolled, but as soon as Calhern entered the room he let out a wolf whistle—MM was dressed in a see-through nightie that, to quote the *Chronicle* journalist, "would never pass a censor board." Even in clothing that did get the nod from censors, Marilyn was able to elicit a similar response.

Following a public preview of *The Asphalt Jungle* at the Picwood Theater in West Los Angeles on February 16, 1950, 282 audience members submitted appraisal cards. 50 described the film as "outstanding," 109 thought it was "excellent," 89 considered it "very good," 25 stated that it was "good," eight thought it was "fair," and a solitary misguided soul asserted that it was "poor." One viewer expressed his enjoyment at watching "the hot blonde," while another demanded, "Let's see more of the blonde."

The Asphalt Jungle garnered four Oscar nominations: Best Black-and-White Cinematography, Best Director, Best Supporting Actor (Sam Jaffe), and Best Screenplay. It won the British Academy Award for "Best Film from any source," and Jaffe was named Best Actor at the Venice Film Festival. Clearly, Marilyn Monroe also became one of the movie's beneficiaries. Her career gained momentum and her struggle to find work diminished; in her small role as Angela Phinlay, Marilyn had a big impact and attracted the attention of the people she needed most: Hollywood's hierarchy.

"Some sweet kid"—Angela Phinlay's seductive wiles don't work when a cop comes knocking at her door.

"I had an awfully good evening," veteran director Howard Hawks wrote to John Huston on March 27, 1950 after attending an industry screening of the film. "*Jungle* is beautifully done and I envy you for it. The girl is a real find."

Whether Hawks was referring to Marilyn Monroe or Jean Hagen is open to conjecture, but within a few years it would be the former who would appear in a couple of his movies, *Monkey Business* and *Gentlemen Prefer Blondes.* Marilyn's star was now beginning its ascendancy, and the hallowed long-term studio contract was just that little bit closer.

The Critics' Views

"One of the most extraordinary crime films of the year is MGM's *The Asphalt Jungle* . . . Marilyn Monroe, as the baby-faced mistress of the rich lawyer who tries to doublecross the crooks, stands out vividly in a small role. She's definitely due for bigger things."

Los Angeles Evening Herald & Express

"In *The Asphalt Jungle* producer Arthur Hornblow presents a striking study of crime, a film that is almost a classic of its type. . . . Marilyn Monroe has the simple directness needed for her spot of Calhern's mistress."

Hollywood Reporter

"Packed with stand-out performances. . . . There's a beautiful blonde, too, name of Marilyn Monroe, who plays Calhern's girlfriend, and makes the most of her footage."

Photoplay

"Marilyn Monroe would fetch the wolves out of any jungle, asphalt or otherwise."

The People

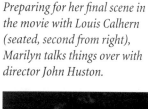

Preparing for her final scene in the movie with Louis Calhern (seated, second from right), Marilyn talks things over with director John Huston.

The Fireball

The Plot

Father O'Hara runs St. Luke's Home for Boys, where pint-sized Johnny Casar is a disruptive hooligan who has a complex because of his height. After running away, Johnny finds some discarded rollerskates that just happen to fit him, and he also stumbles upon a job washing dishes at a bar-restaurant. Police tip off Father O'Hara as to Johnny's whereabouts, and following a chat with the priest, Johnny's boss, Bruno Crystal offers the youngster a place to stay while recommending that he take free skating lessons at the nearby Palamar Rollerbowl. There, Johnny is treated unkindly by obnoxious instructor Mack Miller, before Mack's attractive skating teammate, Mary Reeves, takes the newcomer under her wing.

Johnny excels as a skater and he is soon a member of the local Roller Derby team. Heeding Mary's advice to skate with his head as well as his feet, he outwits, out-hits and outraces his opponents, and when he goes to see Mary and Mack competing in the professional league, he heckles Mack mercilessly and becomes a TV celebrity in the

THE FIREBALL
★½

A Twentieth Century-Fox Release
A Thor Production
Produced by Bert E. Friedlob
Directed by Tay Garnett
Screenplay by Horace McCoy
Original story by Tay Garnett and Horace McCoy
Cinematography by Lester White
Sound by William Fox
Art Direction by Van Nest Polglase
Music by Victor Young
Wardrobe by Richard Staub
Edited by Frank Sullivan
Released: October 7, 1950
Running Time: 84 minutes
Black & White

CAST

Johnny Casar	Mickey Rooney
Father O'Hara	Pat O'Brien
Mary Reeves	Beverly Tyler
Mack Miller	Glenn Corbett
Allen	James Brown
Bruno Crystal	Ralph Dumke
Jeff Davis	Milburn Stone
Shilling	Kenneth Begley
Polly	Marilyn Monroe
Dr. Barton	Sam Flint
Ullman	John Hedloe

Uncredited:

Alan	Larry Holden

Marilyn and Mickey, on location for the scene in which Roller Derby groupie Polly turns up in her finest garb to greet Johnny Casar at the airport.

Flanked by (l–r) Glenn Corbett, James Brown and Mickey Rooney, MM gives the first outing to her own sweater dress that she would also wear for All About Eve, *the* Cold Shoulder *screen test, and* Home Town Story.

process. There is massive public demand for a showdown race between Mack and Johnny, and when Mack reluctantly agrees, Johnny takes to a banked track for the first time and loses badly to the world champion skater. He also loses several well-attended rematches until, with Mary's guidance, he eventually beats Mack and forces his way onto the Bears team.

Unfortunately, after leading the Bears to a championship title, playing for the U.S. national team, and being named "Athlete of the Year," Johnny allows all of the fame to go to his head. He starts carousing, stops training, mistreats Mary, and clashes with team manager Jeff Davis over his egocentric individuality on the track. During an international match between America and Europe, Johnny purposely knocks down his own teammate Mack Miller and causes a dangerous pileup of players from both sides. Now everybody despises him, but just as the out-of-control Johnny knocks Mack out of the rink the following night, he is struck down with polio. Fearing that his career is over, Johnny contemplates suicide, yet with encouragement from both Mary and Father O'Hara, he fights back to make a full recovery and, following a two-year hiatus, returns to the international team. Johnny Casar has at last been humbled by his experience, and just to prove the point he takes the unprecedented step of foregoing the limelight to help a rookie colleague win a big race.

Behind-the-Scenes Facts & Opinions

A top box office star during the late 1930s and early 1940s, Mickey Rooney saw his career go into sharp decline after returning from World War II service, and by the early 1950s he was broke and reduced to accepting stereotyped roles in cheapie films. *The Fireball* was one of them. In fact, when Father O'Hara comments that he's glad Johnny Casar has run away from St. Luke's Home for Boys because "according to his age, Johnny should have been out of here years ago," he isn't kidding—when filming took place in January and February of 1950, the "juvenile lead'" was nearing 30.

Titled *Dark Challenge* while it was in production, *The Fireball* was made under the independent Thor banner of Bert Friedlob and Tay Garnett, with the intention of cashing in on the Roller Derby craze that was then sweeping America. To that end, plenty of live action sequences were inserted into the proceedings, while process shots enabled the actors to appear in close-up. The backgrounds for these were filmed by mounting a camera on a small motor scooter in order to attain the desired speed around the track. Then, when the actors worked in front of the process screen, a mirror was mounted next to the camera lens so that they could follow the rearview action and make the necessary turns.

Such segments aside, there is little else worth watching in *The Fireball*. Tay Garnett's direction is weak, Horace McCoy's script is as hokey as it gets, and while Pat O'Brien turns in his patented portrayal of the tough but kindly priest, Mickey Rooney shamelessly overacts, displaying the kind of exaggerated facial mannerisms that would be out of place even in a silent movie. As for Marilyn Monroe, her husky-voiced performance as Polly, a Roller Derby groupie who is only interested in Johnny's celebrity, is little more than decorative. Of course, it did keep her in work while Johnny Hyde was trying to line up a studio contract, but in terms of Marilyn's visibility it really was like taking one step forward and two back after having appeared in *The Asphalt Jungle*. Fortunately for her, not too many people actually saw *The Fireball*.

The Critics' Views

"An okay actioner idea runs wild in *The Fireball* and results in the programmer classification. . . . Footage is generously sprinkled with rink action and moves along in these portions, but falters in its story and generally proves unsatisfactory."

Daily Variety

"Mickey Rooney sails through the part of the skater with his usual assurance. Pat O'Brien's sensible priest is a likeable performance, and pretty Beverly Tyler does well with her feminine lead. James Brown, Marilyn Monroe, Ralph Dumke, Bert Begley and Milburn Stone figure interestingly in the supporting cast."

Hollywood Reporter

All About Eve

The Plot

Eve Harrington is about to receive the highest theatrical honor that the American stage has to offer, the Sarah Siddons Award for Distinguished Achievement. In attendance are a number of her associates, and while time is frozen just prior to the actress making her acceptance speech, several of these characters proceed to tell us all about Eve.

Her story begins during the Broadway run of *Aged in Wood*, when she attends every performance and camps outside the theater night after night just to catch a glimpse of the star, Margo Channing. Eventually she befriends Karen Richards, who conveniently happens to be Margo's best friend and the wife of playwright Lloyd Richards. When Eve is introduced to these people she tells them about her lifelong love of acting, her financial struggles, and the loss of her husband during World War II. They all empathize, Margo hires Eve as her personal assistant, and thereafter Eve studies her idol's performances from the wings. Nevertheless, while she works her way into most people's confidence, Eve's overzealous nature also provokes skepticism on the part of Margo's maid, Birdie, and eventually Margo herself.

At a birthday party that Eve has thoughtfully arranged for Margo's director-boyfriend, Bill Sampson, the actress's middle-aged insecurities rise to the surface.

If looks could kill, whose gaze would you avoid? Marilyn in exalted company with (l–r) Anne Baxter, Bette Davis, and George Sanders.

Indeed, her jealousy regarding Bill's attention towards Eve boils over, and she drunkenly embarrasses herself in front of the assembled guests, one of whom is the acerbic drama critic Addison DeWitt. Eve, meanwhile, secretly asks Karen to convince producer Max Fabian to audition her for the vacant position of Margo's understudy, and when Margo arrives late at the audition, she discovers not only that Eve has landed the job, but also that she was brilliant when stepping into Margo's shoes to read opposite unsuccessful fellow auditioner Claudia Caswell.

Unable to contain herself, Margo has explosive fights with Lloyd, Max, and Bill, before Karen informs Eve of a plan to give the 40-year-old prima donna her long-overdue comeuppance. Following a weekend in the country with Margo and Lloyd, Karen ensures that their car runs out of fuel on the way to the train station from which Margo must travel to the theater. Eve therefore takes her place on stage that night and

ALL ABOUT EVE

★★★★★

A Twentieth Century-Fox Release
Produced by Darryl F. Zanuck
Directed by Joseph L. Mankiewicz
Screenplay by Joseph L. Mankiewicz
From the story *The Wisdom of Eve* by Mary Orr
Cinematography by Milton Krasner
Sound by W. D. Flick and Roger Heman
Art Direction by Lyle Wheeler and George W. Davis
Music by Alfred Newman
Costume Design for Bette Davis by Edith Head
Wardrobe Direction by Charles LeMaire
Edited by Barbara McLean
Released: November 22, 1950
Running Time: 138 minutes
Black & White

CAST

Margo Channing	Bette Davis
Eve Harrington	Anne Baxter
Addison DeWitt	George Sanders
Karen Richards	Celeste Holm
Bill Sampson	Gary Merrill
Lloyd Richards	Hugh Marlowe
Max Fabian	Gregory Ratoff
Phoebe	Barbara Bates
Miss Caswell	Marilyn Monroe
Birdie	Thelma Ritter
Aged Actor	Walter Hampden
Girl	Randy Stewart
Leading Man	Craig Hill
Doorman	Leland Harris
Autograph Seeker	Barbara White
Stage Manager	Eddie Fisher
Clerk	William Pullen
Pianist	Claude Stroud
Frenchman	Eugene Borden
Reporter	Helen Mowery
Captain of Waiters	Steven Geray

Uncredited:

Well-Wisher	Bess Flowers
Actor in "Hearts of Oak"	Robert Whitney
(Bit Part)	Marion Pierce

Unlike the ineffectual Miss Caswell, Marilyn's career would indeed soon be "rising in the East like the sun..." not to mention the rest of America and then the world.

is a huge success; still, when Addison happens to see her making an unsuccessful pass at Bill, he starts hatching a plan of his own.

Easily ascertaining that Eve's past is far more sordid than she pretends, Addison nonetheless writes a rave review of her performance while making disparaging remarks about Margo. Bill and Karen suspect Eve's complicity in this and they immediately rally to Margo's defense, but Eve is undaunted. She woos Lloyd in an attempt to gain the lead role in his next play, and then tells his wife to ensure this happens or else Addison will reveal how Karen betrayed Margo. Fortunately, this becomes irrelevant when Margo withdraws from the play in order to marry Bill, yet Karen's joy is short-lived, as Eve steals Lloyd away from her.

While Max Fabian holds court with (top of staircase, l–r) Karen Richards, Bill Sampson, and Addison DeWitt, the ruthless Eve sizes up dumb but ambitious Miss Caswell.

Eve's joy is equally curtailed. When she informs Addison that she plans to marry Lloyd, the vituperative critic responds with his own form of blackmail—he tells Eve what he knows about her, and asserts that to keep her past a secret she must "belong to" him. Trapped with a man whom she has used but now despises, Eve has finally been outmatched. Furthermore, shortly after receiving the Sarah Siddons Award and prior to working in the Hollywood that she has previously maligned, she is latched onto by a young hopeful who appears to be every bit as ambitious as she was at the start of this story. Is history about to repeat itself?

Behind-the-Scenes Facts & Opinions

All About Eve is a great film. One of the high points of Hollywood moviemaking, it is a scathing indictment of the New York theater world, delivering Tinsel Town's cynical perspective on Broadway by way of Joseph L. Mankiewicz's seamless direction, his astute and witty script, and some truly unforgettable performances, especially by Bette Davis and George Sanders. Both of these actors give the renditions of a lifetime, squeezing every last drop out of some wonderful dialogue, and the rest of the cast isn't far behind.

"It was a very good cast and we all worked very well together," Celeste Holm told this author. "We just didn't get along very well . . . You know, Bette Davis was her usual rude self"—as she is on-screen in the role of the just-turned-forty bitch-diva with the monumental talent and temperament to match. Indeed, a couple of Davis's exchanges with Hugh Marlowe in the scene where Margo explodes after discovering that Eve is to be her understudy are priceless. Combining terrific acting with Mankiewicz's great lines, the scenes encapsulate all that's best in this movie.

Incensed by Margo comparing him to other playwrights, Lloyd Richards fires back, "What makes you think either Miller or Sherwood would stand for the nonsense I take from you? You'd better stick to Beaumont and Fletcher! They've been dead for 300 years!"
Margo: "All playwrights should be dead for 300 years!"
Lloyd: "That would solve none of their problems, because actresses never die!"

Then, as he is about to storm out of the theater, the writer delivers a parting shot: "I shall never understand the weird process by which a body with a voice suddenly fancies itself as a mind. Just when exactly does an actress decide they're her words she's saying and her thoughts she's expressing?"
Margo: "Usually at the point when she has to rewrite and rethink them, to keep the audience from leaving the theater!"
Lloyd: "It's about time the piano realized it has not written the concerto!"

Davis is so perfectly suited to the Margo Channing character that it is now almost inconceivable to think of Claudette Colbert growling the classic party line, "Fasten your seatbelts, it's going to be a bumpy night." Nevertheless, it was Colbert—another fine but altogether more genteel actress—who was originally cast in the role, only to pull out before the start of filming due to a ruptured disc in her back. Along with Colbert, writer-director Mankiewicz's other early choice for the Margo role was Gertrude Lawrence, while Darryl F. Zanuck initially envisaged Marlene Dietrich in the part, alongside Jeanne Crain as Eve Harrington and José Ferrer as Addison DeWitt.

While Anne Baxter is for the most part excellent as the ruthlessly ambitious Eve, her Mata-Hari-as-Bo-Peep masquerade is so broad and transparent that it is hard to imagine anyone—especially the sharp-witted characters who populate this story—being

*Joseph L. Mankiewicz gives
direction to "a graduate of the
Copacabana School of Dramatic
Art."*

stupid enough to not recognize it immediately. On the other hand, George Sanders is peerless as Addison, imbuing his multilayered character with all the cynicism, sarcasm, and malice that the part demands, while never overacting as others might have been tempted to do. For this, Joseph Mankiewicz must also share in the credit.

"He was the best director in the world," Celeste Holm asserted, "absolutely the very best. He knew everything about the camera. It's so wonderful to work for someone who is utterly in control of his medium. You feel so safe and you're also learning all the time, which is fun. I mean, most directors shoot a long shot, medium shots and close-ups, and then the cutter puts it all together, but Mankiewicz would put his hand over the camera and say, 'Now cut to where you come down the stairs towards the living room.' He'd say, 'I'm not giving the cutter one frame that I don't want in the picture,' so he cut as he went, which was a remarkable feat."

Also remarkable, according to Holm, was the performance that Mankiewicz extracted from Marilyn Monroe in her small but eye-catching turn as Claudia Caswell, an aspiring actress who shares Eve's ambition, but not her talent or her intelligence. For, whereas George Sanders once described Marilyn as being "humble, punctual and untemperamental," Holm's recollection was somewhat different: "She wasn't in the film that often, but it was rather singular that every time she was we had to wait. In his thick [Russian] accent Gregory Ratoff said 'This girl is going to be beeg star,' and I said, 'Why? Because she keeps us all waiting?' She was not very talented and she had a strange delivery, which was something she'd learned from a bad coach. So, I was not that impressed with her, and in fact none of us were, but she was perfect for the part and Mr. Mankiewicz was a good enough director to make her sound as if she knew what she was doing."

All About Eve was adapted from *The Wisdom of Eve,* a short story by Mary Orr that appeared in *Cosmopolitan* magazine in May of 1946, and that Twentieth Century-Fox purchased three years later for $1.25 million. In the story, Margola Cranston is the Margo Channing character (based on real-life stage actress Elisabeth Bergner), and she is married to Englishman Clement Howell. There is no one resembling either Addison DeWitt or Miss Caswell, and the story, narrated by Mrs. Lloyd Richards, ends with her landing Eve Harrington's part in her husband's play, her subsequent success taking her to Hollywood, and the twist of a divorce because Eve is going to marry Lloyd.

On May 10, 1949, Fox acquired a copy of Mary Orr's subsequent radio script, in which Margola is now Margo Cranston and there is a DeWitt character named Ronny Dawson, a famous Hollywood radio commentator who narrates the intro and outro while former stage actress Karen Manners recounts the story. Five months later, on October 26, 1949, Joseph L. Mankiewicz delivered his first adaption of *The Wisdom of Eve,* comprising narrative and a few lines, but not yet a full dialogue script. Titled *Best Performance,* this opens with the theatrical Sarah Siddons Award in place of Hollywood success, and introduces Addison DeWitt, Max Fabian, Bill Sampson, Birdie, and Miss Caswell, along with the introduction: "You all know all about Eve . . . what can there be to know that you don't know?"

Also in evidence for the first time are Margo's "Fasten your seatbelts" line and Miss Caswell's query about producers, "Why do they always look like unhappy rabbits?" Indeed, about 90 percent of the ingredients are already in place, for while Mary Orr's story was interesting, this first adaption is pure dynamite. The title was changed to *All About Eve* on January 6, 1950, and then more parts fell into place in the February 27 screenplay—Margo Channing is now the aging star, while Addison DeWitt murmurs some of his classic lines to Miss Caswell: "You have a point. An idiotic one, but a point," and "Well done. I see your career rising in the East like the sun," not to mention his famous introduction of her as "an actress. A graduate of the Copacabana School of Dramatic Art."

The final script, submitted on March 15, 1950, tightened up certain small parts, yet by the time it was translated onto the screen there were some other not insignificant adjustments: the elimination of a flashback during the party scene meant that, aside from the intro, the story now ran in sequence; crooner Eddie Fisher's brief appearance as a stage manager was cut prior to the film's release, even though his name still appears in the end credits; and one and a half pages of dialogue in which Karen begs Lloyd not to leave her for Eve were scrapped in the middle of production.

"I was in that scene and I was delighted that it was cut," Celeste Holm recalled. "It was an extension to the short segment in which the playwright gets up from bed to take care of Eve. I was supposed to rail about what's happening, but you know, self-pity never works as far as the audience is concerned. At the same time, the crew did not like

Hugh Marlowe. He was a little pompous, and crews can see through all of that stuff. He was also very self-conscious about the fact that he didn't see too well, so they did a terrible thing. They put a light stand with three legs right across the doorway where he was supposed to come in, and he tripped and of course it was hysterically funny. He didn't hurt himself, but it was just one of those ridiculous things that destroyed the take, and all of a sudden Mankiewicz said, 'I'm not going to shoot this scene. I don't think it works.' I also think that's what the crew was trying to say, because I didn't like the scene either. I thought that Karen was too smart to confront Lloyd about what he was doing. Once a guy's headed in the wrong direction like that, conversation's not going to help!"

For her part, Marilyn was initially signed to do a week's work for $500. However, she ended up spending a month shooting her few scenes, including that inside the lobby of the Curran Theatre in San Francisco, just a couple of blocks away from Union Square, where Addison DeWitt advises Miss Caswell that, having failed her big stage audition, her "next move should be towards television." When Caswell asks whether there are auditions for television, DeWitt responds, "That's all television is, my dear. Nothing but auditions."

Miss Caswell is a calculating yet basically dumb blonde, a successor to Angela Phinlay and a forerunner of the numerous other bimbos whom Marilyn would portray during the coming years. Nevertheless, she acquitted herself admirably in the role and managed to attract the attention of Zanuck and some notable critics.

In production from April to August of 1950, *All About Eve* opened to rave reviews, was nominated for 11 Oscars, and, in a year when it was competing with the likes of *Sunset Boulevard* and *Born Yesterday,* won six of them: for Best Picture, Best Director, Best Screenplay, Best Supporting Actor (George Sanders), Best Sound Recording and Best Black-and-White Costume Design.

The Critics' Views

"Dialog is scintillating, characters showy and even extraordinary, direction well nigh perfect and production as fine as anything 20th-Fox has turned out in years. All this adds up to a film which any studio might well be proud of. . . . Bette Davis and Anne Baxter enact the two principal roles. . . . Likewise standouts are Thelma Ritter, Marilyn Monroe and Barbara Bates, in smaller but most effective parts."

DAILY VARIETY

"This flavor of realism—of true life in which tragedy and comedy are not exaggerated beyond acceptable proportions—is the point that makes *All About Eve* such a distinguished motion picture. . . . Marilyn Monroe's chorine is right out of Esquire and grand."

HOLLYWOOD REPORTER

Public Reaction

Costing $1.4 million to film, *All About Eve* earned back $2.9 million during its initial run. Billed as "The most provocative picture of the year!" it also bore the tagline "It's all about women, and their men," yet it was clearly about a lot more than that and is still recognized as a pinnacle of cinematic achievement. Incidentally, in 1971 Anne Baxter would replace Lauren Bacall in the Broadway production of *Applause,* the musical based on *All About Eve,* ironically assuming the role of her film character's rival, Margo Channing.

Screen Test #3: Cold Shoulder

Twentieth Century-Fox
1950
Black & White

Having listened to Johnny Hyde's ongoing promotion of Marilyn, and after being suitably impressed by what he saw of her when viewing rushes of *All About Eve*, Darryl Zanuck agreed to screen-test his former contract player for a movie titled *Cold Shoulder*, scheduled to costar Victor Mature and Richard Conte.

Marilyn had three days in which to prepare with Natasha Lytess for her role as a gangster's moll opposite tough guy Conte, and when the big moment arrived she donned the same tight sweater-dress that she had already put to good use in *The Fireball* and *All About Eve*. According to Richard Conte's later recollection, Marilyn was fully focused when they filmed the test. However, she was also contending with a fairly cliché-ridden script.

The setting is a living room, where Benny is agitated by his girlfriend's surprise visit. Sitting on a couch while she stands in front of a fireplace, he asks her why she has dropped by.

Girl: To tell you, you can't stay here. If those gorillas find you here, what happens to them? [She motions towards a closed door, behind which there are presumably some

"Go ahead! It won't be the first time I've been worked over today!" Marilyn gives it all she's got in her screen test with Richard Conte.

other people.] Nothing? They're just gonna leave them alone? What's the matter with you, Benny? You can't take such a chance.

Benny [rising from the couch]: How did you find out about this?

Girl: Two guys came calling on me, looking for you!

Benny: Who were they?

Girl: I never saw them before.

Benny: Well, when did they come?

Girl: About four o'clock.

Benny [having crossed the room and peered through the curtains covering his front door window]: You dumb broad! You stupid little . . .

Girl: What's the matter?

Benny: They followed you here! Or did you bring them with you? I oughtta . . . [He is about to strike her with the back of his hand.]

Girl: Go ahead! It won't be the first time I've been worked over today! I'm getting used to it. [Benny puts on his jacket and gets ready to leave.] Where are you going? [She grabs his arm.] Benny . . .

Benny exits, leaving his girlfriend looking dejected and disconsolate. FADE.

In truth, while Richard Conte turns in his usual accomplished performance, Marilyn's is full of overstated melodramatics, not least when, with eyes closed, head bowed and suffering written all over her face, she tells the brute that she is "getting used to" being "worked over." Undoubtedly, MM was giving it her all.

"Star Role Goes to Newcomer Once Fired" announced the headline of a small syndicated article by leading Hollywood gossip columnist Louella O. Parsons, on July 18, 1950. "Marilyn Monroe, who packs the same punch Lana Turner did in her early days, gets her first starring role in *Cold Shoulder* with Vic Mature and Richard Conte. Marilyn, who hasn't a relative in the world and who was brought up in an orphanage, is one of the nicest girls in this town and everybody is plugging for her to succeed. She must be proud that she is clicking big in 20th, the studio which once let her go. Marilyn didn't have a big role in *Asphalt Jungle,* but what she did was so punchy that 20th brought her back home at many times what she had received before. I'm told she is excellent in *All About Eve,* which is whispered to be a honey."

Parsons concluded by saying that George Jessel would be producing *Cold Shoulder,* yet that never happened because Darryl Zanuck—possibly as a result of watching the test—shelved plans to make the movie. Conversely, it has been suggested that the test helped secure a long-term contract for Marilyn with Twentieth Century-Fox, but this is doubtful. More likely it was her good performances in *The Asphalt Jungle* and *All About Eve,* together with Johnny Hyde's continued overtures, that ultimately helped swing the deal.

The Television Advertisement: Royal Triton Gasoline

From her first days as a model through to the early years of her stardom, Marilyn appeared in numerous newspaper and magazine advertisements, promoting everything from clothing, makeup, shampoo, and suntan lotion, to beer, cigars, and diet pills. However, the only TV commercial that she is known to have made was one for the Union Oil Company of California, endorsing Royal Triton Gasoline.

Filmed at a time when Marilyn was already raising her visibility courtesy of appearances in *The Asphalt Jungle, All About Eve* and, to a much lesser extent, *The Fireball* and *Right Cross*, the Royal Triton ad was screened during the 1950–51 season and managed to turn the routine of filling a car's tank into a somewhat sensuous experience.

"This is the first car I ever owned," Marilyn tells the men who have just pushed her vehicle into a gas station. "I call it Cynthia. She's going to have the best care a car ever had." This is all well and good, seeing as said car has been allowed to conk out. Still, in her most suggestive manner, the nubile owner orders the pump attendant to "Put Royal Triton in Cynthia's little tummy," before looking straight into the camera and, with a trademark lowering of the upper lip, informing viewers that "Cynthia will just love that Royal Triton!"

Never a great fan of the small screen, and nervous about making a fool of herself on live television or in front of a studio audience, Marilyn would only make two more official TV appearances during her lifetime. After all, at a time when television was making huge inroads into the once-dominant movie market, it was stars such as Marilyn Monroe—in addition to wide-screen processes and gimmicks such as 3-D and Smell-O-Vision—who would lead Hollywood's desperate attempt to regain lost viewers throughout the 1950s and early 1960s.

> The Union Oil Company of California
> 1950
> Black & White

"Cynthia will just love that Royal Triton!"

Right Cross

The Plot

Ailing elderly boxing promoter Sean O'Malley is frustrated that his daughter Pat now takes care of his work, and that rival promoter Allan Goff is trying to steal away his only champion fighter, Johnny Monterez. Pat is in love with Johnny and she promises to deal with the troubling situation, but when Johnny injures his right hand in training, a doctor asserts that the fragile hand could give up on him at any time.

Cynical because of the discrimination that he and his fellow Mexicans have endured in the U.S., Johnny is also concerned about being financially secure enough to marry Pat and support his relatives. He therefore decides to conceal the truth about his hand and align himself with the hugely successful Allan Goff, who is also offering him a ten-year post-retirement deal to work for the Goff Organization. At the same time, Johnny puts his title on the line in order to help Sean O'Malley sell more tickets for the fight that he has already lined up, but when the old man learns that his sole financial asset is defecting to the Goff camp, he suffers a fatal heart attack.

While Pat blames Johnny for this, the champ's best friend, sports reporter Rick Gavery, is tipped off about a flaw in Johnny's boxing style and he informs him about it. Unfortunately, Johnny is unable to correct the problem and he loses the defense of his title. Rick tries to reconcile Johnny with Pat, despite being in love with her himself, but he has a fight with the fallen champ and is floored by a perfect right cross that also breaks Johnny's hand. His career clearly over, Johnny nevertheless patches up his differences with Pat and Rick when they learn about his honorable intentions. At long last, Johnny asks Pat to marry him and she gladly accepts.

Behind-the-Scenes Facts & Opinions

A well acted, solidly directed prizefighting drama, *Right Cross* was originally titled *The Big Money* when writer Charles Schnee submitted his story to MGM on February 22, 1949. The name change would take place in October of that year. In the meantime, according to the first complete script submitted on May 15, the classy enchantress who would be played by Marilyn was "a lovely redhead model" known simply as Dusky, and she also had a far more substantial part than the one which eventually earned MM no on-screen billing.

The Rick Gavery character who chats to Dusky at Hoop's nightclub was originally called Danny Malone, and in addition to the segment in the movie where he tries to convince a skeptical Dusky to accompany him home for some spaghetti, salad, and a bottle of red wine, there were also a couple of follow-up scenes. In the finished film, just as Dusky appears to be falling for his smooth patter, Rick has to leave the club with Johnny. "We'll meet again, I know," he assures her, only to receive a handwritten snub from Dusky on a subsequent visit. However, in the first-draft script, the two make a date for the following night, Danny (Rick) stands her up, and although Dusky is upset, she leaves him her telephone number.

Later on, this same script contains a scene in Danny's apartment that opens with Dusky standing before a mirror, eyes closed, while the roving-eye reporter clasps a necklace—described as "Woolworth inside a Tiffany box"—around her neck. Dusky says it is beautiful, but just as she and Danny start to kiss, he takes a phone call and again says he has to leave. "The Great Torchbearer!" exclaims Dusky. "They ought to call you Little Houdini! Always disappearing!"

Nevertheless, in a final scene outside a police station that also features Johnny and Kit (the original name for Pat), Danny notices Dusky walking up the street and he chases after her. Through the rear window of a car, Johnny and Kit see Dusky swing a hatbox and catch Danny full in the face. Yet, as she walks on, he persists with the smooth talk and takes her arm, and the two of them end up strolling dreamily together, Dusky's head on Danny's shoulder. Johnny and Kit then turn to the camera, obscuring its view of Danny and Dusky. They grin, Johnny takes Kit in his arms, and they kiss. FADE. THE END.

In the June 22, 1949, revised script, Dusky Jones interacts with Rick Morgan, and while their first two scenes together remain intact, the film ends with Rick setting off for a night-club on his own. An October 14 script then eliminates the second scene with Dusky, and has Rick giving the necklace to Pat O'Malley, while in the January 9, 1950, shooting script and August 3, 1950, continuity script, the Dick Powell and Marilyn Monroe characters are known as Rick Gavery and Dusky Ledue (not Ledoux as stated in other books).

Following her mini-triumph in *The Asphalt Jungle, Right Cross* was the second of three films that Marilyn would make for MGM. It was released five weeks after *The Fireball,* yet by all accounts neither did anything for her but earn a little extra money while *All About Eve* was opening Darryl Zanuck's eyes.

The Critics' Views

"Montalban and Miss Allyson do a great deal of kissing while Powell, her real-life hus-band, looks on stoically. He has more patience than a lot of us, perhaps because he is playing a sports writer. Those sports writers!"

Los Angeles Times

"John Sturges directed with neat balance between love-making and leather-pushing, for smooth continuity. The characters come alive. A thin thread of racial conflict seems superfluous. . . . *Right Cross* doesn't let down in action or heart appeal. It depicts some backstage skullduggery with realism. The fight sequences are thrilling and convincing."

New York Daily Mirror

"If you're a good girl I'll teach you the recipe," says Rick Gavery, inviting Dusky Ledue back to his place for some home-cooked spaghetti. "I know the ingredients," she replies.

Home Town Story

HOME TOWN STORY

★★

A Metro Goldwyn-Mayer Release
Produced by John K. Ford and Arthur Pierson
Written and Directed by Arthur Pierson
Cinematography by Lucien Andriot
Sound by William Randall
Art Direction by Hilyard Brown
Music by Louis Forbes
Edited by William Claxton
Released: July 18, 1951
Running Time: 61 minutes
Black & White

CAST

Blake Washburn	Jeffrey Lynn
John MacFarland	Donald Crisp
Janice Hunt	Marjorie Reynolds
Slim Haskins	Alan Hale, Jr.
Iris Martin	Marilyn Monroe
Mrs. Washburn	Barbara Brown
Katie Washburn	Melinda Plowman
Taxi Driver	Renny McEvoy
Kenlock	Glenn Tryon
Berny Miles	Byron Foulger
Uncle Cliff	Griff Barnett
Phoebe Hartman	Virginia Campbell
Andy Butterworth	Harry Harvey
Dr. Johnson	Nelson Leigh
Motorcycle Officer	Speck Noblitt

Uncredited:

(Bit Part)	Dorothy Adams
(Bit Part)	Joseph Crehan

The Plot

Returning to his Midwestern home town after failing to gain reelection to the State Senate, Blake Washburn is bitter over the way that people were "hoodwinked into voting for Bob MacFarland." Consequently, when he resumes his old job as editor of his Uncle Griff's local newspaper, the *Fairfax Herald,* Blake proceeds to use it as a tool to court personal popularity with the voters in the run-up to the next election.

Launching an editorial campaign against big businesses, he investigates the firm owned by the father of Senator MacFarland to see if it is polluting the local river. Then, when this comes to nothing, he focuses his attention on certain companies' excessive profits. However, even though Blake's front-page articles prompt a rise in the newspaper's circulation, they also alienate both his staff and his longtime fiancée Janice Hunt, who advises the wayward editor that he was only ever elected to the Senate because he was a war hero, and that his recent defeat was due to the voters realizing they had made a mistake. To make matters worse, Janice no longer wants to marry Blake, and he then gets into a fight with reporter friend Slim Haskins just as Senator Bob MacFarland's father pays him a visit.

John MacFarland advances his theory that successful companies make large profits for their customers, by providing goods and services that are of value to everyone. Blake doesn't want to know about this, but he is persuaded otherwise after his kid sister Katie is trapped and critically injured in a mine-shaft accident during a school trip to Copper Hill. John MacFarland arrives at the scene with his company's doctor, and after a bulldozer reopens the entry to the collapsed shaft, Katie is driven away in a private ambulance and then rushed to hospital in MacFarland's own plane. On board she receives oxygen from tanks supplied by yet another commercial enterprise, while at the hospital there just happens to be equipment that is powered by MacFarland motors. Following emergency surgery, Katie pulls through, and a grateful and humbled Blake patches up his differences with Slim, starts writing an article that advances John Mac-Farland's more compassionate theory about big businesses, and has his offer of marriage accepted by Janice.

Behind-the-Scenes Facts & Opinions

Financed by General Motors as a means of promoting the free enterprise system and how it benefits the American way of life, *Home Town Story* was acquired by MGM for theatrical release but received virtually no promotion and was instead exhibited at industrial and educational institutions. Nevertheless, some of those who participated in its making were evidently not aware of the picture's raison d'etre.

"I should have learned to read my scripts," Jeffrey Lynn told me in 1994. "I had no idea of the source, and it was only when I learned a while ago that the film was financed by General Motors that I saw it in a new light. Of course, it did contain a little more politicizing than I was used to, but nobody told me anything about it and I didn't look into it at all. I mean, I wasn't against the film's message, but I was against making it and not releasing it. . . . None of us were making very much money, but I suppose we were happy to be working, so we didn't care if General Motors or whoever was paying us."

John K. Ford, head of GM's film division, actually visited Hollywood to supervise production of the movie at the Hal Roach studio in late 1950, where an accomplished cast and crew assembled under the direction of Arthur Pierson, the same man who had helmed Marilyn's second movie, *Dangerous Years*, three years earlier. The result is a B-movie with decent production values and competent performances by the likes of Lynn, Donald Crisp, and Alan Hale, Jr., yet aside from a good action sequence when the mine shaft collapses, *Home Town Story* is nothing but a simplistic propaganda film that relentlessly hammers away at its main message: big business is GOOD, liberal views are BAD.

Subtlety is not the order of the day here, either in terms of Pierson's script and direction or in the appearance of Marilyn Monroe as Iris Martin, the sexy secretary at the offices of the *Fairfax Herald*. Looking as if she has been vacuum-packed into her outfits, including her own sweater dress that she had already worn in *The Fireball, All About Eve,* and the *Cold Shoulder* screen test, MM calls to mind a critic's description of Mamie Van Doren in *High School Confidential* looking like she'd been "shot in the back by a couple of cruise missiles."

Jeffrey Lynn gets an eyeful of the sweater dress that Marilyn had already worn in The Fireball, All About Eve, *and the* Cold Shoulder *screen test.*

"How long do you have to work around here before you stop calling me Mr. Haskins?" Slim asks invitingly. "I always treat men with respect," is Iris's cool reply. "Then they treat me with respect, Mr. Haskins."

Marilyn walks seductively, she talks seductively, and while her acting is forced to say the least, she's undeniably the best reason for watching *Home Town Story.* Then again, it also shows her at an exciting point in her life, for it was during the making of this film that Johnny Hyde's protegée was informed that he had secured her a contract agreement with Twentieth Century-Fox.

"One morning she came running on the set, dancing with the spirit of youth, saying, 'I've got it, I've got it, I've got it,'" Jeffrey Lynn was still able to recall more than 40 years later. "To me, Marilyn was a bubbly sort of person who liked to talk about herself to other people, and who appreciated it when other people were kind to her. Of course, she was just a starlet, and I guess I wasn't too far along myself, but between takes she'd tell me the story of her life. She was very personable and told me about her relationship with her agent, who was madly in love with her and very sick. She told me that she'd seen him the night before and he'd asked her to marry him, but she said, 'No, let's wait until you get well.' He never came on the set, but she was most sincere and I believed her completely."

Given Marilyn's aforementioned physical presence, it's hardly surprising that she was the only cast member to be pictured in the print ad that found its way into a few local papers. On the other hand, the original trailer for *Home Town Story* featured a *Fairfax Herald* front page with a couple of main-character photos that came to life. One of these comprised a Marilyn scene with Alan Hale, Jr., in which the latter asks, "How long do you have to work around here before you stop calling me Mr. Haskins?" "I always treat men with respect. Then they treat me with respect, Mr. Haskins," is the secretary's breathy reply, to which the reporter quips, "Is that a proven theory or something you're just trying out?"

With a chat-up line like that, it's no wonder that Hale ended up on *Gilligan's Island.*

The Critics' Views

"While film handily approaches subject and is well enough made, it is questionable as theatrical entertainment. . . . Marilyn Monroe is standout as secretary."

DAILY VARIETY

"The supporting performances of Alan Hale, Jr., Marilyn Monroe and Barbara Brown are noteworthy, but Melinda Plowman, the precocious moppet in the piece, suffers from bad dialogue direction, her loud, shrill delivery piercing the eardrums like bullets."

HOLLYWOOD REPORTER

"Lynn suffers from the stuffed-shirt, chip-on-the-shoulder character given him in the Pierson screenplay . . . Marilyn Monroe, Barbara Brown and Griff Barnett are up to script demands."

WEEKLY VARIETY

Public Reaction

Bankrolled by General Motors to the tune of just $200,000, *Home Town Story* was the third and final of Marilyn Monroe's movies for MGM. Released after she had already signed a long-term deal with Twentieth Century-Fox, it didn't prompt much public reaction and disappeared without a whimper, only to turn up in Australia of all places when it was revived there following Marilyn's death in 1962.

The Fox Playmate: 1951-1952

DESPITE BEING DEPRESSED over the death of Johnny Hyde, Marilyn did have a lot to look forward to at the start of 1951. With a Twentieth Century-Fox contract pending, she enjoyed the novel prospect of regular film work and thus a regular paycheck, while her supporting role in *As Young As You Feel* would earn her above-the-title billing for the first time.

May 11, 1951, was the effective commencement date of Marilyn's standard seven-year deal with Fox, guaranteeing her an income for 40 weeks of each 52-week period, regardless of whether or not she was actually working. During the first year her salary would be $500 per week, rising to $750 in the second, $1,250 in the third, $1,500 in the fourth, $2,000 in the fifth, $2,500 in the sixth, and $3,500 in the seventh and final year.

> *"I think cheesecake helps call attention to you. Then you can follow through and prove yourself."*
> MARILYN MONROE, 1951.

Neverthless, everything was slanted in the studio's favor. At the end of each year, it was the studio's right to renew or decline the option on Marilyn's contract. She could not work for another studio unless Fox decided to loan her out, and in such cases the profit would go to Fox while Marilyn would just receive her basic salary. At the same time, she was not permitted to earn money from any other source—such as TV, radio, recordings, or the theater—unless Fox gave her the go-ahead, yet if Marilyn ever refused to accept a role that had been allocated to her, she could be suspended without pay, and then have the length of that suspension added to the term of her contract. These were the standard rules, designed by the studios, for the studios, and endured by most contract players over the course of several decades.

Eventually, Marilyn would be among a handful of employees to take on the studio system and help initiate its demise, yet back in 1951 she was grateful for the security offered by her new contract, and hopeful that being assigned a succession of cheesecake roles was all part of a Fox plan to turn her into a star. The evidence in this regard is mixed.

On the one hand, there's the somewhat apocryphal story that Darryl Zanuck was only persuaded to sign Marilyn to a long-term deal after she made a splashy entrance at an exhibitors' party thrown by the studio in April of 1951. Held at the Café de Paris (commonly known as the Twentieth Century-Fox commissary), the party was attended by a variety of studio bigwigs and stars such as Anne Baxter, Susan Hayward, Gregory Peck, Tyrone Power, and June Haver. True to form, bit-part player Marilyn turned up an hour and a half late, yet in her strapless black cocktail gown she immediately attracted all eyes, including those of Fox President Spyros Skouras—once described by director Billy Wilder as "the only Greek tragedy I know"—who took the starlet by the arm and sat her down beside him at the top table.

Venus in a bathing suit—on location in Monterey during the 1952 shoot of Clash by Night *for RKO.*

"If the exhibitors like her, the public likes her," Skouras reportedly told Zanuck, prompting the reluctant production chief to immediately arrange a seven-year contract for the actress. However, this version of events is undermined by the fact that the studio had already submitted a contract to Marilyn's representatives at the William Morris Agency several weeks earlier. The reason for the delay in its signing remains unclear, but it could have been due to an unusual provision that Marilyn was demanding and that she ultimately succeeded in obtaining: Natasha Lytess was to be placed on the Fox payroll and employed as her drama coach.

Accordingly, while it is no secret that Darryl Zanuck didn't rate Marilyn much as an actress—he never would—it is clear that he did spot her box office potential, probably dating back to when he saw the rushes of *All About Eve* the previous year. By October of 1950 she had already been cast in *As Young As You Feel,* and by late December an eye-catching support role was being contrived for Marilyn in another of Fox's lightweight comedies, *The Reluctant Landlord.* (The film was retitled *A WAC In His Life* when shooting commenced in April of 1951, at around the time of the aforementioned exhibitors' party, but it would eventually be released as *Love Nest.*)

Therefore, even though Skouras probably told Zanuck to expedite the contract issue as quickly as possible, the production chief had already committed to signing Marilyn and exploiting what he evidently considered to be her greatest asset: her physical appeal.

"I remember when she came back to Fox, she wanted to play Grushenka in *The Brothers Karamazov,* and she should have," Jean Peters recalled. "She really would have been wonderful, but at that time nobody could see beyond the blonde with the plunging neckline."

Unfortunately, Marilyn didn't always help her own cause in this regard. Max Showalter, like Jean Peters, appeared with her in *Niagara,* and he recounted how MM arrived on location carrying a bundle of books. "One of them was *The Brothers Karamazov,* and she said, 'Have you ever read this?' I said, 'Yes,' and she said, 'Well, why don't you just tell me what it's all about? Then I won't have to read it.' I said, 'No, you read it! It'll be good for you to read it.'"

Nevertheless, contrary to popular opinion and the assertions of numerous biographers, Darryl Zanuck was initially willing to allow Marilyn to prove her talents as a dramatic actress. Sure, in 1951 the sum total of her work assignments for the studio consituted adding sex to the mix of three lightweight comedies—*As Young As You Feel, Love Nest* and *Let's Make It Legal*—yet in the same year she was also being slated for the lead role in a psychological thriller titled *Night Without Sleep* (released as *Don't Bother to Knock*). The fact that Marilyn still had to test for the part before landing it simply indicates that Zanuck wanted to make sure she was ready for the challenge.

"In those days they used to test everything before you got into a film," Jean Peters explained, "and Darryl would spend all night working and reviewing every test. He knew every piece of wardrobe, the makeup, the hair, everything, and he would sit in that projection room with his production people and keep them there until five in the morning."

While Marilyn's performance in *Don't Bother to Knock* would struggle to rise above the limitations of a mediocre movie, there could be no denying her dedication to her craft. By late 1951 she was augmenting the teachings of drama coach Natasha Lytess with private tutorings from Michael Chekhov, trying to absorb the physical and motivational techniques that Chekhov had practiced as a colleague of Konstantin Stanislavsky at the Moscow Art Theatre. Her success in this regard is open to question, but such application singled Marilyn out from the crowd of contract players then at Fox. Then again, she was also fairly unique in various other ways.

"She was only making $500 a week, but she enjoyed a remarkable position because she could come in at any bloody time she wished," noted David Wayne, who appeared with

▶▶ Won't he take the hint? Marilyn with Joseph Cotten in a contrived publicity shot for Niagara, *the film that catapulted her to stardom.*

Marilyn in four movies—more than any other actor—between 1951 and 1953. "I mean, all of the studio personnel were alerted that no matter what time Marilyn came in, nobody was to bark at her or ask her where she had been, and the reason for that was that Joe Schenck, who owned Twentieth Century-Fox, was head-over-heels in love with Marilyn."

The major reason for Marilyn's chronic lateness was her distinct lack of self-confidence, which paradoxically increased along with her success. For, as more important roles placed greater responsibility on her shoulders, and as the Method acting lessons of future years encouraged her to try to assume the inner motivations of the characters she was portraying, she became more paranoid about failure and was often petrified of stepping in front of the camera. Unfortunately, the power that she enjoyed courtesy of contacts such as Schenck only catered to Marilyn's insecurities, giving her the easy option of delaying what she was required to do throughout much of her career; indeed, as the years wore on, she would sometimes not even show up on the set at all. It was a bad habit that she was allowed to indulge right from the start, with highly disruptive—and ultimately destructive—personal consequences. The fact that Marilyn chose to fudge the issue didn't help matters.

"When we were filming *As Young As You Feel*, I was a little pissed off having to wait every day," David Wayne recalled. "One time I said to her, 'Marilyn, I know you have carte blanche to come in anytime you please, and I don't mind, but is there a reason?' and she said, 'Yes, I often have to stay up and comfort Mr. Schenck.' I said, 'Well, I doubt the old bastard can fuck,' and she said, 'I guess not, because he's never bothered me that way.' That's from the horse's mouth. . . . I liked her enormously as just a very nice girl. She wasn't very bright, and in those days she was a piss-poor actress, but she was so protected."

What's more, after she started going out with baseball great Joe DiMaggio in early 1952, and was then confirmed as the nude figure appearing on calendars around the nation (thanks to Tom Kelley having licensed the photos that he'd taken of her three years earlier), Marilyn Monroe also became big news. Before long, idle interest in her evolved into major attention from the public and the critics alike, as evidenced by her appearance on the cover of publications such as *Life* magazine, a weekly mailbag of 5,000 fan letters, and reviewers' descriptions of her as "the box-office delight," "the new blonde bombshell of Hollywood," and "Miss Pash-pie of 1952."

In the summer and fall of 1952, Marilyn appeared in no fewer than five films in the space of just three and a half months; the first of them, *Clash By Night*, was made via Marilyn's loan-out to RKO. All of the breaks were coming her way, and the momentum that was pushing her towards stardom was now accelerating and would soon be irreversible, for as David Wayne observed, "She was being groomed to take over the top spot from Betty Grable, no doubt about it."

The movie that went a long way towards achieving that aim was *Niagara*, which Marilyn began filming on June 6, 1952, just five days after being informed that she had been awarded the costarring role in *Gentlemen Prefer Blondes*—the picture that would truly put her career over the top. Grable had wanted the part of Lorelei Lee, Marilyn got it, yet in so doing she would soon discover that she had boxed herself into a corner of Darryl Zanuck's making. Stardom was about to be hers, but her struggles were far from over.

Supported by MM and Albert Dekker (far right), Monty Woolley (standing) gives an engaging performance as a forced-retiree who wants to get his job back.

Wilson, president of General Motors. There again, the circumstances are also slightly different, with John Hodges making a speech that "resulted in a small stock market and saved the country . . . [and] the whole world, therefore, from what the economic experts all predicted as a devastating depression." Furthermore, the speech convinced the United Automobile Workers union to call off industrial action on June 5, 1948, "the 18th day of their famous strike."

When Lamar Trotti submitted his first treatment of *The Great American Hoax* on June 23, 1950, Thelma Ritter was already considered to be "ideal" for the part of Della Hodges, while other recommendations were for Louis Calhern in the role of Louis McKinley, and for Elisha Cook, Jr. as personnel manager Frank Erickson. The first treatment opens with a theater scene that is not in Chayefsky's story, and it is interesting to note that while this was used for one of the movie's publicity stills, featuring Jean Peters and David Wayne in the foreground, with Marilyn sitting in the row behind, the finished film contains the same scene with Peters and Wayne in different clothes and Marilyn nowhere to be seen. Still, both Peters and Wayne recalled shooting the version in which Marilyn was present.

"We shot that down at the Western Avenue studio of Twentieth Century-Fox, where they had a complete theater," David Wayne said in 1993. "They loaded the set with extras, and that was the first time I realized Marilyn had some power, although I didn't understand why. All of the extras and all of us so-called stars waited and waited and waited the whole morning, and I asked, 'Who are we waiting for?' The assistant director said, 'It doesn't matter. Just sit tight.' Anyway, after we'd all broken for lunch and come back, in she finally came, this very pretty young girl. She didn't have one line, but they told her where to sit, and I said, 'You mean to tell me that we have waited all this time for an extra?' So, we went ahead and shot the scene, and then I realized that something was going on which I didn't know about; this girl had a little power going for her."

Lamar Trotti's first draft continuity script was submitted on October 11, 1950, and as a result of a conference that took place between Darryl Zanuck, Trotti, and Harmon Jones on October 17, the title of the movie was changed to *Will You Love Me in December?*. Monty Woolley, Albert Dekker, and David Wayne were now pegged for the roles that they would play in the film, while other casting suggestions were for Myrna Loy as Lucille McKinley, Barbara Bates as Alice Hodges, and Leon Ames as her father George.

Marilyn Monroe was also confirmed in the part of McKinley's sensuous and plainly-not-dumb secretary, Harriet. "One look at her and we just know that monkey business is going on," noted Zanuck's assistant Molly Mandaville. "In other words, she's quite a gal—and I'm going to watch her like a hawk to see how she does it!"

It was obviously no coincidence that, once Marilyn was cast, the role of Harriet was instantly beefed up. Zanuck had clearly been impressed by her performance in *All About Eve*, and, with Johnny Hyde's encouragement, he was going to start raising her profile with the goal bringing her into the Fox fold. Consequently, at the October 17 script conference, it was suggested that Harriet should appear in the scene where McKinley, his wife, and the fake GM President are at a club. When McKinley spots Harriet entering with another man, he looks miffed, she flees, and the Acme boss leaves soon afterward, implying that they are having an affair. This was duly inserted into the October 27 script, yet at another conference on November 1, Zanuck still felt compelled to tell his writer, "If you can add anything to Harriet's character, please do so." As David Wayne said, this girl had a little power going for her.

The role of Alice, meanwhile, was still up for grabs. "Please see to it that Mitzi Gaynor wears her hair as she did in *My Blue Heaven*," Zanuck stated at the November 1 conference. The eventual outcome would be Jean Peters sporting a short, permed hairdo.

Will You Love Me in December? was retitled *As Young As You Feel* prior to the film's release. At the time of that release, a publicity handout alluding to Marilyn explained that "the azure-eyed, honey-tressed actress with the most provocative chassis to reach the screen since Jean Harlow, has five wardrobe changes—each a sweater of a different type . . . described by the costuming department as: 1. Loose fitting 2. Draping 3. Clinging 4. Tight 5. Gee whizz!!!"

Incidentally, McKinley's teenage son, Willie, was portrayed in the film by Rusty (later Russ) Tamblyn, while the Roger Moore credited in the tiny role of Saltonstall was *not* the same actor who would later star as James Bond, but, rather, a mostly uncredited veteran of more than 30 films (including *Let's Make It Legal*) made between 1937 and 1953.

The Critics' Views

"This unpretentious little picture, which Lamar Trotti has written and produced and which Harmon Jones has directed in a deliciously nimble comic style, is a vastly superior entertainment so far as ingenuity and taste are concerned, and it certainly confronts its audience on a much more appropriately adult plane. . . . Albert Dekker is might amusing as a fatheaded small-business boss, Marilyn Monroe is superb as his secretary. . . ."

NEW YORK TIMES

"Cast and story set amusing situations, but neither explosive nor frequent enough. . . . Curvy Marilyn Monroe is a secretary."

NEW YORK DAILY MIRROR

Love Nest

LOVE NEST

★★½

A Twentieth Century-Fox Release
Produced by Jules Buck
Directed by Joseph Newman
Screenplay by I. A .L. Diamond
Based on a novel by Scott Corbett
Cinematography by Lloyd Ahern
Sound by Bernard Freericks and Harry M.
Leonard
Art Direction by Lyle Wheeler and George L.
Patrick
Music by Cyril Mockridge
Costume Design by Renie
Edited by J. Watson Webb, Jr.
Released: November 14, 1951
Running Time: 84 minutes
Black & White

CAST

Connie Scott	June Haver
Jim Scott	William Lundigan
Charley Patterson	Frank Fay
Roberta Stevens	Marilyn Monroe
Ed Forbes	Jack Paar
Eadie Gaynor	Leatrice Joy
George Thompson	Henry Kulky
Mrs. Quig	Marie Blake
Florence	Patricia Miller
Mrs. Arnold	Maude Wallace
Mr. Hansen	Joe Ploski
Mrs. Thompson	Martha Wentworth
Mrs. Frazier	Faire Binney
Mrs. McNab	Caryl Lincoln
Mr. McNab	Michael Ross
Mr. Fain	Bob Jellison
Postman	John Costello
Mr. Knowland	Charles Calvert
Detective Donovan	Leo Clary
Mr. Clark	Jack Daly
Mr. Gray	Ray Montgomery
Mrs. Braddock	Florence Auer
Mrs. Engstrand	Edna Holland
Mrs. Healy	Liz Slifer
Glazier	Alvin Hammer

Uncredited:

Wine Steward	Tony De Mario

The Plot

After two and a half years of military service in Paris, aspiring novelist Jim Scott returns to New York and the rundown Gramercy Park brownstone that his wife Connie has purchased with most of their savings. The rooming house is mortgaged to the hilt and, despite the revenue from tenants, the couple are running at a loss, yet Connie assures Jim that it is a great investment that will soon pay for itself. Living in the basement, they suffer noises from the drainpipes and the local fire service, and Jim has little time to write while dealing with the tenants' complaints and his wife's jealousy over one of the new people paying them rent, ex-WAC Roberta "Bobbie" Stevens—a buxom blonde who was stationed with Jim in Paris.

Another new tenant, meanwhile, is Charley Patterson, a dapper con man who swindles rich widows out of their money. Connie strongly suspects what Charley is up to, and she is therefore concerned when he woos and marries Eadie, a kindly widow living in the same building. Still, Connie and Jim also have their own problems to think about, not the least of which is the news that their building must either be rewired or condemned. Unable to afford the $800 that the work would cost, Jim insists on selling the property before Charley comes to the rescue by handing over the money and telling the young couple to consider it a year's rent in advance. The police soon catch up with Charley, however, and after he goes to jail, Jim joins him there. Charley has told the authorities that the $800 he paid Jim was hush money, yet this is really just another of the trickster's money-making ploys. In truth, he has been offered $5,000 by a newspaper syndicate for a series of articles on his career, and he wants Jim to be the writer in exchange for half of the fee, while the other half will help the ever-faithful Eadie to subsist until his release.

After recounting his memoirs, Charley then recants his story about the $800, Jim is freed, and the result is a best-selling book entitled *My Life and Loves*. Eighteen months later, Charley returns home to the building that Jim and Connie have totally renovated, and Eadie surprises everyone by giving birth to twins.

Behind-the-Scenes Facts & Opinions

Thin on plot and slight in terms of genuine laughs, *Love Nest* is a pleasant enough way to kill some time, but is little else. While most of the cast members conform to type— June Haver as a sweet but headstrong young wife, William Lundigan as an insipid nice-guy, Marilyn Monroe as a sexy adornment—a pair of more seasoned performers, each in his/her last film, adds some unconventionality to the proceedings: as a suave con man, veteran comedian Frank Fay has an endearingly offbeat demeanor, while 1920s silent film star Leatrice Joy, at the age of 58, nearly steals the show when her character gives birth to twins!

Unimaginatively titled *The Reluctant Landlord* when I. A. L. Diamond began work on the screenplay in December, 1950, it was renamed *A WAC In His Life* when shooting began on April 18, 1951, illustrating how the studio wanted to draw attention to Marilyn's role. The only problem was her lack of screen time; thus the change to *Love Nest*.

As early as December 21, 1950, Darryl Zanuck suggested in a memo to producer Jules Buck, I. A. L. Diamond and Zanuck's assistant Molly Mandaville that they "work Roberta into the last part of the story more," and innocently involve her with Jim after he has a row with Connie and uses Roberta's empty apartment to sleep in a hammock (!). This was incorporated into Diamond's January 9, 1951 "Final Script," and then embellished during another conference on February 7.

When Jim wakes up in the morning, Roberta has reentered her apartment and is in the shower, prompting him to come to his senses because "perhaps it is the kind of shower which reveals the top of Roberta's head—or which reveals something so that Jim realizes it is Roberta in the shower." In the finished film, that something is a shapely leg. Meanwhile, as noted by Molly Mandaville to Jules Buck, director Joseph Newman, Izzy Diamond, and various others working on the movie, "Jim comes tiptoe-ing out just like any philandering husband—*you* know, boys!"

In a party scene that was cut from the movie, Marilyn is seated next to future Tonight Show *host Jack Paar, while above her (l–r) are Frank Fay, 1920s silent film star Leatrice Joy in her last movie, and (fifth and sixth from left) June Haver and William Lundigan.*

Naturally, the brief shower scene was used to maximum promotional effect, appearing in *Love Nest*'s publicity trailer while columnist Sidney Skolsky reported that, during the scene's filming, the crowded set was so quiet "you could hear the electricity." Clearly, Fox believed Marilyn's box office value lay in her looks rather than her acting talent, and this was a view being shared increasingly by the press, the public, and even certain colleagues, including future talk show host, Jack Paar, who portrayed Marilyn's questionable love interest in the movie.

"Looking back, I guess I should have been excited, but I found her pretty tiresome," Paar would later recall. "She used to carry around books by Marcel Proust with their titles facing out, but I never saw her read one. She was always holding up shooting by talking on the phone. Judging from what's happened, though, I guess she had the right number."

The Critics' Views

"Smoocher Fay—and the shape of Marilyn Monroe—are, begging your pardon, the most arresting things. . . . William Lundigan and June Haver are the central couple in this 20th Century-Fox picture, at least insofar as the billing goes. (Fay and Marilyn take care of the cooing, though not to each other.)"

"Frank Fay romps off with honors as the wily middle-aged Romeo. Marilyn Monroe's shapely figure and blonde beauty make her part of the temptress a standout."

"*Love Nest* is a mild variety of comedy which gets a considerable boost from the expert talents—in that line—of Frank Fay. . . . Leatrice Joy is also present in this number. She gives mature warmth to the proceedings. Marilyn Monroe has that other quality."

Public Reaction

Billed as, "The screen's most heart-warming house-warming in years. . . . For everyone who ever built a stairway to the stars, and climbed it kiss by kiss," *Love Nest* cost $765,000 to make and has more than recouped this due to its reputation as one of

Demure during a hat test for the role of Roberta "Bobbie" Stevens, costarring an unidentified hand.

between Zanuck, Bassler and I. A. L. Diamond, and it was Diamond who then took credit for the "Second Revised Final" script of March 28, 1951 before Zanuck did just a little more tweaking—as per a memo of April 4, he altered the title to *Grandma Was a Gold digger*. This, however, didn't insinuate illicit sex (i.e., out of wedlock), and so *Let's Make It Legal* was the eventual choice, enabling the film's promotional trailer to announce, "It's 10% improper! It's 40% illegal! It's 100% hilarious!" while also advising viewers to "See blonde Marilyn Monroe, Miss Cheesecake herself."

There could be little doubt as to how the studio intended to utilize its new signing.

The Critics' Views

"The picture's cast includes two very engaging babies. One is a darling little tot who is as cute a kid as ever sat in a high chair. The other is Marilyn Monroe in a small but showy role. She's definitely not of the Pablum set."

L.A. Examiner

"Gorgeous Marilyn Monroe's in, flittingly. First time I've noticed her diction. It's execrable."

Los Angeles Times

"Claudette Colbert is a capable farceur, but she cannot make *Let's Make It Legal* as merry as it was hoped.... Marilyn Monroe parades her shapely chassis for incidental excitement."

New York Daily Mirror

"Marilyn Monroe is voluptuously amusing as a girl on a husband hunt."

Hollywood Reporter

Public Reaction

Following an outlay of $835,000, *Let's Make It Legal* brought in $1.25 million during its initial boxoffice run.

In her final scene, Joyce serves the drinks and provides the glamor at a men's poker party, just as Marilyn had done for Fox's head of production, Joe Schenck. Macdonald Carey is handing her the glass.

line, her timing and her conception of what a scene was about. I mean, on the set she'd constantly go up on her lines, and it was like acting with a child or an animal. Fritz would become quite impatient, and rightly so; it was just awful. However, Marilyn was very interesting; a calculated sex goddess. When I ran through scenes with her we'd go over them again and again, and occasionally she'd stand in front of me in a tight skirt and blouse with flouncing breasts, and she'd say, 'Do you think men like a little bit of a stomach curve here?' meaning between her crotch and her belly button, and I'd say, 'Well, yeah, that's a normal thing, Marilyn.' It was interesting how she worked at creating that whole persona. She was a very complex kind of a kid."

She was also a kid who knew how to dress, donning her own men's blue jeans for the film because a tighter fit around the hips would better show off her assets. "She was so cute, I adored her," recalled Michael Woulfe, who had spent a week designing a pair of jeans for Marilyn before she informed him of her preference. "If we were having lunch or walking on the lot together, she'd often say something that would break me up, and then she'd say, 'Did you think that was funny?' I'd say, 'Yes, of course,' to which she'd say, 'Why don't you tell Perry Lieber?' Perry Lieber was the head of the publicity department at RKO, and she was therefore telling me to repeat this to him so that he could get it in a newspaper column. She was very aware of every move she made."

As there was little need for any original designs, Michael Woulfe selected most of Marilyn's clothing from stock for *Clash By Night*, yet he would often be present on the set.

"Before filming a scene the actors would all rehearse," Woulfe recalled, "and then, when they were ready to shoot, Marilyn would specifically be asked if she knew what her action was, how she entered the room, who she crossed over to, and so on. She'd say, 'Yes, I come in and I cross over to Miss Barbara Stanwyck, and then to Robert Ryan and then to Paul Douglas, and then I stand here.' They'd say, 'Okay,' they'd check her makeup, and then they'd take a short break to get the lights set, during which Marilyn would dip her finger into a tiny bottle of vaseline that she had hidden nearby, and smear it on her cheekbones. You see, in the play the story takes place on Staten Island, and even when the locale switches to Northern California for the movie there is this thing about the terrible heat and the perspiration. However, when she'd get back on the set and they were ready to shoot, Fritz Lang would see through the finder that there was a sheen on her cheeks, and he'd clap his hands and scream for makeup, causing another delay while they would wipe it off.

"Afterwards, Marilyn would go through this whole thing again, reciting how she should walk, who she should cross over to, and so on. Well, finally at one of these rehearsals, when she said, 'I come in, I cross in front of Barbara, over to Robert Ryan and then over to Paul,' Paul Douglas exploded and said, 'Don't you forget, young lady, I am Mr. Paul Douglas to you!' That created quite a stir on the set, everyone was uncomfortable, again there was a delay, again Marilyn was able to smear the vaseline on her cheekbones, and again they saw it through the finder, but by this time the director was so fed up that he decided to go ahead and shoot the scene. That's why Marilyn's cheeks have a sheen in the movie, and she was right, because part of the story's plot is to do with the heat!"

Which is precisely what MM created prior to the movie's release, when the nude photos that Tom Kelley had taken of her back in 1949 resurfaced on calendars around the country. As acknowledged by co-executive producer Jerry Wald, Marilyn only appeared in *Clash By Night* as a result of her journalist friend Sidney Skolsky virtually browbeating him into handing her the role of Peggy. Wald and partner Norman Krasna subsequently had plenty of reason to be grateful to Skolsky, and so did Marilyn, who garnered plenty of press and public attention as a result of her performance in the film. What's more, its producer was Harriett Parsons, the sister of powerful Hollywood gossip columnist Louella O. Parsons.

Bit by bit, all of the pieces were falling into place.

The Critics' Views

"Before going on any further with a report on *Clash By Night,* perhaps we should mention the first full-length glimpse the picture gives us of Marilyn Monroe as an actress. The verdict is gratifyingly good. This girl has a refreshing exuberance, an abundance of girlish high spirits. She is a forceful actress, too, when crisis comes along."

New York World Telegram and Sun

"In a sort of subplot, *Clash By Night* also gives us a glimpse of Marilyn Monroe and Keith Andes, who play a pair of lovers. Both are quite handsome, but neither can act."

The New Yorker

"*Clash By Night* is an adult picture that tackles a subject heretofore taboo on the screen—adultery—with a strong moral lesson which makes it one of the most important dramas of the year. . . . As for Miss Pash-pie of 1952, otherwise Marilyn Monroe, the calendar girl, clad in dungarees, she proves she can also act and can hold her own with top performers."

L.A. Examiner

Public Reaction

The nude calendar story broke in March of 1952, *Clash By Night* was released that June, and the public turned out in droves to see the film and its controversial star attraction, producing a healthy $1.5 million take at the box office.

Rough-and-tumble lovers —as a tough and sexy dame, Marilyn delivers one of her most natural performances opposite Keith Andes.

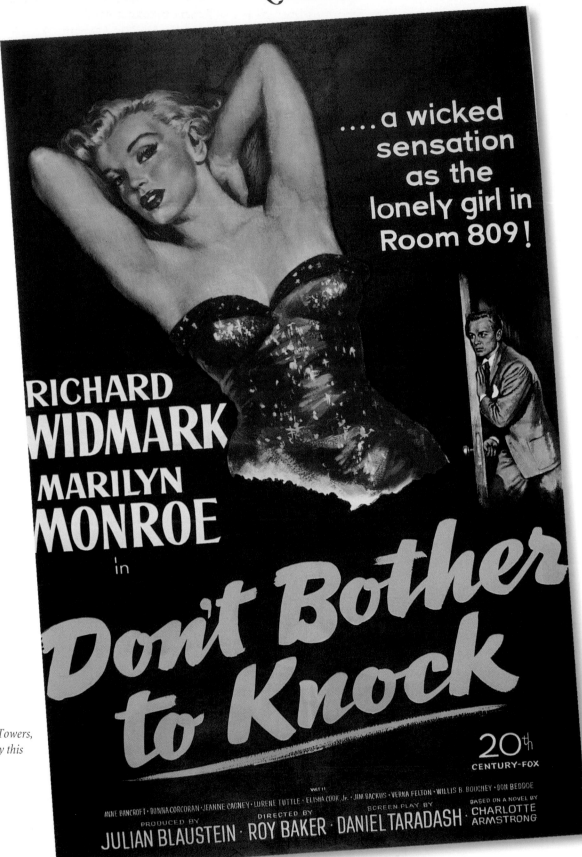

Unfortunately for Jed Towers, Nell doesn't look nearly this alluring in the movie.

The Plot

After Lyn Lesley writes a letter to Skyway Airlines pilot Jed Towers breaking off their relationship, Jed arrives in New York City and checks into the McKinley Hotel where Lyn is a singer. Jed tries to persuade Lyn to change her mind, but she refuses, insisting that he is cynical and uncaring.

Feeling frustrated back in his room, Jed spots an attractive woman on the other side of the hotel courtyard. After figuring out that she is in room 809, he gives her a call and eventually manages to invite himself over. What Jed doesn't realize, however, is that he is involving himself with one highly deranged individual. Her name is Nell Forbes, and she is trying to put her life back together after spending three years in an Oregon mental institution. Thanks to her uncle Eddie, an elevator operator at the hotel, Nell has secured a job babysitting Bunny, the daughter of Ruth and Peter Jones, who are attending an honorary dinner downstairs in the ballroom. Nell doesn't tell Jed that she is minding a child, and neither does she reveal that she is wearing a negligée, jewelry, perfume and makeup belonging to the child's mother. Worse still, when she learns that Jed is a pilot, the delusional woman believes that he is her late fiancé Philip, who died flying a plane during World War II.

The two of them kiss, but Nell's cover is blown when Bunny walks into the room. Perceiving the child as an interfering nuisance, Nells starts threatening her, and she also scares Jed when he notices the huge scars on both of her wrists. Jed wants to see Lyn now that she has finished singing for the night, Nell begs him to stay, and he is then forced to hide in the bathroom when Eddie checks to see how Nell is doing. It doesn't take long for the elevator man to realize that his niece is still disturbed, and this is confirmed when she smashes him over the head with an ashtray after he discovers Jed in the bathroom.

While Jed attends to Eddie, Nell receives a phone call from Mrs. Jones, enquiring if Bunny is okay. Nell assures her that she is, but the child's mother is concerned by the babysitter's strange tone of voice, not to mention a noise that sounds eerily like Bunny crying. Nell subsequently silences the child by binding and gagging her, and when some nosy neighbors come calling she gives them the brush-off, yet Jed sneaks out and Nell's world starts to unravel. She blames Bunny for driving "Philip" away, and looks as if she intends to kill her. Jed, meanwhile, recounts his experiences to Lyn, before rushing back to room 809 in order to investigate why Bunny was so quiet when he made his escape. Mrs. Jones gets there ahead of him, and the two of them subsequently rescue the little girl.

Virtually in a trance, Nell takes the elevator down to the lobby and grabs a razor blade while the hotel staff closes in on her. Then Jed arrives on the scene, and after persuading Nell to hand over the blade, he also convinces her that he is not Philip. The police escort Nell to a hospital, and Lyn, won over by Jed's compassion, now knows that he is the right man for her.

DON'T BOTHER TO KNOCK

★★½

A Twentieth Century-Fox Release
Produced by Julian Blaustein
Directed by Roy Baker
Screenplay by Daniel Taradash
Based on a novel by Charlotte Armstrong
Cinematography by Lucien Ballard
Sound by Bernard Freericks
and Harry M. Leonard
Art Direction by Lyle Wheeler
and Richard Irvine
Music directed by Lionel Newman
Costume Design by Travilla
Edited by George A. Gittens
Released: July 30, 1952
Running Time: 76 minutes
Black & White

CAST

Jed Towers	Richard Widmark
Nell Forbes	Marilyn Monroe
Lyn Lesley	Anne Bancroft
Bunny Jones	Donna Corcoran
Rochelle	Jeanne Cagney
Ruth Jones	Lurene Tuttle
Eddie Forbes	Elisha Cook, Jr.
Peter Jones	Jim Backus
Mrs. Ballew	Verna Felton
Bartender Joe	Willis Bouchey
Girl Photographer	Gloria Blondell
Mr. Ballew	Don Beddoe
Mrs. McMurdock	Grace Hayle
Pat the House Detective	Michael Ross

Uncredited:

Bell Captain	Dick Cogan
(Bit Part)	Bess Flowers
Doorman	Robert Foulk
Maid	Eda Reiss Merin
Elevator Operator	Vic Perrin
Desk Clerk	Olan Soule
Toastmaster	Emmett Vogan

Behind-the-Scenes Facts & Opinions

A so-so psychological thriller hampered by an improbable plot and sometimes laughable dialogue, *Don't Bother to Knock* was hardly the best vehicle in which to showcase Marilyn Monroe's talents as an actress. For one thing, tight budget constraints meant that almost everything had to be shot in a single take, and while director Roy Ward Baker did an admirable job under the circumstances, this didn't provide the first-time leading lady with much leeway to refine her performance (something she would more than make up for on future film assignments!). Then again, the character portrayed by Marilyn is so obviously deranged right from the start that even if her wide-eyed uncle is dumb enough to get her work as a babysitter of all things, you would think that one of the kid's parents would take the requisite 30 seconds to check her out. If they did, they would quickly discover that she's a few slices short of a full loaf, or, as Jed Towers describes her, "silk on one side and sandpaper on the other."

During an initial conference with producer Julian Blaustein on November 16, 1949, Darryl Zanuck suggested that the character of Nell should borrow from that of Ellen, the murderous bride played by Gene Tierney in the 1945 movie *Leave Her to Heaven*, whereby the audience gradually discerns that she is not normal. Characteristically astute, Zanuck emphasized that such an approach was "the only possible chance this story has to be a success." Unfortunately, Blaustein didn't appear to heed his advice.

December 3, 1951—Marilyn tests one of Travilla's simpler designs, and displays what Bosley Crowther of the New York Times *would describe as "a childishly blank expression."*

Don't Bother to Knock was adapted by Daniel Taradash from a Charlotte Armstrong novel entitled *Mischief,* which had originally appeared in *Good Housekeeping* magazine and featured all the main characters who ended up on the screen. In a script conference with Taradash and Blaustein on May 17, 1950, Darryl Zanuck envisaged the film as "A kind of one-night-in-the-life-of-a-hotel story; a sort of minor 'Grand Hotel.'"

Small vignettes involving minor characters would help to achieve this, while Zanuck's secretary, Molly Mandaville, noted: "Please remember that at no time should Nell be identified as or called a <u>Baby Sitter.</u> Everybody has unions these days and possibly the Baby Sitters are organized, too, and it would be awful if our nice picture were to be picked [on] by the Baby Sitters of America. Besides, let's remember that we once made a lot of money out of a baby sitting picture ('Sitting Pretty'), so let's not be ungrateful to the baby sitters of the nation."

Daniel Taradash's "Final Script" of June 13, 1950, incorporated changes that attempt to emphasize Nell's childlike qualities and her lack of any truly murderous instincts, thus ensuring the audience's sympathy for her in particular and emotionally deranged people in general. The "Revised Final" script of October 9 changed the film's title from *Mischief* to *Night Without Sleep,* while during an October 15 conference with Julian Blaustein, Zanuck wisely suggested amending Nell's last name to something other than Munro—given her own mother's history of mental illness, it would be trying enough for Marilyn to portray an insane woman.

After Jed Towers and Mrs. Jones have rescued Bunny from Nell's dangerous clutches, the baby-sitter is left in a desperate state.

Numerous other changes were made before the movie reached the screen, not least a never-filmed opening segment that could have aroused the attention of the censorship board—Just before Nell enters the hotel, she looks at a horse carrying a policeman, prompting the doorman to say, "I never see a dame wasn't a sucker for a cop's horse."

The title *Night Without Sleep* was dropped when Twentieth Century-Fox realized that it had scheduled another film—also directed by Roy Baker—with that name. Meanwhile, for its screen credits, *Don't Bother to Knock* reused Alfred Newman's music from the 1950 Fox picture *Panic in the Streets*, which had also starred Richard Widmark.

While the talented Anne Bancroft is hopelessly miscast in her movie debut, portraying sultry singer Lyn Lesley, Marilyn only partially lives up to her billing in the film's promotional trailer as "America's most exciting personality . . . Every inch a woman . . . Every inch an actress!" In fact, she is far more convincing when just hinting at the madness within, than when, with eyes blazing and arms flailing, she allows her insanity to runneth over.

"Suspense fires the screen as the most talked about actress of 1952 rockets to stardom!" announced the trailer. Well, not quite, although after three more films—and only another six months—that claim would indeed become a reality.

The Critics' Views

"The uncomfortableness, which is all-pervading, seems to grow out of the subject matter and envelop writer, director, cameraman and actors, who jointly and severally appear to be in the grip of a slow-motion blues. . . . Miss Monroe, as the pivotal figure, only increases the uncertainty. She is supposed to be a 'sick girl' and she plays the part like a sick girl. This may have the sound of praise; but when you see her you will be uneasily aware that her portrayal is reinforced by virtually no acting resources whatsoever."

LOS ANGELES TIMES

"All the equipment that Miss Monroe has to handle the job are a childishly blank expression and a provokingly feeble, hollow voice."

NEW YORK TIMES

"In *Don't Bother to Knock* . . . they've thrown Marilyn Monroe into the deep dramatic waters, sink or swim, and while she doesn't really do either, you might say that she floats. With that figure, what else can she do."

NEW YORK POST

Public Reaction

Don't Bother to Knock may have garnered mixed reviews but, released just one week after *We're Not Married* and about six weeks after *Clash By Night*, it was yet another of the films to capitalize on the nude calendar scandal. As such, it helped add to the now-irreversible momentum that was pushing Marilyn towards stardom, and the result was a healthy box-office return of $1.5 million on an investment of just $555,000.

When Uncle Eddie starts interfering, he quickly learns that Jed was right when describing Nell as "silk on one side and sandpaper on the other".

We're Not Married!

WE'RE NOT MARRIED!

★★★

A Twentieth Century-Fox Release
Produced by Nunnally Johnson
Directed by Edmund Goulding
Screenplay by Nunnally Johnson
Adapted by Dwight Taylor
From a story by Gina Kaus and Jay Dratler
Cinematography by Leo Tover
Sound by W.D. Flick and Roger Heman
Art Direction by Lyle Wheeler and Leland Fuller
Music by Cyril Mockridge
Costume Design by Elois Jenssen
Edited by Louis Loeffler
Released: July 23, 1952
Running Time: 85 minutes
Black & White

CAST

Ramona Gladwyn	Ginger Rogers
Steve Gladwyn	Fred Allen
Justice of the Peace Melvin Bush	Victor Moore
Annabel Norris	Marilyn Monroe
Jeff Norris	David Wayne
Katie Woodruff	Eve Arden
Hector Woodruff	Paul Douglas
Willie Fisher	Eddie Bracken
Patsy Fisher	Mitzi Gaynor
Freddie Melrose	Louis Calhern
Eve Melrose	Zsa Zsa Gabor
Duffy	James Gleason
Attorney Stone	Paul Stewart
Mrs. Bush	Jane Darwell
Detective Magnus	Alan Bridge
Radio Announcer	Harry Golder
Governor Bush	Victor Sutherland
Attorney General	Tom Powers
Organist	Maurice Cass
Autograph Hound	Maude Wallace
Irene	Margie Liszt
Mr. Graves	Richard Buckley
Pinky	Lee Marvin

Uncredited:

Justice of the Peace	Harry Antrim
Willie's Sergeant	James Burke
Postman	Harry Carter
MP at Railroad Station	Robert Dane
Twitchell	Ralph Dumke
Wife	Kay English
Man in Radio Station	Eddie Firestone
MP	Robert Forrest
License Bureau Clerk	Byron Foulger
Man in Radio Station	Alvin Greenman
Man at the Miss Mississippi Contest	Dabbs Greer
Ned	Harry Harvey
Chaplain Hall	Selmer Jackson
Counterman	Edwin Max
Beauty Contest Announcer	Emile Meyer
Governor of Mississippi	Forbes Murray
Ruthie	Marjorie Weaver
Postman	O. Z. Whitehead

The Plot

Justice of the Peace Melvin Bush mistakenly marries six couples before his license becomes valid, and when this is discovered two and a half years later they each receive letters notifying them that their unions are null and void. One of the couples is already filing for divorce, but the others must decide how they wish to proceed. . . .

Steve and Ramona Gladwyn are enjoying huge success as the wholesome radio hosts of "Breakfast with The Glad Gladwyn." However, they despise the ad-infested show and absolutely hate each other, so there is great joy when they learn that they are not legally married, followed by concern as they realize this may cost them their $5,000-per-week job.

Next up are Annabel Norris, winner of the Mrs. Mississippi beauty pageant, and Jeff, who serves as a househusband while his wife tries to attain sponsorship for her entry into the Mrs. America contest. Jeff takes care of their baby while Annabel and her money-hungry manager are out on the road, and so he is delighted when he learns that their marriage is invalid, because this means that she is no longer eligible for the Mrs. America contest. Annabel is quick on her feet, however, entering the Miss Mississippi contest and winning that instead!

According to Melvin Bush's recollection, Hector and Katie Woodruff were a pair of chatterboxes when he married them, yet they now have very little to say to one another. Hector has been consistently unfaithful, Katie knows it, and so when he opens the mail and discovers that they are not really married, he starts dreaming about all the romantic escapades that he'll soon be able to enjoy. Then Hector considers what they might end up costing him, and he decides to burn the letter before Katie sees it.

When wealthy entrepreneur Freddie Melrose takes a business trip to New Orleans, his beautiful and overly pampered wife Eve arranges to meet him there, yet this is just a ploy to frame him. A strange woman knocks on the door of Freddie's hotel room and he lets her in, only to realize that he has been set up when a bunch of news reporters follow close behind. Back at his office, Freddie is visited by Eve and her attorney, who inform the businessman that he is being sued for divorce on the grounds of his "adultery," and that if he doesn't part with more than 50 percent of his estate then they will tell the authorities about his illicit "affair." Freddie appears to be sunk, yet after opening his mail he is suddenly more than happy to divulge all of his assets . . . including the letter informing the Melroses that they're not even hitched.

Lastly there is army recruit Willie Fisher, who departs on a train clutching the all-important letter just as his wife Patsy arrives on the platform and shouts out that she is pregnant. Upset that their child will be illegitimate if he dies while serving overseas, Willie goes AWOL so he and Patsy can quickly marry, only to be arrested and jailed aboard a ship. On the dock, however, a tearful Patsy encounters a military man of the cloth, resulting in the grateful couple being wed by means of ship-to-shore radio.

Finally we see Jeff and Annabel Norris, Hector and Katie Woodruff, and Steve and Ramona Gladwyn all happily getting remarried.

Do you think he'll be able to resist much longer?
David Wayne takes it on the cheek in the second of
four films that he and Marilyn appeared in.

Filming her first scene in the movie, Marilyn justifies David Wayne's assertion that "she just could not be badly photographed. It was impossible."

Facts & Opinions

An episodic comedy comprising five interwoven sequences, *We're Not Married!* utilizes a stellar cast and achieves mixed results. Best of the bunch is the segment featuring the pair of radio hosts whose on-air conviviality contrasts sharply with their off-air animosity. Ginger Rogers and Fred Allen are superb as the bickering couple, and the scene in which they broadcast their massively successful breakfast show—consisting of non-stop product endorsements—is an absolute gem. By comparison, most of the other segments are moderately entertaining—although it is amusing to see multi-married Zsa Zsa Gabor cast somewhat according to type as a glamorous gold digger—while that concerning the AWOL soldier is plain daft. (It does, however, include a brief appearance by Lee Marvin in just his third film.)

Dwight Taylor adapted *We're Not Married!* from a story by Jay Dratler and Gina Kaus entitled *If I Could Re-Marry,* in which Marilyn's Annabel Norris character is called Janie McKay and is described as "blonde, big-eyed and big-Russelled," no doubt alluding to the top-heavy attributes of screen star Jane Russell. However, McKay also has a very run-down appearance and is in no way a beauty queen. Taylor submitted his working script on June 11, 1951, and while it is episodic like the original story, it is also considerably different from the finished film.

Nunnally Johnson was subsequently recruited to whip the story into shape, and his October 16, 1951, First Draft Continuity Script closely resembles the action that appears on the screen. Indeed, by Johnson's own admission, Marilyn's beauty queen character was only contrived so that she could be seen in a pair of bathing suits, for

Scriptwriter Nunnally Johnson specifically contrived the role of Annabel Norris so that Marilyn could be seen in a pair of bathing suits.

Cary Grant and, especially, Ginger Rogers are excellent in their schizoid roles as a couple of rejuvenated middle-agers, and Charles Coburn is also wonderful as the bumbling company boss who is eager to profit from the elixir of youth. However, it is most often the scenes featuring Marilyn Monroe as Oxley's daft secretary, Lois Laurel, that steal the picture.

To begin with, it is obvious that the old boy hardly employs the voluptuous young dimwit for her skills behind the desk. "Miss Laurel, find someone to type this," he tells her. "Oh, Mr. Oxley, can't I try again?" she asks plaintively, to which he replies, "No, it's very important. Better to find someone to type it for you."

Equally classic are the segments in which the revitalized Barnaby Fulton decides to impress Miss Laurel by diving off the high board at a local swimming pool, only to hit the water stomach-first, and that in which he takes her on a wild car ride (along Pico Boulevard, just seconds away from the Twentieth Century-Fox lot, and around the adjacent Cheviot Hills neighborhood; meanwhile, the Fox front office exterior doubles as that of the Oxley Chemical lab).

Miss Laurel craves the intellectual Barnaby's attention, but during his more sober moments he is not in the least bit interested. He describes her to his wife as "half-infant," to which Edwina responds, "Not the half that's visible," for it has to be said that, whenever she appears, Marilyn lights up the screen with her bubbly personality and figure-hugging outfits. Nevertheless, William Travilla would later admit that, of all the costumes he designed for her over the course of eight movies between 1952 and 1956, the only one that Marilyn disliked was the beige jersey wool dress with pleated full-circle skirt that she wore for her opening scenes in *Monkey Business*.

"It's true that Marilyn hated that pleated dress," confirmed Bill Sarris, who was then Travilla's assistant and later his business partner. "She'd shove the skirt between her cheeks."

For her part, Ginger Rogers is terrific in the scene where Edwina and Barnaby are back in their old honeymoon suite at the Pickwick Arms Hotel. Regressing to a point that starts to disturb him, she tells her husband to go in another room while she undresses, cries because she misses her mother, and then picks a petty fight that she later forgets about while Barnaby spends the night in the laundry room. When I interviewed Rogers shortly before her death in 1995, she described Cary Grant as "just a dream come true," while director Howard Hawks—whose off-screen voice is heard during the film's opening credits—was "very inspirational." Marilyn, on the other hand, was—surprise, surprise—"late every day. She always kept everyone waiting, but she knew all of her lines." Hawks would later assert, "The more important she became the more frightened she became. . . . She had no confidence in her own ability."

Revitalized by the youth serum, Edwina confronts Barnaby about his friendship with Miss Laurel. Earlier he had described the secretary as "half-infant," prompting Edwina to respond, "Not the half that's visible."

It seems that Marilyn wasn't the only one to delay proceedings. Ginger Rogers recalled, "When we were getting ready to shoot the scene towards the end of the movie, where the chimp is messing with the potion in the laboratory, he got away from his handlers and went scampering along the catwalk above the set. The crew and the handlers went up there on ropes and ladders, and they were running up and down trying to catch this monkey, but it took them a long time before they were able to do so. That was quite a sight."

As it happens, no primates were involved in Harry Segall's original story, *The Fountain of Youth,* from which *Monkey Business* was adapted. Segall submitted a working script on July 2, 1951, featuring Clay and Rhonda Ogden instead of Barnaby and Edwina Fulton, and thereafter I. A. L. Diamond took charge of the screenplay, renaming it *Darling—I Am Growing Younger* while introducing a chimp into the proceedings. In Diamond's "Working Script" of October 9, 1951, a teenager named Shirley vied for Clay's attentions, but following a conference with Darryl Zanuck and producer Sol Siegel, she evolved into Joyce, the niece of Clay's boss, described as "a young woman of perhaps 28—an Ava Gardner type—a real siren in an adult manner."

By the time of the December 11, 1951, revised screenplay, this siren was far more Marilyn-like—"young, blonde and voluptuous"—her name was Lois Laurel, and she was Oxley's secretary. The other main characters' names also matched those in the finished movie, as did the basic plot, yet Zanuck still wanted to build up the parts of both Lois and the monkey, so Charles Lederer was brought in to make some more changes. His January 11, 1952, working script incorporated the car and skating scenes involving Barnaby and Miss Laurel, yet even after the film went into production during the late winter and early spring of 1952, more revisions were made on the set.

At this point, Ben Hecht was contributing to the story line, adding lines such as Oxley's "find someone to type this," and replacing the skating sequence with one set in a record store in which Barnaby and Lois stand in a booth and listen to "hip" discs, while discussing them with other young people. This was shot but never used—the skating scene was retained. However, some additional skating footage, in which Lois helps Barnaby to his feet after he falls over, was omitted from the movie but included in the promotional trailer.

Suffering from recurring appendix trouble, Marilyn left the set of *Monkey Business* during early March and checked into Cedars of Lebanon Hospital. After a week she was able to return to work, taking antibiotics to help to delay the necessary surgery until the following month.

The Critics' Views

"Not having seen Miss Monroe before, I know now what that's all about, and I've no dissenting opinions to offer. She disproves more than adequately the efficacy of the old stage rule about not turning one's back to the audience."

NEW YORK HERALD TRIBUNE

"Marilyn Monroe . . . poses and walks in a manner that must be called suggestive. What she suggests is something that this picture seems to have on its mind much of the time, with or without the rejuvenation."

NEW YORK POST

"Marilyn Monroe can look and act dumber than any of the screen's current blondes."

NEW YORK DAILY NEWS

Public Reaction

Marilyn undertook a promotional tour for *Monkey Business,* and was the only leading member of the cast to attend its world premiere at the Stanley Theater on Atlantic City's famous Boardwalk. In the event, the film posted a modest profit during its initial run, earning around $2 million in return for an outlay of $1,615,000.

A few seconds of Lois helping Barnaby to his feet were omitted from the movie but included in the promotional trailer.

Niagara

Marilyn Monroe
and "Niagara"
a raging
torrent of
emotion
that even
nature can't
control!

20th CENTURY-FOX presents

Niagara

TECHNICOLOR

STARRING

MARILYN MONROE · JOSEPH COTTEN · JEAN PETERS

WITH CASEY ADAMS · DENIS O'DEA · RICHARD ALLAN · DON WILSON · LORENE TUTTLE · RUSSELL COLLINS · WILL WRIGHT

PRODUCED BY CHARLES BRACKETT · DIRECTED BY HENRY HATHAWAY · WRITTEN BY CHARLES BRACKETT, WALTER REISCH AND RICHARD BREEN

Publicity material for Niagara emphasized the movie's two main attractions.

The Plot

Ray and Polly Cutler's belated honeymoon at Niagara Falls is disrupted when they arrive to find that their reserved Rainbow Cabin is still being occupied by George and Rose Loomis. The Cutlers take another cabin, but they are soon very aware of the rocky relationship between the overly neurotic George and his overtly sexy young wife, who chooses to tease her husband rather than be intimate with him.

On a visit to the Falls, Polly sees Rose locked in a passionate embrace with handsome hunk Ted Patrick, and although Polly keeps this to herself, George strongly suspects that his wife is being unfaithful. What he doesn't know is that Rose and her lover are actually planning to murder him, and their plan is put into effect when Rose piques George's curiosity and has him follow her to the local bus station, where she mingles with the crowd while Ted shadows George with a view to getting him alone and killing him. Back at the Rainbow Cabins, Rose tells the Cutlers that George has gone missing and they duly inform the police, yet when she is subsequently called to the mortuary to identify the body of her dead husband, Rose has a terrible shock. The sheet is pulled back from the face, she passes out, and the reason for this soon becomes clear.

Polly Cutler encounters George Loomis both at the motel and by the Falls, and he confides to her that he has killed his wife's lover in self-defense. Now he intends to run away, but first he stalks Rose, who, realizing that she is in deep trouble, buys a bus ticket to leave Niagara. This attempt is thwarted, however, when the border between Canada and the States is blocked, and with her options fast running out Rose flees to the top of the Carillon Tower, where she is trapped by George and mercilessly strangled.

Hijacking the Cutlers' hire boat, George makes his escape with Polly trapped on board. However, with Ray and the police in hot pursuit, the vessel runs out of gas and it is drawn into the current of the Falls. At the last moment, George manages to help Polly climb out onto a rocky ledge, before he and the boat are swept fatally over the

NIAGARA

★★★★

A Twentieth Century-Fox Release
Produced by Charles Brackett
Directed by Henry Hathaway
Screenplay by Charles Brackett, Walter Reisch, and Richard Breen
Cinematography by Joe MacDonald
Sound by W. D. Flick and Roger Heman
Art Direction by Lyle Wheeler and Maurice Ransford
Edited by Barbara McLean
Music by Sol Kaplan
Costume Design by Dorothy Jeakins
Released: January 23, 1953
Running Time: 89 minutes
Technicolor

CAST

Rose Loomis	Marilyn Monroe
George Loomis	Joseph Cotten
Polly Cutler	Jean Peters
Ray Cutler	Casey Adams
Inspector Starkey	Denis O'Dea
Ted Patrick	Richard Allan
Mr. Kettering	Don Wilson
Mrs. Kettering	Lurene Tuttle
Mr. Qua	Russell Collins
Boatman	Will Wright

Uncredited:

Motorcycle Cop	Henry Beckman
Taxi Driver	Harry Carey, Jr.
Young Man	Robert Ellis
Canadian Customs Officer	Neil Fitzgerald
Young Man	Bill Foster
Dancer	Gloria Gordon
Straw Boss	Winfield Hoeny
Carillon Tower Guide	George Ives
Taxi Driver	Arch Johnson
Doctor	Lester Matthews
Sam	Sean McClory
Morris	Norman McKay
Detective (Bit Part)	Patrick O'Moore
	Marjorie Rambeau
Husband	Tom Reynolds
Motorcycle Cop	Willard Sage
Mrs. McGrand, Landlady	Minerva Urecal
Wife	Nina Varela
Guide	Gene Wesson
Policeman	Carleton Young

MM'S SONG

"Kiss" By Lionel Newman and Haven Gillespie

After Marilyn had repeatedly been asked to back away from the curtain while filming the shower scene, she did at least emerge with a towel wrapped around her.

M a r i lyn stretched out alluringly in front of the Falls—in the movie's opening credits, Peters' name appears above the title but below the names of Marilyn Monroe and Joseph Cotten.

"Marilyn had the more interesting part but I felt that we were equal," Peters recalled. "You know, I didn't feel that I was in a Monroe vehicle, but that all changed when the film came out!"

One thing that did not change, however, was Marilyn's habitual tardiness on the set, even though in Henry Hathaway she was up against a director who could be extremely tyrannical when the mood took him.

"He always had to have his whipping boy," said Max Showalter. "He started with me, blowing up and calling me every name under the sun when I took two to three takes for a scene at the Falls, but I called his bluff and walked right off the set. After that he had two other whipping boys: Denis O'Dea [Inspector Starkey] from the Abbey Theatre and Russell Collins [Mr. Qua] from the New York stage. Hathaway always loved to pick actors who had gotten brilliant reviews and were up for Tony Awards in New York, and then bring them out and really just lash into them. Denis O'Dea and Russell Collins were sometimes shaking so badly that they could hardly remember a line. He was cruel to people, yet he was a hell of a good director."

"Hathaway was not an angel," agreed Paul Wurtzel, who was in charge of the special-effects work on *Niagara*. "He was the toughest director in Hollywood. It wasn't unusual for him to fire an entire electrical crew, grip crew or effects crew if he didn't like them. A very peculiar man, and yet he could be a nice man." He was also a man whose temper and geniality were tested fully when dealing with the enigmatic character of Marilyn Monroe.

"He'd call her 'Clabberhead'," Max Showalter recalled. "He'd say, 'Alright, Clabberhead,' and Marilyn would ask, 'What does that mean?' I said, 'Well, all I know is that back in Kansas, where I come from, we'd put milk and butter in a big churn and make what we called clabber.' She said, 'Well, I don't know why he calls me that,' and I said, 'Well, I don't know either.'"

"He could be really mean," asserted Jean Peters. "There was one day after lunch when we were shooting at the studio, and all of us—Joe, Casey, Marilyn and I—were scheduled to take part in this scene. One hour went by, two hours went by and no Marilyn, and Henry used to smoke a cigar, holding it between his teeth so that it would point skywards, and he was storming up and down the stage. We were all saying, 'Oh God, this is going to be a slaughter! He's going to kill her.' And she finally arrived on the set, walked right past him, flung her arms up in the air and said, 'Oh, I'll have to have my makeup checked,' before sailing into her dressing room. Henry just gave up!"

A meticulous craftsman, Hathaway had mapped out the precise length of every movie segment before shooting even began. "I was supposed to walk up some stairs, knock on a door and open it," Jean Peters recalled, "and Henry said, 'Jean, you've got to get there faster. I've only allowed four seconds for this,' and he had. That was the way he operated, but you couldn't do that with Marilyn, so it probably aged him. However, he also ended up loving her."

Not without reason. Richard Allan, who portrayed Rose's lover Ted Patrick, recalled filming the scene in which he and Marilyn kissed by the Falls under the close scrutiny of their intimidating director: "Just before the shot she said, 'Now, when he says "Action!" pull me to you and kiss me passionately,' and I said, 'Well, sure!' So he said, 'Action!' and we went into this great big embrace, kissing very passionately, and he said, 'Cut! Cut! Jesus Christ, I can't print that!' So I said, 'Well, Mr. Hathaway, you show me how you want me to do it.' I knew that's what he wanted to do, so he did, and

◄◄ *June 1952—in a spectacular setting, MM poses as the siren who "sang of love just as she lived for love, like a Lorelei flaunting her charms as she lured men on and on to their eternal destruction."*

then when we got the shot I went up to him and I said, 'I'm sorry I took so long to get that,' and he said, 'Oh, that's alright, Richard!'"

Max Showalter, meanwhile, had been assigned by Darryl Zanuck to reside in the room next door to Marilyn on location and watch over her. She in turn asked Max to never lock the door between their rooms at the General Brock Hotel—apart from the times when Joe DiMaggio was visiting—and he complied.

"I remember it was just before she shot her first scene," Showalter recalled. "In the middle of the night, stark naked, she came in and jumped on my bed and said, 'Please don't do anything to me but just hold me.' Nudity meant nothing to her at all, but she was quivering and she said, 'Just help me with my lines. Help me.' So I said, 'Alright, sure.' There was a quality about her that made you want to help her, and I really loved her and felt sorry for her.

"But then I was doing this scene with Jean Peters, where I'm photographing her as she is sunbathing and Marilyn appears and is supposed to say, 'I'm sorry, but have you seen my husband?' Well, we were rehearsing this scene and Marilyn was looking beyond me, and finally I said, 'Who are you looking at?' She said, 'Oh, I'm looking at you.' I said, 'No, you're not,' and she said, 'Don't ask me to look in your eyes or I'll forget my lines.' I said, 'But Marilyn, we're playing a scene,' and she said, 'I know, I know,' and finally Henry Hathaway said, 'Will you stop telling her what to do? Just let her do it her way!' Marilyn had this pedantic style of speech, but then I noticed that she was looking over at [her drama coach] Natasha Lytess, who was moving her mouth to the words, 'have you seen my husband?' Marilyn was watching Natasha and saying the words exactly as she was, and that was very difficult to work with. She didn't look at me, so it was almost like playing with a blind lady."

Overall, however, Max Showalter asserted that, no matter the number of takes needed to satisfy Marilyn's requirements, "it was magic that came out, and sometimes I wondered if she really knew which was the magical moment. On the set I personally felt that she couldn't even compete with the talent that Jean Peters had, but there was a glow about Marilyn and what came across was incredible."

Adding to that glow was the "face" that Marilyn and personal makeup artist Whitey Snyder had been working on for several years. "By that time we both knew exactly how she wanted to look, and we used that look for several pictures in a row," Snyder explained in 1994. "Slowly but surely we changed the eyebrows and the eye shadow and things like that, but the look was established."

"Wherever Marilyn went while we were at the Falls, the crowds were just going crazy watching her," added Max Showalter. "However, she never fraternized with the rest of the company. After a day's shooting we'd always go up to Joe Cotten's room and have drinks, but Marilyn was never there. On the other hand, I remember her standing stark naked in front of her room window which looked out over the street, and saying, 'Come in and look! Why are all of those men looking up here?' I said, 'Well, why the hell do you think they're looking up here? You haven't got a stitch of clothing on, you're standing in the window, so they're all down on the street looking up at you!' She said, 'Oh, they are?' I honestly think it was innocent."

Meanwhile, the crew members also caught an eyeful during filming of the unforgettable scene in which Marilyn sings "Kiss" wearing an electrifying red dress that Joseph Cotten's character describes as "cut down so low in front you could see her kneecaps." Shot at the studio on June 25 and 26, this enabled Marilyn to redefine seductiveness in song, yet Max Showalter would recall that of more immediate interest to many present on the set was her lack of underwear.

"After about 10 or 15 takes of her writhing about in this dress, the crew just covered her from the waist down in a horse blanket," he told me. "By this time they were shoot-

ing the close-ups, and what with her being naked and the dress riding clear up to her waist they obviously decided that they had seen enough!"

Nevertheless, they would see more when shooting the scenes where Marilyn was under the bedsheets or taking a shower, when she again had to be prevented from showing too much flesh. "Henry Hathaway kept asking her to back away from the shower curtain, but she couldn't help pressing up against it," Showalter recalled. "The special effects department therefore had to go over the film and darken it down."

Meanwhile, right up until—and including—the final shooting script of May 15, 1952, "Kiss" was not slated as Marilyn's musical contribution. Instead, she was supposed to sing along to a "magnificent orchestration" of Cole Porter's "Night and Day."

Richard Allan and Marilyn find it difficult to remain serious while filming the scene in which they kiss by the Falls.

For reasons that are now unclear, this was replaced at the last moment by Lionel Newman and Haven Gillespie's new composition. Ironically, in the script, just before she starts singing along to the Night and Day record, Rose responds to Ray Cutler's question, "You kind of like that song, don't you Mrs. Loomis?" by asserting—as she does in the film—that "There isn't any other song."

Well, in this case there was just *one* other, and when it was announced that Marilyn's rendition of "Kiss"—one different from the version in the film—was to be released as a single, co-composer Lionel Newman suggested that MM's lips be imprinted on the disc. However, in light of the storm of protests by women's groups over Marilyn's overt sexuality in *Niagara*, MGM decided to veto the idea and avoid further controversy.

A report in the February 11, 1953, edition of *Variety*, leading with the line, "The berth of a sexboat is not necessarily a downy one," explained how not only organized groups but also individual females were "deploring the effect Miss Monroe's frank characterization has had upon their children, husbands or sweethearts, as the case may be." While MGM Records felt that in Marilyn's new renditions of both "Kiss" and the standard, "Do It Again," it had two "very hot" sales items, Fox felt that their release should be cancelled, as they were "a little too incendiary at this time."

And all of this over a woman who had informed journalist Sidney Skolsky on the set of *Niagara* that all she wore to bed was Chanel No. 5. One thing was for sure: love her or hate her, Marilyn Monroe was now Hollywood's most bankable ticket, and Fox was wasting no time in rushing her into her next starring vehicle. On June 1, 1952, the day of her 26th birthday, the studio gave its new sensation the role of Lorelei Lee.

▶▶ *All smiles with Henry Hathaway, "the toughest director in Hollywood," who called Marilyn 'Clabberhead' on the set but afterwards referred to her as "the best natural actress I've directed."*

The Critics' Views

"Two of nature's greatest phenomena, Niagara Falls and Marilyn Monroe, get together in *Niagara* and the result is the sexiest, tingling-est, suspensful-est film in lo, these many months. . . . Here is the greatest natural star since Jean Harlow. . . She assaults your eyes and your nerves. She peppers your imagination."

L.A. Examiner

"Perhaps, after all, it is Miss Monroe's good fortune that she is in the same movie as the Niagara Falls. For now it can be said that her limited performance suffers only by comparison with the stupendous dramatic effects created by God, and Technicolor. Her thespianic talents scarcely measure up to her physical equipment—but this, of course, is not news."

Cue

"Marilyn Monroe, whom Hollywood has been ballyhooing as a new-day Lillian Russell, takes a fling at big-league melodrama in *Niagara* and demonstrates a wide assortment of curves and a tendency to read her lines as if they were written in a tongue she is not entirely familiar with."

The New Yorker

Public Reaction

Despite—or perhaps because of—the audible audience gasps when Marilyn shimmied her way towards the Falls, *Niagara* grossed a healthy $2.35 million return on an outlay of $1,670,000 during its initial run. Today it is still among MM's most popular films.

After You Get What You Want You Don't Want It: 1953–1954

O
N FEBRUARY 9, 1953, Marilyn Monroe won the Photoplay Award as Hollywood's "Fastest Rising Star." Sewn into a Travilla-designed gold lamé dress with a neckline that plunged down to her waist, she made headline news when Joan Crawford condemned her appearance as a "burlesque show" to Associated Press syndicated columnist Bob Thomas. On the other hand, Fox stablemate Betty Grable rallied to Marilyn's support, telling Aline Mosby of the Los Angeles *Daily News* that Crawford and her like were just jealous of the newcomer. "Marilyn's the biggest thing that's happened to Hollywood in years," Grable asserted. "The movies were just sort of going along, and all of a sudden—zowie!—there was Marilyn. She's a shot in the arm for Hollywood!"

As it happens, Betty was about to costar with that shot in the arm at the same time as she was being usurped by her. Painfully aware that, in light of her snubbing for *Gentlemen Prefer Blondes,* the choice roles were now being fashioned for Marilyn, Grable bowed to the inevitable, and following a showdown with Zanuck on July 1, 1953, tore up her contract with five years still remaining. "Honey, I've had it," she told Marilyn. "Go get yours. It's your turn now."

By this time, Marilyn was receiving upwards of 25,000 fan letters each week. *Redbook* named her "Best Young Box Office Personality," and she and Jane Russell immortalized themselves on the forecourt of the Chinese Theater on Hollywood Boulevard by signing their names, and placing their hands and feet, in wet cement. *Blondes* would make Marilyn an international superstar, and she in turn would serve as one of the film industry's main assets—along with innovations such as CinemaScope—in its fight against the incursions of television.

> *"I never had a chance to learn anything in Hollywood. They worked me too fast. They rushed me from one picture into another. It's no challenge to do the same thing over and over. I want to keep growing as a person and as an actress, and in Hollywood they never ask me my opinion. They just tell me what time to show up for work."*
>
> MARILYN MONROE, 1954

Performing "After You Get What You Want You Don't Want It" in the film There's No Business Like Show Business—*hat-check girl Vicky must have saved a long time for this particular costume.*

At the Turnabout Theater in the spring of 1953, Marilyn studied with acting coach Michael Chekhov and mime artist Lotte Goslar, while continuing her private tuition with Natasha Lytess. Yet, ignoring her aspirations to be a serious dramatic actress, Darryl Zanuck and his cronies now assigned Marilyn some of the limpest roles of her starring career: as a saloon singer in the Western adventure *River of No Return,* and then as a burlesque singer in *Pink Tights.* She reluctantly accepted the first assignment, quickly regretted it, then rejected the second assignment and was placed under suspension by the studio.

A remake of the Betty Grable pictures *Coney Island* (set in New York) and *Wabash Avenue* (set in Chicago), *Pink Tights* was supposed to costar MM and Frank Sinatra. Marilyn, however, wasn't prepared to be shoehorned into yet another stereotyped role, and neither was she charmed by the news that Sinatra would be earning $5,000 a week, precisely four times her own salary. Thus, she didn't report for work on December 15, 1953, and then reiterated her determination eight days later by flying out of Los Angeles to spend Christmas in San Francisco with Joe DiMaggio.

Fox waited until the holidays were over before suspending its hottest star without pay on January 4. Marilyn let it be known that money wasn't the major issue here; she just wanted to take a look at the script in order to assess its suitability. This, of course, wasn't in the rules laid out by the good old studio contract, which basically stipulated that the employee would accept any role that was assigned—or else. Nevertheless, Marilyn no longer felt either the need or the desire to play by the rules. Having taken the fast track to stardom by doing whatever Fox had required of her, she now knew that she had developed some muscle, and she was prepared to flex it if Fox wouldn't allow her to exert some measure of control over her own destiny.

Zanuck, of course, knew that he had no legal obligation to do this, but with a $2.2 million production on the line, he sent Marilyn the script. She read it and rejected it. Now both sides dug in, although the studio boss, while stressing that "The picture is written and designed for her," did blink first. After his recalcitrant star made international headlines by marrying Joe DiMaggio in San Francisco on January 14, Zanuck's wedding gift was a lifting of her suspension and a return to the payroll. The couple would be honeymooning down in Palm Springs for the next few days, so January 20 would be a reasonable date to start rehearsals for *Pink Tights,* wouldn't it? By January 26, Marilyn was back on suspension.

"The part isn't good for me," Marilyn told columnist friend Sidney Skolsky at the time. "It's as simple as that. Of course I'd like a salary adjustment, but right now I'm more interested in getting a good script so I can make a good picture."

The following day the newlyweds arrived in Japan, where Joltin' Joe was scheduled to watch some exhibition baseball games. There the press and public went wild for Marilyn, and shortly afterwards she accepted an invitation to entertain troops still stationed in Korea. This she did between February 16 and 19, before returning to the States with her suddenly second-fiddle husband on the 24th.

On March 8, 1954, Marilyn was yet again feted by *Photoplay* magazine, this time for her performances in *Gentlemen Prefer Blondes* and *How to Marry a Millionaire.* Then, at the end of the month, she officially signed with the Famous Artists agency, whose cofounders Charles Feldman and Hugh French had been handling her career for some time, even though Marilyn had still been obliged to pay the William Morris agency its commission until the end of 1953.

Famous Artists represented a number of actors and actresses under contract to Twentieth Century-Fox, and Feldman enjoyed a good relationship with the studio's top brass. Consequently, it was soon agreed that Marilyn would no longer have to appear in *Pink Tights*—which was later scrapped altogether—as long as she would play a

smaller (yet equally trite) part in the Irving Berlin musical extravaganza *There's No Business Like Show Business.* Marilyn had been written into the story line the previous December specifically to boost its box office appeal, but she only accepted the assignment because of the studio's pledge that she would be given the costarring role in the film version of the Broadway hit *The Seven Year Itch.*

Fox verbally promised to give her a $100,000 bonus for appearing in *Itch,* while also agreeing to pay drama coach Natasha Lytess, vocal coach Hal Schaefer, and choreographer Jack Cole to work with her on *Show Business.* What's more, a new, more financially rewarding seven-year contract would be implemented in August of 1954. Round One to Marilyn—at least in terms of her dealings with the studio.

Now residing in a rented house on North Palm Drive in Beverly Hills, Marilyn reported for work on *There's No Business Like Show Business* in late May, and as with *River of No Return,* she quickly regretted it. Joe DiMaggio didn't like the idea of his wife

With Robert Strauss and Tom Ewell in The Seven Year Itch.

being anything but an obliging housewife, he objected to the flashing of her semi-clothed body before the cameras, he resented her ongoing association with acting coach Natasha Lytess, and he took particular exception to the close relationship (professional and personal) that she formed with singing coach Hal Schaefer.

Suffering from anemia, bronchitis, and the side-effects of sleeping pills—upon which she increasingly depended—Marilyn began to crack up under all the pressure. She was often emotional and disoriented on the set, as well as dispirited about the part that she was playing in such a lightweight film.

"I was put into these movies without being consulted at all, much against my wishes," she would tell the *New York Herald-Tribune* the following year with regard to *River of No Return* and *There's No Business Like Show Business*. "I had no choice in the matter. Is that fair? I work hard, I take pride in my work, and I'm a human being like the rest of them. If I keep on with parts like the ones [Fox] has been giving me, the public will soon tire of me."

Stuck in back-to-back vacuous movies, Marilyn gave back-to-back vacuous performances, although Natasha Lytess had to shoulder a fair amount of the blame for her protegée's often ridiculously affected acting style. That having been said, it would also be equitable to give Lytess much of the credit for Marilyn's outstanding performance in

The Seven Year Itch, which began filming within days of work being completed on *Show Business.* In truth, however, the peerless on-screen results were almost certainly due to the strong directorial and cowriting contributions of Billy Wilder, in conjunction with MM's alternately amazing and alarming ability to match the standard of material, good or bad.

When principal photography on *The Seven Year Itch* wrapped on November 4, 1954, Marilyn's agent—and the film's coproducer—Charles Feldman threw a party in her honor at Romanoff's restaurant in Beverly Hills. Among the star-studded lineup of guests that evening were Marilyn's childhood idol Clark Gable, as well as Gary Cooper, Susan Hayward, Humphrey Bogart, Lauren Bacall, William Holden, Loretta Young, Jimmy Stewart, Claudette Colbert, Clifton Webb, Doris Day, Billy Wilder, Jack Warner, Samuel Goldwyn and, yes, Darryl Zanuck. "I feel like Cinderella," Marilyn told journalist Sidney Skolsky after arriving an hour late. "I didn't think they'd all show up."

"This party was a big deal to Marilyn," Skolsky wrote a few days later, "because it signified in its peculiar Hollywoodian manner that the elite of the town had finally accepted her."

Darryl Zanuck and *Seven Year Itch* playwright George Axelrod both complimented Marilyn on her "magnificent" performance in the film, even though its completion coincided with the disintegration of her relationship with Twentieth Century-Fox. In fact, Zanuck had been increasingly vocal about her absences, tardiness, and inability to remember her lines, and he was also frustrated with Marilyn's constant whining about wanting to be handed some serious dramatic parts. After all, the tried and trusted formula had worked so far, hadn't it? And if it ain't broke, then why fix it?

Marilyn, on the other hand, was fed up with Zanuck overlooking her talents and aspirations, while under-appreciating the efforts that were earning Fox millions of dollars at the box office. By making noise about her to his colleagues and to the press, the head of production was trying to put the onus on Marilyn to make the first concession. However, neither he nor his honchos could have anticipated her plans to make a clean break—from a disastrous marriage that had reached the point of no return during the filming of *The Seven Year Itch;* from an unpopular and increasingly demanding acting coach who was now more of a liability than an asset; from an environment that seemed designed to stifle rather than encourage artistic expression; from an agency she suspected was being too amenable towards her employers; and from the studio system that was methodically strangling her personal and professional development.

For several of the remaining few months of 1954, while lawyers searched for contractual loopholes that would enable Marilyn to forgo her commitment to Fox, she and photographer Milton Greene finalized plans to form an independent production company that would afford them creative leverage and a larger slice of the profits. Greene, a top celebrity photographer, had first befriended Marilyn several years earlier, and it was he who had suggested forming an enterprise that would enable the partners to select viable projects, obtain the necessary financing, oversee the writing, hire the preferred cast and crew, and generally guide each undertaking through to completion. The only problem was that neither of them had any production experience whatsoever.

Marilyn Monroe was, therefore, taking a giant leap into the unknown when, just before Christmas of 1954, she donned a black wig and dark glasses, booked a ticket in the name of Zelda Zonk, and flew to New York, where Milton Greene was awaiting her. Nothing less than the career for which she had worked so very hard was on the line, yet Marilyn wouldn't return to Hollywood for more than a year, and when she did it would be strictly on her own terms.

Gentlemen Prefer Blondes

The Plot

Following a nightclub performance, entertainers Dorothy Shaw and Lorelei Lee are visited backstage by wealthy dimwit Gus Esmond. Lorelei informs Dorothy that she and Gus are planning to sail on the Ile de Paris so that they can get married in Europe, but Gus's father is suspicious that Lorelei is just interested in his son's money, and when Gus can't make the trip, Lorelei takes Dorothy as her chaperone. In so doing, she hopes to make Gus jealous and lure him to Europe, away from his father's influence, yet what she doesn't know is that the elder Esmond has hired a private detective, Ernie Malone, to monitor her activities.

Aboard the ship, while Dorothy hangs out with the muscle-bound male athletes who are en route to the Paris Olympics, Lorelei makes a beeline for Sir Francis Beekman, the elderly owner of a South African diamond mine. Beekman, affectionately known as "Piggy," only has eyes for Lorelei, she only has eyes for his riches, and this plays right into the hands of Detective Malone, who secretly photographs the pair just as Piggy is clutching the wily blonde gold digger to demonstrate how a python kills a goat by squeezing it to death. Dorothy has been growing close to Malone, but when she sees him using the camera, she informs Lorelei, and they eventually retrieve the incriminating photo.

▲ *Jane Russell and Marilyn in the French "Two Little Girls From Little Rock" segment that was cut from the movie. A few seconds of footage were included in the film's promotional trailer.*

▶ *A lobby card utilized an inaccurately colorized black-and-white still of the omitted "Little Rock" scene.*

Piggy is extremely grateful for this, and he rewards Lorelei by acceding to her request for his wife's diamond tiara. The only problem is that Malone has recorded this transaction with a hidden tape recorder, and he forwards the information to both Lady Beekman and Esmond Sr.

After arriving in Paris and shopping at the city's most chic stores, Lorelei and Dorothy try to check into a swank hotel, only to be greeted by Malone, Lady Beekman and her lawyer, who demand the return of the tiara. Insisting that it was a gift, Lorelei refuses, thus placing herself in trouble with the law, and then also discovers that Gus has cancelled her letter of credit. With their vacation in tatters, Dorothy and Lorelei land jobs as the headlining act at the Chez Louis nightclub, where Gus visits them just before a gendarme arrives with a warrant for Lorelei's arrest. Dorothy persuades her to return the tiara, but they then discover that it has been stolen.

While Lorelei works her magic on Gus so that he'll cough up the money to bail her out of trouble, Dorothy appears in court disguised as "Madamoiselle Lee" and works her magic on Malone. She confesses that she is in love with him, prompting Malone to locate Piggy and show the judge that it is the old man who lifted the tiara. Gus's father, meanwhile, arrives in Paris to confront Lorelei, but it doesn't take her long to win him over, and as the ship sails back to New York there is a double wedding between Lorelei and Gus, and Dorothy and her private dick.

Behind-the-Scenes Facts & Opinions

Gentlemen Prefer Blondes is not a great movie, but it does have some outstanding moments and an all-time classic musical segment that amply justify its celebrated status.

Tommy Noonan's asinine performance as Marilyn's rich beau is more annoying than amusing, and song-and-dance sequences such as "Anyone Here For Love?"—in which Jane Russell checks out a bunch of bare-bodied muscle-men while they provide a demonstration of early-1950s aerobics—are pretty hokey. Nevertheless, Russell herself is first-rate as Lorelei's streetwise sidekick Dorothy Shaw, and so is Charles Coburn as Lord "Piggy" Beekman, a monocled magnate with a roving eye. Marilyn Monroe, on the other hand, steals the show. Stunningly attractive in a variety of dazzling Travilla costumes, she imbues not-so-dumb Lorelei Lee with the breathless voice and exaggerated lip and eye movements that have served as rich material for generations of Marilyn impersonators. Together with her appearances in *The Seven Year Itch* and *Some Like it Hot,* this performance is the perfect embodiment of the self-contrived MM persona, but Marilyn wasn't immediately pegged for the role.

At the start of 1952, Carol Channing was briefly in the running after Twentieth Century-Fox had spent half a million dollars securing the rights to make *Gentlemen Prefer Blondes.* With her saucer-shaped eyes and raspish voice, Channing had been a sensation as Lorelei in the Broadway stage version of Anita Loos' original 1925 novel. That novel, serialized in six parts as *Gentlemen Always Prefer Blondes* in *Harper's Bazaar* magazine, had been made into a silent black-and-white film starring Alice White and Ruth Taylor in 1928, and then adapted by Loos and Joseph Fields for the 1949 stage musical. However, neither Darryl Zanuck nor his assigned producer, Sol Siegel, felt that Carol Channing had sufficient name recognition for the movie, and so they soon began considering other actresses with proven box office allure.

First on the list was Fox's reigning queen, Betty Grable, who made it clear to Zanuck that she wanted the part of Lorelei Lee. Zanuck was more than aware of Grable's abilities as a singer, dancer, and comedienne, yet by early 1952 there was a fast-growing

GENTLEMEN PREFER BLONDES

★★★★

A Twentieth Century-Fox Release
Produced by Sol C. Siegel
Directed by Howard Hawks
Screenplay by Charles Lederer
Based on the musical Comedy by Joseph
Fields and Anita Loos
Cinematography by Harry J. Wild
Sound by E. Clayton Ward and Roger Heman
Art Direction by Lyle Wheeler
and Joseph C. Wright
Music and Lyrics by Jule Styne and Leo Robin
"When Love Goes Wrong" and "Anyone
Here For Love?"
by Hoagy Carmichael and Harold Adamson
Choreography by Jack Cole
Costume Design by Travilla
Edited by Hugh S. Fowler
Released: July 31, 1953
Running Time: 91 minutes
Technicolor

CAST

Dorothy Shaw	Jane Russell
Lorelei Lee	Marilyn Monroe
Sir Francis Beekman	Charles Coburn
Detective Malone	Elliott Reid
Gus Esmond	Tommy Noonan
Henry Spofford III	George Winslow
Magistrate	Marcel Dalio
Esmond Sr.	Taylor Holmes
Lady Beekman	Norma Varden
Watson	Howard Wendell
Hotel Manager	Steven Geray

Uncredited:

Sims	William Cabanne
Winslow	Harry Carey, Jr.
Dancer	George Chakiris
Proprietor	Jack Chete
Coach	John Close
Cab Driver	George Davis
Purser	Charles DeRavenne
Ship's Captain	Jean Del Val
Passport Official	Robert Foulk
Pritchard	Alex Frazer
(Bit Part)	Robert Fuller
(Bit Part)	Larry Kert
Grotier	Henri Letondal
Headwaiter	Alphonse Martell
Featured Dancer	Matt Mattox
Peters	Ray Montgomery
Anderson	Alvy Moore
Phillipe	Leo Mostovoy
Dancer	Fred Moultrie
Evans	Robert Nichols
(Bit Part)	Ron Nyman
Pierre	Alex Paix
Passport Official	Ralph Peters
Waiter	Rolfe Sedan
Captain of Waiters	Harry Seymour
Steward	Philip Sylvestre
Ed	Charles Tannen
(Bit Part)	Lee Theodore
(Bit Part)	Dick Wessel
Court Clerk	Max Willenz
Stevens	Jimmy Young

MM'S SONGS

"Two Little Girls From Little Rock" (with Jane Russell) by Jule Styne and Leo Robin

"Bye, Bye Baby" by Jule Styne and Leo Robin

"When Love Goes Wrong" (with Jane Russell) by Hoagy Carmichael and Harold Adamson

"Diamonds Are A Girl's Best Friend" by Jule Styne and Leo Robin

buzz about Marilyn Monroe, and after Zanuck heard a recording of her sexily singing "Do It Again" for the U.S. marines at Camp Pendleton, he began to envisage Marilyn in the role. What's more, in the second year of her contract, she would cost only $750 per week instead of Betty Grable's $150,000 per film. (This would subsequently equate to a total of about $9,000 for the December 1952 to February 1953 shoot, while Jane Russell would indeed receive $150,000 for her work.) On June 1, 1952, her 26th birthday, Marilyn was informed that she had landed the part of Lorelei Lee.

At that point, wholesale changes were being made to the musical by screenwriter Charles Lederer. Out of the 18 songs being performed in the stage version—including numbers involving Lorelei such as "It's Delightful Down In Chile," "Homesick Blues," "Button Up With Esmond," and the title number "Gentlemen Prefer Blondes"—only three of the Jule Styne/Leo Robyn compositions made it into the finished film: "Bye, Bye Baby," "A Little Girl From Little Rock" (amended to "Two Little Girls From Little Rock" so that Jane Russell could accompany Marilyn), and "Diamonds Are A Girl's Best Friend."

Furthermore, the last-named song had two verses excised due to lyrics that were then considered too racy for the screen. The first of these ended with the lines "But buyers or sighers/They're such Goddam liars," while the second verse was even more 'risqué': "Some girls find/Some peace of mind/In a trust fund that banks recommend/But if you are busty/Your trustee gets lusty . . ."

Charles Lederer's June 20, 1952 outline opens in the present day, with Lorelei and Dorothy in their fifties, reminiscing about their 1924 Parisian adventure, but this idea was eliminated by the time of Lederer's first screenplay just ten days later. (In the movie the time setting is vague—the athletes are clearly on their way to the Paris Olympics, which were staged there in 1924, yet the fashions are straight out of the 1950s.) Anita Loos' niece, Mary Loos, simultaneously penned a "Working Script" with husband Richard Sale, incorporating more of the original songs, yet this was passed over in favor of Lederer's work, and he continued to submit revised screenplays. His September 25 "Temporary Script" was the first to contain a complete storyline, and although it suggested opening with the "Diamonds" number over the main titles, it was fairly similar to the movie.

"I want to say that I think this is some of the best dialogue I have ever read in any script," Darryl Zanuck commented during a September 27 conference with Lederer, Sol Siegel, and director Howard Hawks, while suggesting that the film should open with Lorelei and Dorothy arriving at the dock, where they are ogled by the Olympic team. "Suppose the ship hit an iceberg and sank, which one would you save from drowning?" asks one of the athletes, to which another replies, "Those girls wouldn't drown. Something about them tells me they can't sink." In the finished movie, this is amended to the less suggestive "Those girls couldn't drown."

Lederer's 'Revised Final' script of November 10, 1952, incorporated numerous changes that do appear in the film, and several others that didn't quite make it. By now, in addition to the aforementioned triplet of songs retained from the Broadway show, there were new ones composed by Hoagy Carmichael and Harold Adamson, including "When Love Goes Wrong" and "Anyone Here For Love?" These two ended up on screen, but certain others didn't.

Lorelei was scheduled to sing "When The Wild Wild Women Go Swimmin' Down In The Bimini Bay," while Dorothy had three scripted sequences in which she sang "My Conversation" to and with Detective Malone, but both numbers were nixed by Zanuck before the start of production. Another musical segment was filmed (but later cut) that took place on the boat, after Lorelei and Dorothy have discovered that Henry Spofford

◀◀ *The French-language "Little Rock" sequence would have immediately followed "When Love Goes Wrong" and preceded "Diamonds Are A Girl's Best Friend". It was cut because Darryl Zanuck felt that the picture would be unbalanced by having too many musical interludes.*

III is a young boy. Lorelei dances with Lord Beekman and "generally gives him the works," but when he tries to kiss her she laughs, pushes him away, and sings "Down Boy."

This was cut from the released film, although the very end of the segment did survive, showing Marilyn dancing with Charles Coburn and wearing a gold lamé dress that was adapted from one that Ginger Rogers had recently worn in *Dreamboat*. "She literally had to be sewn into that dress because she wanted it to look like a second skin," recalled Bill Sarris, who was then the assistant to designer Billy Travilla. "She really loved it, and she would later wear it to the Photoplay Awards."

Meanwhile, there were other musical sequences that were filmed and cut from the movie just before its release. One, entitled *Four French Dances*, was not a song, as has been asserted in other books, but simply a quartet of orchestral arrangements. On the other hand, a segment in which Marilyn and Jane sport Napoleon-style hats with black bustiers and yellow trimmings, accompanied by similarly attired chorus dancers and a backdrop painting of the Eiffel Tower, featured the pair singing a French-language version of "Two Little Girls From Little Rock." The soundtrack to this number was later discovered in the Fox vaults, but not the footage, although a few seconds of it do appear in the film's promotional trailer.

"In those days it was standard practice at Fox to wait one year after the release of a picture, and then we would junk all of the outtakes and all of the trims," explained James Blakeley, who was an assistant editor on *Gentlemen Prefer Blondes*. "We'd throw them away because of storage problems and because we never thought we'd use them again. In fact, when I graduated from editing and was put in charge of post-production, I would issue a 'letter of destruction' with my signature on it, saying that it was okay to throw away a specified list of trims and outtakes. These would then be dumped in large barrels and taken away."

Thanks to this short-sighted policy, cut footage has often only been retrievable if it exists in foreign release versions.

"Back then, we had our own self-contained editing department, and like practically every major studio in town we also had our own trailer department," Blakeley explained. "Someone from there would come to us before we had got in our first cut and say, 'Look, I've read the script, and I'd like to have this scene and that scene,' and we'd make him a duplicate negative so that he could make the trailer even before we finished the picture. That's how scenes that were cut before the picture's release—and which were eventually junked—occasionally ended up in the trailer, because they wanted to get that trailer into the theaters well before the film was released."

Both "Down Boy" and the French-language "Two Little Girls From Little Rock" were cut because Darryl Zanuck felt that the picture would be unbalanced by having too many musical interludes. Indeed, as illustrated by the appearance of Lorelei and Dorothy in yellow-trimmed black bustiers when Gus first encounters them backstage at the Paris nightclub, the Little Rock sequence would have immediately followed "When Love Goes Wrong" and preceded "Diamonds Are A Girl's Best Friend." "I can't say for certain, but those decisions probably came down to Darryl Zanuck, who in my estimation was a marvelous editor," said James Blakeley. "He never cut any film himself, but he had an innate ability to know a good cut, and he would be the one to say, 'Well, I think we ought to do this and we ought to do that,' because in those days his word was final."

"Diamonds Are A Girl's Best Friend" was never destined for the trim bin. Probably the single most identifiable film sequence pertaining to the career of Marilyn Monroe, it is the perfect blend of stunning art design and outstanding choreography, shot in long takes that required very few edits, and forever enshrined by Marilyn's inimitable performance.

George Chakiris, who would win a Best Supporting Actor Oscar a decade later for

Marilyn models the costume that Travilla originally designed for the "Diamonds" number. However, in light of the nude calendar scandal, the Fox front office ordered him to "cover her up!" The outfit was never used. Given the feathers and the tail, Jack Cole's choreography and Joseph Wright's set would have probably been considerably different for the "Diamonds" sequence.

his performance as Bernardo in *West Side Story,* was a 19-year-old dancer at the time of *Gentlemen Prefer Blondes,* and he was able to observe Marilyn firsthand from his vantage point as a participant in the "Diamonds" segment.

"Jack Cole was clearly Marilyn's favorite choreographer," Chakiris told me in 1994. "She loved him and he was absolutely perfect for her. He was one of the great choreographers not only for film but for the stage as well, and for the musical numbers he took over the direction. The work was very demanding and he was very demanding. We rehearsed three weeks or more for the 'Diamonds' sequence, and it took three days to shoot. The last day they went overtime, because Jack had to go back to New York to do a show, so instead of working until six o'clock I believe we worked up until nine, and then Jack raced off to the airport."

During the shoot of "Bye, Bye Baby," even though Jack Cole and Howard Hawks were happy with the first take, Marilyn apparently demanded another ten before she herself was satisfied. "Marilyn was always concerned about herself, how she looked, and it didn't matter what everybody else was doing," confirmed Ron Nyman, who was one of the chorus dancers for that number. "It had to be right for her." Marilyn's frequent lateness on the set also didn't help matters, and so when the studio brass asked how production could be sped up, Hawks' terse reply was "three wonderful ideas: Replace Marilyn, rewrite the script and make it shorter, and get a new director."

"Square-cut or pear-shaped, these rocks don't lose their shape. . ."— Watched over by George Chakiris (top right), MM delivers her inimitable performance of "Diamonds Are A Girl's Best Friend."

According to Jane Russell, most of Marilyn's colleagues didn't fully appreciate the extent of her insecurities, and as a result they had little idea as to how they should handle her. "Marilyn was very sweet and very shy, and nervous about going out on the set," Russell told me in 1994, "so I used to just stop by her dressing room and say, 'Come on, it's time to be there,' and she'd get up and come with me. I think if there had been someone to do that on a lot of other films she would never have been late. She was just scared."

George Chakiris agreed with this notion, citing Marilyn's conduct during filming of the "Diamonds" sequence as being hardly that of a prima donna:

At the very beginning, where she is in the round chaise with the guys all around her, whenever she made a mistake or Jack shouted 'Cut,' she didn't go to a mirror to check her makeup, and she didn't go to her dressing room and wait to be called. She did what we did: she went right back to her starting position. She was working very hard, she obviously cared a great deal, and she really didn't for one moment behave like a star. Someone would go up to her, perhaps, and fix her hair a little bit or touch up her makeup, but that was not what she would do. She was working, and I must say she was very conscientious and really just wonderful. She cared deeply about wanting everything to be the best it could be. . . . At that time, Natasha Lytess was present during the entire filming. Between takes, Jack Cole was talking to Marilyn, and while I couldn't hear what he was saying, I could see that he was telling her something about the number. She was facing him, listening to him, and directly behind him—unbeknown to him, but facing her—was Natasha Lytess, who was very quietly shaking her head 'no.' So, there was Marilyn Monroe, facing both of them and trying to be nice to both of them at the same time. I remember that so well. She had such a sweetness about her."

Meanwhile, the now-legendary shocking pink dress that Marilyn wore for the "Diamonds" sequence was not the one that Travilla originally designed. "The costume that Bill initially dressed Marilyn in was like a leotard with all of these rhinestones, and it was very nude looking," recalled Travilla's then-assistant Bill Sarris. "This was after the calendar had come out, and it didn't take long before Bill received a call from Zanuck's office saying, 'Cover her up.' So, they threw that out and he designed the shocking pink dress. That used a very heavy fabric and it was not fitted; they just belted it in. The other one was never filmed, but there's a still shot of Marilyn wearing it. A couple of years later Bill used that design for Betty Grable when she was doing her Las Vegas act."

So much for the best laid plans. However, an even quicker improvisation came about towards the end of filming the "Anyone Here For Love?" sequence, when, as per the tirelessly rehearsed routine, Jane Russell bent down at the edge of the swimming pool so that the dancers could dive over and around her into the water. The problem was, one of them clipped Jane on the head with his foot and she rolled into the pool, even though her tumble did look intentional.

"It was an accident, and we had to go back and re-shoot the whole number, but they ended up using that footage," Russell confirmed. "We had a long time in those days to rehearse the numbers, and we'd worked every day for a couple of months. I wasn't supposed to end up in the pool at all, but it turned out better the way it happened, although the poor dancer got fired. I mean, it didn't hurt." Ron Nyman, who managed to avoid Jane Russell with his own well-executed dive, added, "The guy's name was Ed Fury, he caught her by accident, and the reason he was fired is because he then insisted on getting a co-choreography credit. . . . Anyhow, I guess it was late morning and they told everybody to take two hours for lunch, because they had to dry Jane off and get her hair restyled. Then, when we got back from lunch, Jack Cole's assistant Gwen Verdon was in the same black outfit as Jane's and they had two guys on either side hauling her out of the pool. Jack was looking at how the clothes and makeup reacted to the water, and then he and Howard Hawks decided that this would work, so they kept the shot of Jane falling into the pool and created a different ending by having her emerge from the water."

A comedic high point of the film occurs towards the end, when Esmond Sr. (wonderfully portrayed by Taylor Holmes) finally encounters Lorelei and makes it clear that she is nothing but a gold digger. She insists that she loves Gus, prompting the indignant old man to ask, "Have you got the nerve to stand there and expect me to believe that you don't want to marry my son for his money?" "It's true," she says, before responding to the question "Then what *do* you want to marry him for?" by calmly stating, "I want to marry him for *your* money!"

The same scene includes a line suggested by Marilyn that not only reveals her grasp of the Lorelei character, but also neatly summarizes her own real-life predicament. "I thought you were dumb!" exclaims Esmond Sr., provoking Lorelei to explain, "I can be smart when it's important, but most men don't like it."

It is doubtful that the Fox hierarchy paid any attention to this subtle rejoinder, but in time their sexist underestimation of Marilyn's mental astuteness would come back to haunt them.

The Critics' Views

"In her own class is Marilyn Monroe. Golden, slick, melting, aggressive, kittenish, dumb, shrewd, mercenary, charming, exciting sex implicit . . . Miss Monroe is going to become part of the American fable, the dizzy blonde, the simple, mercenary nitwit, with charm to excuse it all."

MOTION PICTURE HERALD

"There is the amazing, wonderful vitality and down-to-earthness of Jane Russell . . . AND—there is Marilyn Monroe! Zounds, boys, what a personality this one is! Send up a happy flare. . . . Her natural attributes are so great, it's like a triple scoop of ice cream on a hot August day, to realize she is also an actress—but, by golly, and Howard Hawks, she is . . . . She'll do more for 20th Century-Fox than their discovery of oil on the front lot."

L.A. EXAMINER

"The pneumatic aspects of Marilyn Monroe and Jane Russell are examined extensively in *Gentlemen Prefer Blondes,* and while it is plain that both ladies are most pleasantly configured, it is also apparent that neither of them have more than a glancing acquaintance with the business of acting."

THE NEW YORKER

Public Reaction

Produced for $2.26 million, and enticing audiences to see "the world's most fabulous gold-digging blonde," *Gentlemen Prefer Blondes* was Marilyn's largest-grossing film to date—and the third biggest of her entire career—scooping a cool $5.1 million at the box office during its initial run.

Gentlemen Prefer Blondes *put Marilyn's career over the top, yet thanks to her Fox contract she earned about $9,000 for the December 1952 to February 1953 shoot while Jane Russell's take was $150,000.*

A dream sequence depicts Pola's fantasy about being gifted jewels during a Middle Eastern trip with her eye-patched suitor, J. Stewart Merrill (Alex D'Arcy).

wardrobe lady looked at Natasha like she wanted to kill her. Back then I don't recall any other actors having their coach on the set. Directors generally don't like coaches on the set, they don't care for them at all, and they don't like mothers on the set either!"

Jean Negulesco was no exception. On April 13, 1953, sick of Marilyn demanding countless retakes until her coach gave the nod of approval, he banned Natasha Lytess from the set. The next day, Marilyn had a sudden attack of bronchitis and failed to show up, and before long Lytess was invited back . . . at a higher salary. "Monroe cannot do a picture without her," agent Charles Feldman advised his staff in a memo. "The coach threatens to quit unless she is compensated in a substantial manner."

And so the tiring process continued. "Marilyn was frightened, insecure," Lauren Bacall wrote in her 1978 autobiography, *By Myself*. "During our scenes she'd look at my forehead instead of my eyes."

Bacall also described how, thanks to the all-important judgment of Natasha Lytess, scenes often required 15 or more takes, meaning that Marilyn's fellow actors had to be good in all of them as there was no way of knowing which one would be used. "Not easy—often irritating," admitted Bacall. "And yet I couldn't dislike Marilyn. She had no meanness in her—no bitchery. She just had to concentrate on herself and the people who were there only for her."

According to Lauren Bacall, she and Betty Grable agreed to make things as easy as possible for Marilyn, so that she eventually came to trust them. However, this was to be Grable's last film under her Fox contract, which she tore up with five years remaining in recognition of the fact that Marilyn was being groomed to assume her title as "Queen of the Fox Lot."

In *How to Marry a Millionaire,* Loco wrongly asserts that some music on the radio is being played by trumpeter-bandleader Harry James, who was then Betty Grable's husband, and there are several other inside jokes sprinkled throughout the movie: trying to persuade J. D. Hanley that she has always liked older men, Schatze Page says, "Look at Roosevelt, look at Churchill, look at that old fellow what's-his-name in *African Queen. . . .*" (Lauren Bacall's husband, Humphrey Bogart, was 25 years her senior.) When Pola models a red swimsuit (of which there is a little more close-up footage in the movie's publicity trailer), she is introduced with the line, "You know, of course, that diamonds are a girl's best friend, and this is our proof of it," while for leisure reading during a plane trip she has a book entitled *Murder by Strangulation,* the fate suffered by Marilyn's character in *Niagara.*

The film's closing scene—around the counter (l–r) are Betty Grable, Rory Calhoun, Lauren Bacall, Cameron Mitchell, myopic Marilyn, and neck-braced David Wayne.

Mark overhears this, he loses all respect for his father, despite the latter's insistence that he shot a man who was trying to kill his friend. The journey continues, Kay catches a cold as a result of getting soaked, and Matt, although he appears uninterested, takes tender care of her. Kay, confessing that she and Harry aren't actually married, quickly falls for Matt, and even when he brutally tries to force himself upon her, she isn't put off.

After overcoming a wild bobcat, greedy fortune hunters, arrow-totin' Indians, and the raging waters, Matt, Kay, and Mark arrive safely in Council City. Kay meets with Harry, who assures her that he will talk to Matt, yet as soon as he sees him Harry pulls out a gun. Still unarmed, Matt looks as if he is about to meet his maker, until Mark uses a rifle from a store to kill Weston with a shot in the back. Having saved a life in the same fashion as his father once did, Mark is now able to identify with Matt, and the two reconcile. Kay, meanwhile, takes a job in the local saloon. However, after she finishes a performance, Matt slings her over his shoulder and tells her that she is going home with him and Mark.

"Moderately high barometric pressure will cover the, er, north, east and . . . the Deep South!" Marilyn lights up the screen with her sizzling rendition of "Heat Wave." And to think—Ethel Merman had previously been slated to perform this number. As usual, Marilyn imbues Travilla's revealing design for the "Heat Wave" number (above) with even more sex appeal in the movie.

business to join the priesthood. At a Four Donahues engagement down in Florida, Vicky—now renamed Vicky Parker—is the support act and Tim makes a strong play for her, but with producer Lew Harris planning to showcase her in a Broadway revue, Vicky is far more focused on a career than a full-time relationship. Still, Harris does offer to feature Tim and Katy in the same show, and although their mother is already miffed with Vicky for performing a song that she herself had intended to sing, Molly nevertheless gives them her blessing.

Tim proceeds to date Vicky, but he gets jealous when she spends professional time with Lew Harris, and he drunkenly infers that she is sleeping with the producer in order to advance her career. On the show's opening night, Tim drinks some more, gets into a car accident, and ends up in hospital. While Molly fills in for him by partnering Katy on stage, Terry reprimands his irresponsible son and slaps him in the face, as a result of which Tim checks out of the hospital and disappears. Molly blames Vicky for the sorry situation, but Terry blames himself and he takes an extended leave to search everywhere for Tim.

Eventually, on the long-running revue's closing night, Molly and Vicky reconcile after Katy stresses that Tim was the cause of his own troubles. Steve, now an army chaplain, shows up backstage, and then while Molly steps before the footlights, Navy recruit Tim appears in the wings, as does a relieved Terry. For the first time in years, the Five Donahues perform together on stage, and during the show's grand finale they are joined by Vicky.

Behind-the-Scenes Facts & Opinions

Conceived as a tribute to the music of Irving Berlin, *There's No Business Like Show Business* utilizes a wafer-thin story about the trials and tribulations of a close-knit showbiz family in order to run through no fewer than 14 of Berlin's songs. A few of the production numbers are standouts—most notably "A Man Chases A Girl," which features virtuoso dancing by Donald O'Connor; Marilyn's electrifying and risqué performance of "Heat Wave"; and of course Ethel Merman's classic, barnstorming rendition of the title song, which leads into the kind of glitzy, cast-of-thousands finale that no real-life theater stage could ever accommodate. Nevertheless, for all of the overblown production values, the picture's overall effect is more cloying than engaging, with a script that has as much corn as a truckload of Green Giant.

As assembled by producer Sol Siegel, the talent in this movie is an extremely mixed bag: Merman and O'Connor are both in top form; Dan Dailey and Mitzi Gaynor are also fine, although Dailey really overdoes things when required to emote; Marilyn looks terrific in some stunning Travilla costumes, and compensates for exaggerated acting by cranking up the power when singing and dancing; and Johnnie Ray . . . well, what to say about Johnnie Ray, except that as an actor the early 50s pop sensation has a dazzling smile. When singing a ballad in his trademark crying voice, the "Nabob of Sob" (as he was then idiotically dubbed) wiggles his lower jaw as if it has been hinged to move sideways, while it's anyone's guess as to why he was cast in a bizarre role that sees him becoming a priest!

Still, Darryl Zanuck apparently envisaged a bright future for him on the big screen. "When you next come out here, I will show you the Johnnie Ray test," Zanuck wrote in a letter to Irving Berlin on December 17, 1952. "He is more than a singer; he is a wonderful performer."

Nine months earlier, Lamar Trotti had come up with a basic story outline and some cast suggestions of his own: The troupe's mother figure should be "a Thelma Ritter type," the father "a somewhat younger Jim Barton," the eldest boy intriguingly "a Dan Dailey

When Vicky rehearses with the band, Tim discovers that her repertoire includes "Heat Wave," which his ma Molly Donahue has been planning to perform.

type," the sister "a Betty Grable type," to be courted by "a Fred Astaire type," while the "Donald O'Connor type" younger brother is in love with "a Mitzi Gaynor type."

"With this wide sweep we ought to be able to use twenty-five or thirty song numbers," Trotti optimistically noted. His June 12, 1952, "Writer's Working Script" then expanded the family to include four children—Tim, Al, Katy, and Steve—while providing for a narration by the man himself, Irving Berlin. On June 17, Lamar Trotti submitted a "First Draft Continuity Script," and following a conference with Zanuck, Berlin and director Walter Lang six days later, he started preparing a "Temporary Script," but then on August 28, 1952, Trotti died suddenly of a heart attack, aged 51.

In Darryl Zanuck's aforementioned December 17 letter to Irving Berlin, he dedicated himself to continuing Lamar Trotti's work, and to that end listed an ideal cast: Dan Dailey as Terry, Jane Wyman as Molly, Donald O'Connor as Al, Johnnie Ray as Steve, R. J. (Robert) Wagner as the youngest son Tim, and Mitzi Gaynor or June Haver as Katy.

"With a cast like this you can see that we are headed for one of the all-time great box office attractions," the studio boss assured the composer, while reiterating that he also wanted Berlin to sit at the piano and narrate. "You are show business and this is a story of show business told through the medium of one family."

The playing-and-narrating concept would be retained until just before the start of production. Meanwhile, I. A. L. Diamond was to be assigned the rewrite, yet on January 3, 1953, Zanuck received a memo from Sol Siegel stating that, while he thought Diamond was a good writer who would become better in time, for a rewrite it would be wiser to use someone of more experience and greater stature. Zanuck may have considered this, but for the time being he was prepared to give Diamond a chance, and the result was a screenplay in which the Tim character sings "Heat Wave" (Robert Wagner singing "Heat Wave"?) and then dies in World War II.

After a second attempt by Diamond in early February, Phoebe and Henry Ephron were then recruited to come up with a story line that was much closer to that of the finished film. At the same time, it was suggested that Ethel Merman should sing "Heat Wave." By May, Johnnie Ray was cast as Al. Before the start of production, this character would evolve into producer Lew Harris, Ray would play Steve, and Donald O'Connor would displace Robert Wagner as Tim. However, it wasn't until the Ephrons' "Final Script" of December 17, 1953, that the role of Vicky was created especially for Marilyn Monroe, at which point the singing of "Heat Wave" was thankfully assigned to her. (In the film, the Ethel Merman character intends to perform the number, and she fumes when she is obliged to let Marilyn's character do it instead. As a riposte, Merman was supposed to sing "Anything You Can Do, I Can Do Better," but this scene ended up being cut from the movie.)

Quite simply, Zanuck wanted to add the studio's hottest property to the cast of *Show Business* in order to boost its box office potential, and he lured Marilyn by promising her the starring part in Fox's upcoming filmization of George Axelrod's hit Broadway play, *The Seven Year Itch.* She in turn complied not only because she coveted that role, but also because, after Fox suspended her for refusing to appear as a turn-of-the-century singer in *Pink Tights,* this was a way of both sides making amends. Besides, Marilyn's January 14, 1954 marriage to Joe DiMaggio began to unravel even before the honeymoon was over, and by May 29, although suffering from anemia and bronchitis, she was more than a little glad to report to the studio for the start of filming.

Unfortunately, DiMaggio's sexist and sometimes brutal disapproval of his wife's career, together with Marilyn's newly acquired dependence on sleeping pills, conspired to create problems on the set. Often groggy and confused, she sometimes broke down in tears under all of the pressure that she was feeling.

"She was a hell of a nice kid," Donald O'Connor asserted in a 1994 interview. "I'd known Joe since 1938, and I felt for him and I felt for Marilyn. She was having a very, very difficult time."

Indeed she was. DiMaggio was resentful of drama coach Natasha Lytess' influence over his wife—even though Donald O'Connor insisted that, during his scenes with Marilyn, "Natasha was always in the background. She was rarely on the set,"—and he was increasingly jealous of the close relationship she was enjoying with vocal coach Hal Schaefer. Matters came to a head on August 27, when the baseball great showed up to watch the filming of the "Heat Wave" number, then stormed off in protest over what he considered to be Marilyn's lewd and disgusting exhibitionism. On the next take she broke into a sweat, went up on her lines and slipped over, before ultimately pulling herself together and perfecting a routine that is now an integral part of the Monroe legend.

"A front of warm air is moving in from Jamaica," Marilyn intones as she frolics around in exotic headwear, a strapless bikini top and an open flared skirt. "Moderately high barometric pressure will cover the, er, north, east and . . ." "Where else?" ask the chorus dancers. "The Deep South!" she responds with a bump, while pushing the skirt between her gaping legs. "Hot and humid nights can be expected." *That's* for sure.

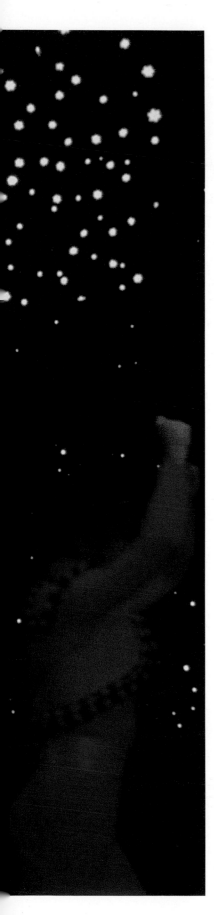

"One of the things that Jack Cole very often did with female stars was throw in little bits of dialogue," explained George Chakiris, who had worked with the choreographer when dancing in the "Diamonds Are A Girl's Best Friend" sequence of *Gentlemen Prefer Blondes.* "He would insert humorous little asides with sexual innuendos or undertones, and these were kind of surprising at the time, but they were always in good taste."

Chakiris participated in the film's grand finale, yet he was originally also scheduled to take part in the "Heat Wave" sequence as choreographed by Robert Alton, who was contracted to take charge of all the dance numbers in *There's No Business Like Show Business.* Accordingly, Alton—who, like Jack Cole, was one of the most respected choreographers of his time—rehearsed the "Heat Wave" routine and then invited Marilyn to watch it being performed.

Chakiris recalled in 1994, "The way he did it was to use four boys including me, along with a girl standing in for Marilyn—so that he could present it to her—and a guy who partnered her. We worked for about four weeks in one of those wonderful big rehearsal halls that no longer exist at Fox, and once the number had been choreographed and it was ready to present to her, she came in at about two or three in the afternoon, simply dressed, no makeup, and very quietly watched.

"Marilyn was very sweet and she was nice enough to see what Bob Alton might have done for her, but it can't have been what she wanted because she subsequently had Jack Cole choreograph the number instead. I loved working for Robert Alton, but I have to say that she was right. The number that Jack Cole did for her was better. His style was very different to Alton's. It was sexier, and I guess you could say it was more modern in terms of the feel."

Meanwhile, Jack Cole was not the only member of Marilyn's "team" with whom she insisted on working. Very attached to William Travilla, whom she would call at all hours of the night (much to his wife's annoyance), Marilyn stood firmly by his side when the costume designer clashed with the producer of *Show Business.* "Bill was very easygoing, but he got into some sort of thing with Sol Siegel and he walked off the film," recalled Travilla's then-assistant, Bill Sarris. "Well, Marilyn walked off the set too. She wouldn't continue unless he did her clothes, so they brought him back just to dress her, while Miles White was brought in to finish things up with everyone else."

Still, such displays of solidarity aside, Marilyn was characteristically late on the set even when she did have all of the desired people around her. "When she was filming 'Lazy' with Mitzi Gaynor and Donald O'Connor, they were there ready to shoot at nine o'clock in the morning, and Marilyn wasn't ready until about three in the afternoon," George Chakiris recalled, while Ron Nyman—who participated in some of the movie's other musical sequences—stated that after Marilyn did show up, she still managed to delay proceedings.

Nyman recalled, "She was on the couch while Donald O'Connor and Mitzi Gaynor were dancing their asses off, and all Marilyn had to do was get up and say, 'Wrong number.' Well, every time it got to her bit the director would call, 'Cut. Do it again,' and after 50 takes of this Donald and Mitzi were just wiped out. At that point, Bob

Johnnie Ray, Mitzi Gaynor, Dan Dailey, Ethel Merman, Donald O'Connor, and Marilyn Monroe descend the stairs while singing the title number in the film's lavish finale.

While autographing some publicity photos, Marilyn shoots the breeze with Johnnie Ray, whose screen test had prompted Darryl Zanuck to enthuse, "He is more than a singer; he is a wonderful performer."

Alton and Walter Lang said, 'Marilyn, come over here,' and they sat behind me with Natasha Lytess. I leaned back and I could hear them say, 'Marilyn, in this scene you're like a bubble. You burst.' She said, 'I do?' and they said, 'Yes. Now go out and do it.' Well, she went out and she did it in two takes. That night I had dinner with the director and I said, 'I don't know what I would do if someone said that to me. I mean how does that bubble burst?' and he said, 'Ah, that's just the way you talk to her.' Obviously, it worked."

Unfortunately, Walter Lang wasn't always so understanding. He and cameraman Leon Shamroy had worked with Marilyn eight years earlier, when she filmed her first screen test for Twentieth Century-Fox, yet on the set of *There's No Business Like Show Business* Lang reportedly disparaged her at every opportunity.

"He was a strange guy," asserted Donald O'Connor, who had worked with Lang on the 1953 picture *Call Me Madam,* costarring Ethel Merman and again featuring the music of Irving Berlin. "His claim to fame was that he wasn't a good director, but all of his pictures made money. To tell you what he was like, we were doing the sequence where Marilyn is rehearsing with the band. Thanks to her bouffant hair and high heels she looked taller than me—even though she was about five-foot-five and I'm five-nine—so Lang came over to me and asked if I'd stand on an apple box. I said, 'Why don't you ask her to take off her shoes?' and he said, 'I'm afraid to.' I went to Marilyn and I said, 'Marilyn, this idiot's afraid to ask you to take off your shoes, but I'd feel very strange working with you, standing on an apple box.' She said, 'Oh Christ, the guy's nuts.' So, she kicked off her shoes and everything was fine."

Not quite so straightforward, on the other hand, was the show-stopping "A Man Chases A Girl" sequence, which O'Connor described as "one of the best numbers I've ever done." Dancing amid fountains and statues that come alive, O'Connor acquitted himself memorably, yet what neither he nor the costumer anticipated was that his suit would shrink under the hot studio lighting when soaked in the spraying water. O'Connor recalled, "The legs of my pants would rise about six inches, my sleeves would rise, and they didn't make enough jackets and pants for me. I had to wait in the wardrobe department to get outfitted again, but the day we shot that scene the air conditioning went off and I had the toughest stuff to do, so it was pretty difficult."

Having recently signed an exclusive contract with RCA Records, Marilyn was not permitted to appear on the official *Show Business* soundtrack recording released by Decca Records in 1954. Instead, Broadway star Dolores Gray performed MM's numbers, while Marilyn recorded separate versions for the RCA extended-play release *Songs From 'There's No Business Like Show Business,'* which featured "Heat Wave," "Lazy," "After You Get What You Want You Don't Want It," and a track entitled "You'd Be Surprised," which is performed by Dan Dailey in the movie. It is not clear whether Marilyn was originally slated to sing it.

Over schedule, the filming of *Show Business* wrapped in late August of 1954, at which point Marilyn immediately flew to New York to commence location work on *The Seven Year Itch*.

The Critics' Views

"You'll see a new Marilyn Monroe in this picture . . . the kid has learned to act . . . And she has learned to read comedy lines as though she knew what they meant."

HOLLYWOOD REPORTER

"Miss Monroe's s.a. treatment of her vocal chores must be seen to be appreciated. It's not going to chase 'em away from the b.o. On the other hand, as a song salesgirl, per se, she'll never have to worry Miss Merman. She's more competitive to Mae West in her delineating."

WEEKLY VARIETY

"When it comes to spreading talent, Miss Gaynor has the jump on Miss Monroe, whose wriggling and squirming to "Heat Wave" and "Lazy" are embarrassing to behold."

NEW YORK TIMES

Public Reaction

The lavish production numbers, expansive cast, expensive costumes, and overlong schedule, all added up to the most costly film of Marilyn Monroe's entire career. In return for a $4.34 million budget, *There's No Business Like Show Business* grossed $4.5 million during its first run, meaning that, despite healthy attendance figures, the movie initially failed to break even after publicity and distribution costs had been deducted.

The Seven Year Itch

THE SEVEN YEAR ITCH

★★★★½

Twentieth Century-Fox Release
Produced by Charles K. Feldman
and Billy Wilder
Directed by Billy Wilder
Screenplay by Billy Wilder
and George Axelrod
Based on the Original Play
by George Axelrod
Cinematography by Milton Krasner
Sound by E. Clayton Ward
and Harry M. Lennard
Art Direction by Lyle Wheeler
and George W. Davis
Music by Alfred Newman
Piano Concerto #2 by S. Rachmaninoff
Costume Design by Travilla
Edited by Hugh S. Fowler
Released: June 17, 1955
Running Time: 105 minutes
CinemaScope and DeLuxe Color

CAST

The Girl	Marilyn Monroe
Richard Sherman	Tommy Ewell
Helen Sherman	Evelyn Keyes
Tom MacKenzie	Sonny Tufts
Mr. Kruhulik	Robert Strauss
Dr. Brubaker	Oscar Homolka
Miss Morris	Marguerite Chapman
Plumber	Victor Moore
Elaine	Roxanne
Mr. Brady	Donald MacBride
Miss Finch	Carolyn Jones

Uncredited:

Ricky Sherman	Butch Bernard
Indian Girl	Dorothy Ford
Waitress	Doro Merande
Indian	Ron Nyman
Train Station Gateman	Ralph Sanford
Woman in Train Station	Mary Young

The Plot

When his wife Helen and bratty son Ricky leave the summer heat of New York City for the cooler climes of Maine, Richard Sherman stays behind and vows not to smoke, drink, or chase women like the rest of the male pack. An unimposing 38-year-old man with a florid imagination, Sherman works for book publisher Brady & Co., creating sensational titles and lurid covers for 25¢ reprints of literary classics. However, although he can only fantasize about women lusting after him, his far-flung dreams take a step towards reality when, on his first night alone, the sensuous new tenant in the upstairs apartment agrees to join him for a drink.

Immediately, Sherman's pledges go out of the window as he smokes, imbibes alcohol, and sets about trying to woo the 22-year-old model with tall Martinis and Rachmaninoff's *Second Piano Concerto*. She reciprocates by contributing a packet of potato chips and a bottle of champagne, and all goes well until, during a joint rendition of "Chopsticks" at the piano, Sherman makes a clumsy pass at The Girl.

Feeling stupid and guilty after they fall on the floor, he asks her to leave, yet he is still full of self-recrimination the next day. Instead of doing his work, Sherman reads how "the urge-curve in the middle-aged husband rises sharply during the seventh year of marriage." This so-called "seven year itch" reportedly afflicts 91.8 percent of married males during the summer months, and when a psychoanalyst provides no solution, Sherman imagines The Girl telling the entire nation about his lecherous behavior.

"A married man, air conditioning, champagne and potato chips—it's just a wonderful party!"

One of the most famous scenes in the history of the movies— Richard Sherman watches admiringly as air blasting through the subway grating provides The Girl with temporary relief from the summer heat.

Back home, Sherman's determination to stay away from his neighbor is quickly forgotten when he convinces himself that Helen is having an affair with handsome writer Tom MacKenzie, whom she ran into on the train ride to Maine. As "retaliation," therefore, he takes The Girl out to dinner and a movie, and after seeing *The Creature From the Black Lagoon* the two of them kiss outside the theater. They then return to Sherman's air-conditioned apartment.

Asking if she can spend the night there rather than in her own stuffy abode, The Girl ends up sleeping in Sherman's bed while he dozes on the sofa, and the next morning he imagines Helen returning home and shooting him after learning of his "affair." The Girl manages to calm Sherman down, and when he admits to being dull and unworthy of his own fantasies, she also tells him that his kindness and modesty are far more exciting than the vanity of good-looking men.

Fitting that description is Tom MacKenzie, who is flattened by Sherman's fist when he comes calling for a toy paddle that little Ricky left behind. His pride and sense of reality restored, Sherman now decides to hand-deliver the paddle and spend the next two weeks with his wife and child, while telling The Girl that she can stay in their apartment until they return.

Filming on New York's Upper East Side, September 1954.

Behind-the-Scenes Facts & Opinions

An acerbic, funny look at marital infidelity during the ultra-conservative Eisenhower years of the 1950s, *The Seven Year Itch* was toned down considerably in its translation from stage to screen, but it is still a wonderful movie with a terrific script and outstanding performances by the two lead actors.

As a sweet, sexy and charmingly innocent model who cools off by keeping her undies in the icebox, thinks that everything is "just elegant," and recognizes classical music "because there's no vocal," Marilyn is completely endearing. She not only looks delectable, but she also displays a first-rate flair for comedy. This is one of her very best performances, and as such it stands as the best reason for not attempting to remake the film. Tom Ewell, on the other hand, although not boasting quite the same physical attributes, is equally fine as the plain-faced everyman who dreams about shedding his domestic lifestyle for that of a stud.

Ewell had originated the role of Richard Sherman in the hit 1952 Broadway production of *The Seven Year Itch,* opposite Vanessa Brown as The Girl. Yet, after Billy Wilder approached George Axelrod about purchasing the screen rights, and Fox weighed in with around half a million dollars, the director/coproducer/cowriter's initial instinct was to try out a little-known actor whom he had seen in another Broadway play.

That actor's name was Walter Matthau, who filmed a black-and-white screen test with Gena Rowlands in New York on June 15, 1954, focusing on the scene where Sherman hastily prepares to entertain The Girl in his apartment and she then arrives. Wilder liked what he saw and he was ready to hand Matthau the role, but the studio wasn't prepared to take a chance on an inexperienced newcomer, and so the director then filmed a color test of the same scene with Tom Ewell. He got the part.

Clearly able to spot talent, Billy Wilder would return to Walter Matthau just over a decade later when starring him opposite Jack Lemmon in *The Fortune Cookie.* However, even though the aforementioned screen test confirms that Matthau would have been excellent as Richard Sherman, and that as a result he probably would have achieved stardom several years earlier than he eventually did, he still would have been hard pressed to outdo the efforts of Tom Ewell, who shares some timeless scenes with Marilyn Monroe.

One of these is a dream sequence where The Girl, outfitted in a figure-hugging tiger-pattern dress, falls under the spell of Sherman as a Noel Coward-esque smoothie when he serenades her with Rachmaninoff's *Second Piano Concerto.* "It shakes me, it quakes me, it makes me feel goose-pimply all over," she enthuses, before he stops playing and tells her, "now I'm going to take you in my arms and kiss you, very quickly and very hard."

Both actors are superb as the melodramatic participants in Richard Sherman's fantasy. Meanwhile, other standout sequences in which Marilyn shows deft comic timing include that in which Sherman thinks about seducing The Girl as they play "Chopsticks" at the piano, and the segment where she gives a performance of her Dazzledent toothpaste TV ad and talks about sticking her big toe in the bath faucet.

In George Axelrod's original play, Richard Sherman actually sleeps with The Girl. However, thanks to the self-imposed Production Code, which existed to ensure that filmmakers didn't provoke moral outrage and alienate moviegoers, motion pictures still didn't enjoy the same amount of freedom as the theater during the 1950s. Consequently, Axelrod and cowriter Billy Wilder removed all explicit references to adultery from the screenplay of *The Seven Year Itch,* and when Darryl Zanuck and Wilder's coproducer Charles Feldman foresaw censorship trouble over a scene in which a maid finds a hairpin in Sherman's bed, they removed that too.

The result was that, from Axelrod's perspective, the story lost its whole raison d'être, for as he would later assert with regard to the central character, "if he hasn't had the affair with The Girl he's got nothing to feel guilty about, so the picture really doesn't make very much sense."

Actually, it does, for there is still much comic value to be derived from Sherman getting so immersed in his fantasies that he starts to feel guilty about them and become paranoid about the consequences. Nevertheless, at the behest of the studio and the censors, much of the sharper dialogue had to be replaced, although Axelrod and Wilder did draw the line when Catholic organization the National Legion of Decency tried to assert pressure and make script suggestions.

As late as July 23, 1954, with the start of shooting just a few weeks off, the screenplay was still incomplete, ending at the point where The Girl descends a previously sealed-off staircase between her apartment and Sherman's and prepares to spend the night at his place. The August 10 "Final Script" then completed the story, yet even after filming commenced in early September there were numerous rewrites taking place.

"That was very usual," Billy Wilder told me in 1994. "Very often I would still be working on the third act with my collaborator while I was already on the soundstage shooting the first or second act. That way I could get a feel for the characters. We'd have a perfectly good idea as to how we were going to end the story, but this wouldn't be final and the dialogue would only be sketched out. So, quite often, I'd start with a script that was 70 to 80 percent complete, and then have Saturday and Sunday to rewrite and correct a scene that I had already shot, or to work on the ending of the picture."

In the finished film there are numerous dream sequences in which Sherman fantasizes about passionate escapades, his romancing of The Girl, her informing people about how she was molested by him, and the consequences that he might suffer as a result of his misdeeds. Nevertheless, several more were scripted, and some were actually filmed, before being discarded at the editing stage. For example, between the sequence where The Girl is in a bathtub with her toe stuck up the faucet, informing a plumber about Sherman's evil ways, and that in which she tells the nation about him on TV, there were two additional scenes.

The first of these had the plumber telling what he has heard to a woman on a subway car, while two waitresses from a vegetarian restaurant where Sherman has eaten gossip about him. The second scene was set at New York baseball venue, Yankee Stadium, where the pitcher, "Lopat," pitches a ball, and the catcher, "Yogi Berra", calls time, walks to the mound, takes off his mask and, rubbing the ball, initiates a short conference by telling Lopat about the piano bench episode. "No kidding," says Lopat, to which Berra responds, "Well, it figures. The guy's got the seven year itch!" By now the umpire has joined the discussion, and saying that he was on the subway when he first heard about the incident, he asks, "Anybody know who the poor girl was?" "I don't know her name," replies Berra, "but she's on the Dazzledent program. The one with the teeth . . . on television!"

"They are standing on the mound and talking, and people think they are discussing what kind of a pitch he wants," Billy Wilder explained. "I shot part of the scene during a game at Yankee Stadium, using a long lens so that nobody was bothered, and then I filmed the close-ups later on in New York. However, the scene laid an egg, and being that we had already made the point in other little fantasy sequences, we said, 'The hell with it.' It was just one of a series, and this one did not work."

Yet another cut dream sequence was that filmed on October 25, 1954, in which Robert Strauss portrays a gangster and Marilyn plays his moll, Tiger Lil, looking like a slimmed-down version of Mae West. This was intended to lead on from the segment towards the end of the movie where Sherman discovers that The Girl is no longer

October 25, 1954—Tom Ewell and MM film a dream sequence in which Sherman envisages The Girl as a gangster's moll. This was one of several segments cut from the movie.

asleep in his bed and, unaware that she is in the shower, assumes that she and the janitor Mr. Kruhulik are rifling through his bank safety deposit box.

The aforementioned cut scenes were excised from the picture for artistic reasons, yet there were also others that, due to complaints about their sexual innuendo, were replaced with alternate takes after the film was simultaneously premiered in New York and previewed in Los Angeles on June 1, 1955. In the version subsequently released to theaters, the short scene of Marilyn in the bathtub fades with her saying, "Then suddenly he turned on me, his eyes bulging. He was frothing at the mouth, just like the Creature From the Black Lagoon!" As originally shot and screened, however, this is immediately followed by the elderly plumber dropping his wrench into the tub, groping around in the water to retrieve it, and saying "I'm sorry," to which The Girl calmly responds, "That's alright."

Then there is the most famous scene in the movie—or of any movie, for that matter—featuring The Girl standing over a subway grating outside the movie theater and enjoying the cool breeze blasting up her skirt. The released version of the film shows her saying, "Isn't it delicious?" the first time the skirt billows up around her thighs, before exclaiming, "Oh, here comes another one!" and experiencing a second pleasant draft, at which point Sherman asks her to tell him more about the "kissing-sweet" qualities of Dazzledent toothpaste. As originally filmed and premiered, the same shots of Marilyn saying "Oh, here comes another one!" and the breeze going up her skirt are followed by her telling a leering Sherman, "This is even cooler . . . must be an express. Don't you wish you had a skirt? I feel so sorry for you in those hot pants."

Who ever said making movies isn't tiring work?

These two "long-lost" scenes resurfaced nearly half a century after the film's release when researchers at Fox viewed a print of *The Seven Year Itch* that was supplied for foreign release. Post-production chief James Blakeley told me back in 1993: "I've talked to some people at the studio relative to restoring old pictures, and they have found that certain segments that were removed from the American version might still be in a foreign version somewhere. You see, when we make a picture we make an original negative that we keep in this country, and so we then make a duplicate negative to send to other parts of the world. Therefore, if we take out certain things for our own release, they might still exist overseas."

It might be worth checking out those foreign prints. Still, it is ironic that the aforementioned scenes were considered too racy, when certain then-risqué dialogue did make it past the censors—entering his three-unit apartment building near the start of the movie, Sherman refers to "those two guys on the top floor; interior decorators or something," while Marilyn's entrance a short time later sees her halfway up the staircase in a skintight cotton dress, asking Sherman, "Would you mind pressing it again?" "Press what?" he asks. "The button," she replies, referring to the entry-hall buzzer. "My fan's caught in the door." Being that her curvaceous derriere is sticking out when she says this, Sherman briefly hesitates before realizing that she is talking about the cable of her electric fan.

The legendary skirt-blowing scene combines footage shot on location in New York and on a soundstage at Twentieth Century-Fox—when MM and Tom Ewell walk out of the Trans-Lux Theater and the camera pans down to show her skirt billowing upwards, this is on Lexington Avenue in New York, near the 52nd Street intersection. Thereafter—as can be determined by the different store-window background—shots of the pair talking, and of Marilyn enjoying a second blast of cool air, derive from retakes filmed in Hollywood. This was due to the actors having been distracted, and their voices obliterated, by the cheers, shouts, and wolf-whistles of several thousand New Yorkers as Marilyn—sporting two pairs of white panties—stood above a real subway grating and smiled her way through multiple takes during the early morning hours of September 15, 1954.

"I think they really used the wind from the subway train," said Paul Wurtzel, who was then Fox's head of special effects. "At least, we never sent anyone to New York from our department for that segment, so I don't think that anybody rigged it. The location shoot was partly unsuccessful because there was just too much noise and commotion. We did not have the techniques then that we have now to dub voices, and Marilyn was horrible with the facilities that we did have, so we had to duplicate the set according to what the art director showed us and reshoot the scene back at the studio.

"I was standing inside a wind tunnel under the stage where the subway grating was, and on cue we'd remove this sliding top to create the effect of the train going by and blowing up Marilyn's skirt. Well, that scene took all day, what with Billy Wilder filming it over and over and over again, and there I was underneath her. Marilyn had a habit of squatting down and talking to me, and I can confirm that she was wearing tight panties . . . very tight."

The now-legendary fully-pleated white halter dress that Marilyn wore for the scene was designed by William Travilla, who was working on the Jane Russell/Jeanne Crain movie *Gentlemen Marry Brunettes* when he got the call to design ten costumes for *The Seven Year Itch.*

"Bill was leaving for London in a couple of weeks, so he designed that whole picture over the course of a weekend in the studio that I had in my apartment," recalled Travilla's then-assistant, Bill Sarris. "In those days you were not allowed to show cleavage, but Bill always talked about how, because of the way Marilyn's breasts were, you could cut a dress fairly low and still not show breast. Then again, Bill would also take a little half-ball button and sew it inside the costume where the nipple would be, so it looked like she had a titty hard-on all the time. They had all kinds of tricks. Anyway, for *Itch* the wardrobe department quickly made up the clothes at the studio, and he was able to leave for London. That was a real rush job, and when he worked out the design for the

While Marilyn talks to director Billy Wilder during a break in filming, her ever-present drama coach Natasha Lytess lurks in the background. The Seven Year Itch, however, would be the last project on which the women would work together.

skirt-blowing scene I'm sure he didn't think it was going to become the most famous dress in the world."

The massive promotional value of the New York shoot didn't escape the Fox publicists, yet this was hardly of interest to Joe DiMaggio when, standing alongside columnist friend Walter Winchell, he watched in disgust while thousands of people ogled his wife in her underwear. "What the hell's going on here?" he demanded of Winchell, who had encouraged him to attend the filming. Later on, in a suite at the St. Regis Hotel, a row between Marilyn and Joe turned ugly and he became violent. The next day, they returned to Los Angeles. Within three weeks she was filing for divorce.

Suffering from exhaustion and a heavy cold as a result of the chilly night spent filming outside the Trans-Lux Theater, Marilyn missed four days of work during late September, and when she did show up at the studio it was evident that she was in bad shape, both physically and emotionally. Medication and sleeping pills were having their effect, as was the strain of her crumbling marriage, yet Tom Ewell recalled that Marilyn still gave every scene her best effort.

"She was wonderful," Ewell told me shortly before his death in 1994. "Oh my God, she was great; so professional and so polite. Billy Wilder was wonderful too. He was the best director I ever worked with."

Judging the results of some on-set publicity shots during a break in filming the Tiger Lil segment.

He had to be. On bad days Marilyn would break down, fluff lines, and require numerous retakes of short scenes. On good days, she could be letter-perfect on the first take of a much lengthier and more demanding sequence, such as that towards the end of the film where The Girl refutes Sherman's notion that she's excited by a man who struts around with an "I'm so handsome you can't resist me" look on his face: ". . . there's another guy in the room, way over in the corner. Maybe he's kind of nervous and shy, and perspiring a little. First you look past him, but then you sort of sense he's gentle and kind and worried, and he'll be tender with you, nice and sweet. That's what's really exciting." As her relationship with Joltin' Joe hit the rocks, these tenderly delivered words may well have echoed Marilyn's own true sentiments.

Verbally offered a $100,000 bonus by Twentieth Century-Fox for her work on *The Seven Year Itch*, Marilyn would have to wait more than a year to receive it after principal photography was completed 13 days over schedule on November 4, 1954. (Final retakes were filmed on January 9, 1955.) However, the intervening months would bring significant changes in both her personal and her professional life, and by the time she would step in front of a movie camera next, Marilyn Monroe would be exercising far more control over the career for which she'd fought so hard.

The Critics' Views

"*The Seven Year Itch* is as merry a romp as ever screened—up to a point. Never has Marilyn the Marvelous been so well photographed, wonderfully dressed, nor presented as such an understanding young comedienne. She truly is a knockout. And that's the trouble, even as in the film. Because, excellent and funny actor though he is, Tom Ewell, next to her, presents all the sex appeal of a wet sandwich."

L.A. Examiner

"Marilyn is just about perfect in the role of the pleasantly vacuous and even more pleasantly curved heroine. . . . In the supporting cast, Oscar Homolka is a standout as a psychiatrist and Victor Moore, searching for a wrench in the depths of Marilyn's bubble bath, makes a bit a thing of joy."

Hollywood Reporter

"There are occasions when Tom Ewell evokes a laugh or two, but when Marilyn Monroe turns up as a young lady too substantial for dreams, the picture is reduced to the level of a burlesque show."

The New Yorker

Public Reaction

Proclaimed to be "The funniest comedy since laughter began" by its own publicity trailer, *The Seven Year Itch* was accorded a star-studded premiere at Loew's State Theater in Time Square, New York, on June 1, 1955, Marilyn's 29th birthday. Escorting her to the event was Joe DiMaggio, who had to walk under a 52-foot-high cutout of his bare-thighed, up-skirted wife as he entered the venue.

The $1,500 poster would eventually be replaced with a less revealing image after the theater received complaints (from DiMaggio?), yet the public didn't seem to mind the film, spending around $5 million at the box office to make it Fox'ss biggest hit of the summer.

Running Wild, Mighty Bold: 1955-1962

1 N 1955, Marilyn put her hands on the wheel and tried to take charge of her own destiny. Having already extricated herself from a disastrous marriage, she was also estranged from her long-term partner, Twentieth Century-Fox, and in an environment far removed from that which she had known all her life she laid the groundwork for her autonomy and her serious consideration as an actress.

In so doing, given the conformist and often prejudicial attitudes of the times, Marilyn was striking a blow for female independence. After all, while she was perceived in many circles as an enfant terrible and often mocked by the press, few could deny her determination or the eventual results of her efforts. What is more, by walking out on her contract and virtually holding Fox to ransom, she was playing an integral role in the demise of the repressive Hollywood studio system.

"Actors are pretty insecure people, so they generally seek a secure position, and the studio system gave them a certain amount of security," actor David Wayne explained. "However, they put you under a seven-year contract, and it was their option to renew it every year, so in reality the actors weren't as secure as they might have felt. When business wasn't too good, they'd start 'cleaning the stables', as they called it. They'd get rid of all their contract players, and the way they would do that was to send you either a terrible script or a good script with a tiny part, hoping that you would say, 'Screw you, Darryl Zanuck. I'm not going to do that and you can go ahead and fire me!' Which is usually what happened."

Announcing the formation of Marilyn Monroe Productions, with herself as president and Milton Greene as vice president, MM asserted that she was "tired of the same old sex roles. I want to do better things. People have scope, you know." Thus, after flying to Hollywood in early January to shoot retakes for *The Seven Year Itch,* she returned to the East Coast and from there fired salvos at Fox, stating that broken clauses meant she was no longer under contract, while the studio fired back that she most certainly was, and that she would be penalized if she didn't play the part of a stripper in *How to Be Very, Very Popular.*

> *"Later in her career she had the power to say, 'If I have to do 50 takes, I don't care, and nobody else should care either.' Because by then she knew that she was something, and she truly was something."*
>
> DAVID WAYNE, 1993

A pensive look during a problematic time. On location in Reno, Nevada, for her last completed film, The Misfits, *Marilyn sits beside her masseur Ralph Roberts, who had a small role in the movie as an ambulance attendant.*

This was an empty threat and Marilyn knew it. Besides, she didn't appear to care one way or the other, for by now she was digestng the sights and sounds of New York City, taking in Broadway plays, and attending the Actors' Studio, where Lee Strasberg had gained both respect and notoriety coaching people in the then-controversial "Method" style of acting. Derived from the teachings of Konstantin Stanislavsky at the Moscow Art Theatre, Method acting basically requires performers to draw on personal experiences in order to evoke real emotions, assuming a character's frame of mind rather than simply learning the lines and playing the part.

Marilyn certainly had plenty of experiences to draw on, not to mention demons to exorcise, and under Strasberg's guidance she set about discarding the overly mannered MM persona that she had worked hard to create, replacing it with a more multi-dimensional and realistic approach to her craft. As writer Mary Loos observed, "She would rather have been Anna Karenina than Marilyn Monroe."

A mid-1950s-style Hollywood publicity shot intended to promote The Prince and the Showgirl, *which is set in London in 1911.*

All of this signaled the end of Marilyn's relationship with Natasha Lytess, and, when she was ready to return to Hollywood, the start of a new one with Lee Strasberg's wife, Paula. From now on it would be the "Lady in Black" who would serve as Marilyn's ever-present coach, motivator, and adjudicator on the set.

At the end of 1955, with absolutely no one to replace her—certainly not the much-touted Sheree North, who had ended up appearing in *How to Be Very, Very Popular*—Fox caved in to Marilyn's demands and agreed to provide her with a far more equitable new contract. Over the next seven years she would only have to appear in a total of four films, for which she would be paid $100,000 each, in addition to $500 per week expenses during production. Marilyn would have story line, directo, and cinematographer approval, she could make a picture at another studio for each one that she made at Fox, and she could also perform on record and radio while making up to six TV appearances annually.

On the set of Billy Wilder's comic masterpiece Some Like It Hot.

Thus armed, Marilyn returned triumphant to Hollywood in early 1956, the same year that Darryl Zanuck became an independent producer and was replaced by Buddy Adler as Twentieth Century-Fox's head of production. Furthermore, she would subsequently live up to all of the hype—and far exceed most people's expectations—by way of her critically acclaimed performances in *Bus Stop,* directed by Joshua Logan, and *The Prince and the Showgirl,* costarring and directed by Sir Laurence Olivier. The latter, filmed in England and released by Warner Brothers, was the first to be made under the Marilyn Monroe Productions banner, but as things turned out it would also be the last, for by the latter part of 1956 storm clouds were already casting a shadow over Marilyn's bright hopes.

To start with, she had formed a business venture with Milton Greene, and together they had set about refashioning her career. Then Marilyn had hooked up with Lee and Paula Strasberg, both of whom began to exert their own brand of influence, before playwright Arthur Miller also entered onto the scene. He and Marilyn married on June 29, 1956, prompting the famous headline "Egghead Weds Hourglass," and thereafter a three-way struggle ensued between the husband, the drama coaches, and the business partner for control of the prize asset.

Max Showalter had already witnessed how Marilyn reacted when just two of the parties applied pressure during the filming of *Bus Stop:* "There was Milton Greene on one side and Paula Strasberg on the other, each clawing into Marilyn because they wanted dominance over her. They hated each other, and it was just pulling her to pieces. She came to me and said, 'Oh, I wish I could just get away from everybody and we could go and have dinner together someplace.' This was the first time Marilyn had ever said that to me. She didn't when we were filming *Niagara.* You could tell that she was frustrated."

Marilyn was herself suffering from a variety of physical ailments and emotional problems. She applied herself diligently when she turned up on the set, but she didn't turn up very much, and by breaking all of her previous records for absenteeism she managed to bring the walls of the Pico Boulevard studio crashing in on her. The Fox executives were determined to show some muscle in the face of what they regarded as costly shenanigans by their wayward stars, and to that end it would be much easier to make an example of Marilyn Monroe than, say, Elizabeth Taylor, who was earning a record $1 million plus $50,000 per week overtime in exchange for causing all sorts of delays on Cleopatra. Taylor was nevertheless vital to a production that had to be completed in order to have any hope of recouping its outrageous costs.

Marilyn was therefore fired from *Something's Got to Give* in early June, and although the photos of her semi-nude swimming pool scene attracted plenty of attention when they were published in *Life* magazine that same month, her death on August 5, 1962, was widely perceived as following on the heels of professional disgrace. Accordingly, Twentieth Century-Fox didn't make much noise about the fact that, just a few days earlier, the irreplaceable Marilyn had been hired to resume work on *Give,* at several times her former salary.

"She was very excited about going back to work," recalled Marilyn's stand-in, Evelyn Moriarty. "I spoke to her on the phone and she told me about how they were going to shoot Dean Martin's close-ups first, and then her close-ups. She was really up. She also told me that she had to finish this picture at Fox because she was going to do *I Love Louisa* for United Artists and three pictures in Europe, two of them with Brigitte Bardot."

I Love Louisa would eventually be produced by Fox and released in 1964 as *What a Way to Go!* starring Shirley MacLaine and an all-star cast. Meanwhile, other projects that Marilyn was considering shortly before her death included *Harlow,* eventually filmed with Carrol Baker and released by Paramount in 1965, and a musical version of *A Tree Grows in Brooklyn,* which had been proposed to Marilyn by composer Jule Styne, who would be writing the songs for *I Love Louisa.*

The two of them scheduled a meeting in New York for August 9, 1962, having agreed that Frank Sinatra might be good in the costarring role. This wasn't the first time that someone had come up with the idea of pairing Marilyn with Frank—it had previously been suggested for movies such as *The Girl in Pink Tights, Some Came Running,* and *Can-Can*—and the thought of them working together is somewhat amusing. After all, Frank was notorious for refusing to film more than a couple of takes, whereas Marilyn . . .

Had she lived, Marilyn would have continued to receive numerous movie offers. How she would have fared is open to conjecture. However, what is beyond doubt is the contribution that she made to the silver screen and popular culture. "Marilyn Monroe was a legend," Lee Strasberg eulogized at her funeral. "In her own lifetime she created a myth of what a poor girl from a deprived background could attain. For the entire world she became a symbol of the eternal feminine."

The TV Interview: Person to Person

Having announced the formation of Marilyn Monroe Productions back on January 7, and with the Twentieth Century-Fox situation very much in limbo, MMP's president and vice president set about recasting the star's public image from that of an empty-headed sexpot to that of a sophisticated businesswoman and serious actress. To that end, being interviewed by Ed Murrow on his Friday night show appeared to be the right political move.

The format of *Person to Person* was very straightforward: by way of a live hookup, celebrities would chat with Ed and show him around their homes while he sat comfortably in the CBS studio in New York. Two celebrities, often in different parts of the country, would fill each seemingly casual—yet carefully rehearsed—half hour: one during the first 15 minutes, the other thereafter. Yet, what complicated matters was the fact that, in the days before TV cameras could be easily moved around, the interviewees' homes were virtually taken over by a technical crew running cables from room to room.

From Marilyn's perspective this was no problem, since she was staying with Milton Greene and his family at their rambling 16-room, 150-year-old house—a converted barn and stable—in Weston, Connecticut, about an hour's drive from Manhattan. On the other hand, what did bother her was the prospect of appearing on live television, with no chance to film retakes if she said the wrong thing. As airtime approached her trepidation increased, for appearing alongside not only Milton but also his young wife Amy, Marilyn was concerned that her simple makeup and plain clothing would make her look drab by comparison. A cameraman's reassurance that millions of viewers would think she was beautiful only served to heighten her anxiety, before the aptly named producer, Fred Friendly, calmed her down by saying, "Just look at the camera, dear. It's just you and the camera—just you two."

CBS
Produced by Fred Friendly
Directed by Don Hewitt
Hosted by Edward R. Murrow
Featuring:
Marilyn Monroe, Milton & Amy Greene, Sir Thomas & Lady Beecham
Broadcast: Friday, April 8, 1955, 10:30–11:00 P.M.
Black & White

Marilyn looks typically relaxed when posing for still photographers before her one and only TV interview. During the actual broadcast she would appear a little more nervous.

The broadcast commences with Ed Murrow announcing his guests, who will include conductor Sir Thomas Beecham and his wife at home in New York during the second half of the show. After an outside shot of the Greene residence, Milton shows his host the cover photos that adorn his photographic studio, before walking into the kitchen where Amy and Marilyn are both seated at the table. Looking demure while speaking in a quiet, breathy voice, Marilyn talks about her modeling appearances on the covers of numerous men's publications "but never *Ladies Home Journal*," and of how she met Milton Greene on a film set when he was on assignment for *Look* magazine.

The small-talk then continues with Murrow asking Amy a set of idiotic and embarrassing questions that must have mortified the house guest: "Does Marilyn know her way around the kitchen? Is she very much help around the house?" "Yes, she is," Amy replies somewhat disingenuously. (MM was never going to win any prizes as a happy homemaker.) "She's sort of an ideal guest. She's not trouble to anyone, and she picks

Marilyn's preoccupation with herself caused some tensions on the set, but she shared an excellent on-screen chemistry with Don Murray, whose film debut earned him an Academy Award nomination as Best Supporting Actor.

Exhausted from his prize-winning exploits at the rodeo, Bo falls asleep during the trip, and this provides Cherie with another chance to escape when the bus makes a stop at Grace's Diner. Unfortunately, a heavy blizzard means that the bus is staying put, and when Bo wakes up he barges into the diner and hauls Cherie over his shoulder with the intention of finding the nearest minister. At this point, the burly bus driver has seen and heard enough, and when Bo won't listen to reason, he challenges the young bully to a fistfight. Naturally, Bo accepts, and the middle-aged man duly hands him his first pummeling.

The next morning, humbled and embarrassed, Bo bows to pressure from Virge and apologizes to all concerned, including Cherie, who in turn confesses that she is not nearly as innocent as the cowboy has assumed. For his part, Bo confirms his own naiveté, while asserting that he still loves Cherie regardless of how many men she has been with. These are the kindest words that the abused hillbilly girl has ever heard, and after enthusiastically accepting Bo's renewed proposal of marriage, Cherie and her now-courteous man leave for Montana without Virge, who is just happy that his ward no longer needs him.

Behind-the-Scenes Facts & Opinions

Based on William Inge's 1955 Broadway play—and adapted specifically for Marilyn by *Seven Year Itch* author George Axelrod—*Bus Stop* is a fine comedy-drama boasting excellent performances by a seasoned cast, as well as those by newcomers Don Murray and Hope Lange, who married that same year.

Treated with gentleness and respect for the first time in her life, Cherie gladly accepts Bo's offer to wrap up in his jacket as they set off for life together on his Montana ranch.

In the role of Cherie, an abused, tired-looking nightclub singer with a checkered past and uncertain future, Marilyn delivers a multifaceted performance that finally made the critics sit up and acknowledge her talents as an actress. In less-than-glamorous costumes that Marilyn herself selected, she is alternately sweet, sad, vulnerable and wistful, with a sex appeal that emanates more from within.

"I've been goin' with guys since I was about 12," Cherie tells Elma as they travel on the bus towards Montana. "I almost married a cousin of mine when I was 14, but Pappy wouldn't have it. . . . Them Ozarks don't waste much time. . . . Naturally I'd like to get married and have a family and all of them things. . . . Maybe I don't know what love is. I want a guy I can look up to and admire, but I don't want him to browbeat me. I want a guy who'll be sweet with me, but I don't want him to baby me either. I just gotta feel that whoever I marry has some real regard for me, aside from all that lovin' stuff."

What Marilyn projects in this scene is real. However, some additional dialogue was edited from the film to quicken the pace, and she would subsequently feel that this helped cost her an Oscar nomination. Don Murray, on the other hand, did get nominated for an Academy Award as Best Supporting Actor for his *Bus Stop* debut, playing an innocent but red-hot-blooded cowboy who handles a woman as if he's herding cattle.

Murray screen-tested for the part of Bo Decker and landed the role after Josh Logan had seen him on Broadway in the play *Skin of our Teeth*. "I think I got more from him as a director than performers usually get from directors," Murray said of Logan four decades later. "He was very, very specific in terms of so many things that he wanted me to do. I really have a great deal to thank Logan for, and not only for casting me. He really was a tremendous help in creating that performance."

Armed with her Method acting techniques, new coach Paula Strasberg, and a lucrative Fox contract that gave her story line, director, and cinematographer approval, Marilyn had originally wanted *Bus Stop* to be directed by John Huston, the man who had elicited what she considered to be one of her best performances in *The Asphalt Jungle*. Huston, however, was unavailable, so Marilyn then endorsed agent Lew Wasserman's suggestion to contact Joshua Logan, the playwright and stage and movie director, who had gained a scholarship to the Moscow Art Theater and studied under Konstantin Stanislavsky during the early 1930s. Logan was one of the 16 men on MM's list of approved directors, yet he initially balked at the *Bus Stop* assignment, telling Lew Wasserman, "But Marilyn can't act!"

Wasserman advised him to consult Lee Strasberg, her coach at the Actor's Studio, and when Strasberg subsequently singled out Marilyn as being—along with Marlon Brando—one of the two greatest talents he had ever worked with, Logan changed his mind. Soon, like numerous others both before and after, he would have to endure Marilyn's lateness, temperamental nature, and erratic work, yet he would ultimately concur with Strasberg's opinion, stating, "I finally realized that I had a chance of working with the greatest artist I'd ever worked with in my life, and it was Marilyn Monroe. I couldn't believe it."

Eileen Heckart, who is wonderful as Cherie's gritty sidekick Vera in *Bus Stop*, had previously worked with Joshua Logan on the Broadway production of *Picnic*. "He was one of those directors who, once you got the part, made you feel that only you could do it," Heckart told me in 1994. "He had that wonderful quality of adoring you while you were there working."

Nevertheless, the accomplished actress was also a firsthand witness to how Logan's adoration of Marilyn was put to the test during filming. "There was one scene in the bar with Arthur O'Connell and Marilyn and me where we had 39 takes," she recalled. "Josh came to me after about the 37th take and said, 'Do something!' and I said, 'Well, aside from saying her lines, I don't know what I could possibly do.' You know, Arthur and I didn't care anymore; let's just get something in the can!

"Her nervousness about not being able to produce is what made her late and unable to remember her lines. I think she knew herself very well in terms of what she could do and what she did best, but for me Marilyn was a movie star, she wasn't an actress. I mean, she wasn't stage trained and to that extent she had no craft. However, because of her wondeful, magnetic quality on-screen, people put up with the lateness and the nonsense."

According to Don Murray, Marilyn didn't appear to have a problem remembering her lines, but simply staying focused. "She would say just a few words and then lose her concentration," he said. "That meant whatever take she didn't completely fall apart on, they might use, and within the first couple of days I recognized that. I said to myself, 'Hey, Don, you've got to be at your best on every take.'"

This same predicament was faced by all of Marilyn's colleagues. "When you played opposite her in a scene she wouldn't look in your eyes," Eileen Heckart observed, "and when you were doing a close-up and talking to her she'd be licking her lips, gazing around and trying to remember to say the lines to you. There was nothing in her performance that you could take from or use, and I think the reason she didn't give as an actress is because she didn't know how. After four or five takes she was friendly and funny if something went wrong, but then she'd get so uptight herself that she'd start to take it out on other people."

Just ask Don Murray, who suffered a facial laceration as a result of Marilyn's frustration when filming the scene where Cherie is trying to get away from Bo in the saloon, and then gets mad at him when he grabs at her dress and rips a piece off.

"There was no indication in the script that she should hit me," Murray explained. "Marilyn, however, felt like she should pound on my chest, which was fine, but the first time she did this I wasn't prepared for it, so when she pushed me I moved out of the light and camera range. Josh Logan told me to just hold my ground and let her do whatever she wanted to do, but when we tried it again she put her head down as she hit my chest, and she bounced off me and fell on the floor. I thought she'd hurt herself, so I got down and lifted her up—not bothering to stay in character—and when she got up she was a little dazed, and she turned around and walked away.

"Josh Logan had told the cameraman, 'Never turn off the camera unless I say, "Cut." No matter what happens, keep going.' He knew that he had to put together a performance in tiny little snips. So, the cameraman kept rolling while I was picking her up and talking to her in my natural voice without the accent, and when Marilyn came back on the set she said, 'Was that alright? Can you use it?' Josh Logan turned to the cameraman and said, 'How much did you get of that?' and the cameraman said, 'Well, I think I got most of it, except when she fell on the floor and went out of camera range. Most of it's usable.' I said, 'Wait a minute, wait a minute. It might have been okay for Marilyn, it might have been okay for the camera, but it certainly wasn't okay for me, because I was worried about her and I stopped playing the Bo character. So, we'll have to do it over.' Well, she got mad at me and said, 'Oh my God, can't you ab-lib?' Not ad-lib, but ab-lib.

"Anyway, we did the scene over, and this time—after I ripped off the tail of her dress and she grabbed it back and told me off—instead of putting her head down and rushing at me, she lashed my face with the dress. I got a cut on the eyelid and Marilyn ran off, and although it didn't hurt much, I was really angry because it was very unprofessional. So, I followed her to bawl her out, and Josh Logan ran, got in front of me, and made me laugh by telling me the story about the Roman general who won all the wars by avoiding the battles. At that point I forgot about the whole thing, and after that it was a non-incident. When Marilyn came back on the set she had totally calmed down and she was fine. She didn't apologize—and I didn't expect her to or want her to—but the next day she came to me and started talking about another scene we'd done, and everything was okay."

The scene that Marilyn was now referring to was the one in which Bo blusters his way into Cherie's hotel bedroom and wakes her up so that they can head out for the rodeo and the marriage that he has planned. Told that it is after nine o'clock in the morning, Cherie says that she didn't get to bed until five, at which point Bo exclaims, "Five? No wonder you're so white and pale!" However, in one particular take, this wasn't quite what Don Murray said.

"Marilyn was very nervous when she acted," Murray recalled. "She'd break out into a rash all over her upper body, which they would cover with makeup. Well, in this scene I

could see the red rash through her makeup, and I guess that distracted me, because instead of saying 'so white and pale,' I said 'No wonder you're so white and scaly . . . .' A Freudian slip, I guess. When Marilyn reminded me about this later on, she said, "You know what you were thinking about, don't you?' I said, 'What?' She said, 'You were thinking about sex.' I said, 'How did you get that?' She said, 'Well, a snake is scaly, and a snake is a phallic symbol! You know what a phallic symbol is, don't you?' and I said, 'Know what it is? I've got one!' She didn't laugh at that. It kind of went over her head."

Meanwhile, true to form, Marilyn also seemed oblivious to many of the basics of movie acting, such as hitting her marks, staying within camera range, and only displaying what was desired on-camera. As a result, Josh Logan instructed Don Murray that, whenever he and Marilyn were being filmed above the waist, he should put his hands on her hips and move her back into position. Furthermore, when shooting the aforementioned bedroom scene, Marilyn was naked under the sheets, and she kept exposing herself everytime she turned to deliver some dialogue. The solution: Her costar was told to subtly keep the sheet tucked in. "It was really weird. Here I was doing my first film, with a famous movie star who had done plenty of films, and I was having to hold her on her marks and tuck the sheet in while trying to play my character," remarked Murray, who nonetheless was convinced that Marilyn was "a superb screen actress."

"Those were the days when censorship meant that you could do very little in love scenes," Murray continued. "Well, one day we had to redo the love scene at the end of the film because Marilyn had opened her mouth during the kiss, but it was difficult for her to get it right, because every time we kissed, her lips would automatically part.

"For that same scene Josh Logan said, 'I want an extreme close-up of just the two of their heads.' So, the cameraman set it up and he said, 'Josh, this isn't going to work. On the CinemaScope screen the heads are going to look too big. It'll be startling to the audience.' Logan said, 'I don't care. As long as you can get it in focus, I want it.' So, they set it up, and Josh Logan looked through the lens and said, 'Yeah, that's good. That's what I want.' The cameraman said, 'But it doesn't work, Josh. The frame is cutting off the top of Don's head,' to which Marilyn said, "Well, the audience knows he has a top to his head. It's been established!"

Filming on *Bus Stop* commenced in March of 1956, at locations in Phoenix, Arizona and Sun Valley, Idaho. Possibly as a result of the sharp change in temperature between the desert and mountain terrains, Marilyn contracted bronchitis and was admitted to hospital for a few days in early April. The following month, interior scenes began shooting at Fox, yet Marilyn's dependence on sleeping pills still hindered production, as did her insecurities.

"She had it in for the assistant director," Eileen Heckart recalled. "He would call Marilyn to the set every day for a scene, so she told him, 'When I look out of my dressing room door I want to see you standing on your tippy-toes.' Well, I've got to tell you, for the whole run of the picture that man was on his toes every time he called Miss Monroe to the set."

Insisting that Hope Lange's hair be dyed a darker shade of blonde so that it didn't detract from her own light tresses, Marilyn also didn't bother to hang around for the young woman's close-ups, meaning that Lange had to shoot these opposite a male stand-in. Still, at least there was no chance of the two women's skin tones clashing on-screen—thanks to Milton Greene's suggestions, Marilyn's complexion in *Bus Stop* was utterly pasty. However, her longtime makeup artist Allan "Whitey" Snyder refuted the popular notion that Greene actually conceived her facial appearance for the picture.

"That's bullshit," Snyder told me. "Milton Greene was a pain in the butt. He worked his way in there and he kind of represented her, but he didn't design her makeup. Marilyn and I had a meeting before the shoot began, and she decided that, being a chanteuse who was asleep all day, in the nightclub all night and never seeing the sun, she had to be absolutely white. Well, Milton Greene came up with the idea of putting clown white on her, but hell, I used a little clown white and mixed that with some other colors to make it a little more natural. Otherwise it would have been too damned white. I think it was still too white, but she wanted it that way. I tried it a shade or two darker and it made her look so much prettier—her teeth stood out better—but I was overruled and so I thought, 'What the hell, I don't care.'"

Happy at the start of production, on location in Phoenix, Arizona, March 1956.

Meanwhile, with Natasha Lytess now totally off the scene, Lee Strasberg's wife Paula was the coach of choice, at least as far as the star pupil was concerned. Fox didn't want to pick up Strasberg's huge salary and Joshua Logan initially barred her from the set, yet Marilyn prevailed, the studio paid Paula an astounding $1,500 per week—more than the crew members, composer, and most actors—and she was there behind the cameras every day.

"A lot of directors would have resented Paula Strasberg being there, but to Josh Logan's credit he collaborated with her very, very well," Don Murray recalled. "I don't know what he thought about it, but on the set there was never any friction between the two of them, and it never seemed to create any problems. He used her work with Marilyn to his advantage."

"She was constantly stroking Marilyn and telling her that she was the most beautiful, most talented person in the world," added Eileen Heckart. "I guess Marilyn needed that to function. Paula had spent weeks working with Marilyn on her Okie accent, and she wouldn't let her drop it at any point. She was afraid that she couldn't be consistent, so she spoke in that Okie accent all of the time while we were doing the picture."

Production of *Bus Stop* wrapped towards the end of May 1956. When watching the first previews, Marilyn's colleagues would be astounded by the grace and beauty of her performance, for as Eileen Heckart explained, this had been so disjointed on the set:

"Paula Strasberg came to me on the last day of filming and said, 'Say something marvelous talent-wise to Marilyn!' I said, 'Paula, I can say I enjoyed meeting her and being on the picture, but if you expect me to say something marvelous, I'm not being cruel but I just can't do it. Working with her was too hard.'"

The Critics' Views

"Hold onto your chairs, everybody, and get set for a rattling surprise. Marilyn Monroe has finally proved herself an actress in *Bus Stop*. She and the picture are swell!"

New York Times

"There has been a good deal of comment and some knowing laughter about Miss Monroe's attempts to broaden her native talents by working at her acting. It should be some satisfaction to the lady that she now has the last and very triumphant laugh. . . . The celebrated attractions are still happily there but they have been augmented by a sensitivity, a poignancy and an apparent understanding that Miss Monroe did not display before."

Hollywood Reporter

"Yipee! Hurray for *Bus Stop!* . . . this is Marilyn's show and, my friends, she shows plenty in figure, beauty and talent. This girl is a terrific comedienne. . . . Her stint at the Actors Studio in New York certainly didn't hurt our girl."

L.A. Examiner

Public Reaction

Produced for $2.2 million, *Bus Stop*—sometimes titled *The Wrong Kind of Girl* when it first aired on TV—earned $4.25 million during its initial run.

The Prince and the Showgirl

THE PRINCE AND THE SHOWGIRL

★★★★

A Warner Brothers Release
An L.O.P. Presentation of a Film by Marilyn
Monroe Productions, Inc.
Produced and Directed by Laurence Olivier
Screenplay by Terence Rattigan
Based on Terence Rattigan's Play
The Sleeping Prince
Cinematography by Jack Cardiff
Sound by John Mitchell
and Gordon McCallum
Art Direction by Carmen Dillon
Music by Richard Addinsell
Choreography by William Chappell
Costume Design by Beatrice Dawson
Edited by Jack Harris
Released: July 3, 1957
Running Time: 117 minutes
Technicolor

CAST

The Regent	Laurence Olivier
Elsie	Marilyn Monroe
The Queen Dowager	Sybil Thorndike
King Nicolas	Jeremy Spenser
Northbrook	Richard Wattis
Maisie Springfield	Jean Kent
Hoffman	Esmond Knight
Fanny	Daphne Anderson
Betty	Vera Day
Major Domo	Paul Hardwick
Valet with Violin	Andrea Melandrinos
Lottie	Margot Lister
Maud	Rosamund Greenwood
The Ambassador	Aubrey Dexter
Lady Sunningdale	Maxine Audley
Call Boy	Harold Goodwin
Maggie	Gillian Owen
Head Valet	Dennis Edwards
Dresser	Gladys Henson
The Foreign Office	David Horne
Theatre Manager	Charles Victor

MM'S SONG

"I Found a Dream" words by Christopher
Hassall, music by Richard Addinsell

The Plot

On the day before the 1911 coronation of King George V and Queen Mary, the regent of Carpathia, Grand Duke Charles, arrives in London with his son King Nicolas VIII, and his mother-in-law the queen dowager. Carpathia is a powerful Balkan nation whose allegiances could tip the balance of power in Europe, and the British are concerned that Carpathia's 16-year-old pro-German king will be assuming power from the Regent in 18 months time. Northbrook, deputy head of the Foreign Office's far eastern branch, is therefore assigned to be the Regent's personal equerry and ensure that he gets "whatever he wants."

On his first night, this turns out to be a visit to see the musical *The Coconut Girl*, where the royal widower sets eyes on American bit-part player Elsie Marina, and invites her to a midnight dinner at the Carpathian embassy. Escorted there by Northbrook, Elsie soon learns that the arrogant grand duke has already eaten, and while he appears more interested in attending to business, she proceeds to get tipsy on vodka and champagne. Wise to his intentions, Elsie makes fun of the grand duke's clumsy attempts at seduction, and although he is furious and tells her to leave, he then has second thoughts and decides to make a more concerted attempt to woo her.

This time around, Elsie falls asleep just as His Grand Ducal Highness thinks that he is making progress, and the next morning, after clashing with his son over the arrest of political opponents in Carpathia, the irate regent informs Northbrook that the previous night was "an unqualified nightmare." Elsie wakes up in the embassy to discover that she is madly in love with the royal ruler, and although he gives her the brush-off, the showgirl is appointed by the queen dowager as her lady-in-waiting and duly accompanies them to the coronation at Westminster Abbey.

A radiant Elsie Marina greets his Grand Ducal Highness. Through the lense of cinematographer Jack Cardiff, Marilyn looked better than ever.

An anachronistic publicity poster for a film that takes place in London at the time of the 1911 coronation of King George V.

Fanny (Daphne Anderson) attends to the showgirl who has just been invited to dine with a prince.

In the meantime, Elsie has overheard and understood a phone conversation in German in which the regent's son was planning to overthrow his father. Subsequently invited by Nicky to the coronation ball, Elsie persuades him to abandon his coup in return for a motorbike and free elections, and afterwards at the embassy she convinces the father to accede to these demands. The regent falls in love with the showgirl and wants her to join him in Carpathia, yet Elsie insists that they should wait for 18 months, at which point he will have handed over power to his son and she will be free of her obligations to *The Coconut Girl*.

Behind-the-Scenes Facts & Opinions

A slow-paced film that suffers from a slightly stuffy feel due to its formal setting and period costumes, *The Prince and the Showgirl* is nevertheless well worth watching thanks to a witty script, superb photography, and wonderful interaction between the two stars. Olivier is very amusing as the pompous, arrogant, and volatile Balkan ruler, although with no one to rein him in while directing this movie, he is very much in

"Actor" mode throughout, hamming it up for all he's worth. Marilyn, on the other hand, easily steals the movie as an endearingly sweet and natural American showgirl with a solid head on her shoulders. That's right, for once she portrays someone of above average intelligence, and the part suits her perfectly.

Marilyn's relaxed, consummate performance is full of subtle nuances. Terrific when tipsy, and highly believable when dealing with her explosive suitor and his scheming son, she conveys so much by way of slight facial expressions and delicate body movements. In light of this, and given the on-screen chemistry between "Larry" and "Sweetie"—as they called one another prior to the start of filming—it is difficult to imagine all of the misery that took place behind the scenes. Yet, take place it did, and a number of relationships would never be the same.

On the one hand, Marilyn was caught in the crossfire between husband Arthur Miller and business partner Milton Greene, each of whom wanted to hold sway over her, and each of whom distrusted the other. Greene, who was keeping Marilyn supplied with a steady diet of uppers and downers in his role as executive producer, had originally intended for her to sing in the movie. Miller, in his role as Svengali, vetoed this idea, and, with the exception of one song, Marilyn complied.

Then there was Paula Strasberg, whose whopping $1,500 per week salary during the filming of *Bus Stop* paled in comparison to the $25,000 plus expenses and overtime (totalling around $38,000) that she was receiving for ten weeks of work on *The Prince and the Showgirl*. Since Marilyn Monroe Productions was footing much of the bill for the movie, this money would be coming out of Marilyn's pocket. Arthur Miller consequently detested Paula Strasberg—as well as her husband Lee, who was basically serving as her business manager—and so did Laurence Olivier, whose direction of Marilyn was curtailed when she consistently deferred to the black-garbed coach's opinions.

Everyone, it seems, wanted a piece of Marilyn, and the effect was completed by others in the entourage that surrounded her in England, including agent Irving Stein, Milton Greene's wife Amy, and friend-cum-secretary Hedda Rosten.

Greeted by Olivier, his wife Vivien Leigh, and the rabid British press after arriving at London Airport on July 14, 1956, the recently married Millers based themselves at Parkside House, a Georgian mansion located not too far from Pinewood Studios. Wardrobe and makeup tests took place at Pinewood on July 18–20, prior to a rehearsal period commencing on the 30th and the start of filming on August 7. Almost immediately there were tensions.

In trying to be friendly when introducing her to the rest of the cast, Olivier patronized his costar by referring to her as "a delightful little thing." Then, during rehearsals, he told her, "All you have to do is be sexy, dear Marilyn." This sort of treatment was not well received by a woman who, just a short time later, would read an entry in her husband's diary in which he concurred with Laurence Olivier's opinion that she was a "troublesome bitch." The discovery of this enlightening opinion would spell the beginning of the end of the Millers' marriage.

Olivier's own antipathy towards Marilyn was, like that of his directorial predecessors and successors, related to her lateness on the set—which would reach new heights during the course of this project—and her inability to deliver the right lines on cue. The fact that she swallowed sleeping pills at night and drank gin for breakfast really didn't help, and although Olivier tried to abide by director Joshua Logan's warning not to "order her about, because it'll throw her and you won't get anything out of her," he was eventually worn down. "You never told me what to do when I'm explaining a scene to her and she walks away from me in mid-sentence," Olivier would later complain.

"We would do take after take after take, and Marilyn would fluff and forget her lines,"

veteran actor whose heyday was the 1920s and early-1930s, is a standout as the wealthy philanderer, Osgood Fielding III, an archetypal dirty old man young beyond his years.

Tony Curtis, on the other hand, turns in the best performance of his career, portraying "Junior" as—in his words—a "half-assed Cary Grant," right down to the laid-back facial expressions and flat-sounding, slightly Americanized English accent. Both he and Joe E. Brown, however, are outshone by the tour-de-force contribution of Jack Lemmon, for whom this project marked the beginning of a long and highly successful working relationship with Billy Wilder.

While Tony Curtis' "Josephine" is strictly a man in drag (his female voice dubbed in by "Man of a Thousand Voices" Paul Frees), Lemmon has to contend with an over-the-top character who all but becomes the woman he is impersonating. The trick here is to assume convincing female mannerisms without ever appearing overtly effeminate, and Lemmon, a very fine actor, achieves this brilliantly.

"If it had not been Billy Wilder who came to me with the idea of playing this role I would have hesitated a great deal," Lemmon stated in 1994. "Tony's character was saner whereas mine was from the moon, and the key for me was to never, ever think, because Jerry does not act; he only *re*acts. He reacts to women, and we make that very clear. He's lusting all the time—if he saw the ugliest broad in the world he'd want to rape her—and Billy was very wise in asserting that. So I didn't hold back and I trusted Billy to tell me if I did go overboard, because if I ever worried about it I knew I'd be dead."

A female impersonator named Barbette was employed to refine the female walk and posture of Messrs. Curtis and Lemmon, but after two days he quit when, in order to ensure some differentiation between the characters, "Daphne" refused to be as cute and convincingly feminine as "Josephine." Nevertheless, some lessons had been learned.

"Barbette was really fascinating," Lemmon recalled. "He explained that, if you want to exaggerate walking like a woman, cross your feet one in front of the other and your hips will swivel. You can't help it . . . Still, I wouldn't do it!"

Scenes such as those when "Daphne" entertains Sugar in his sleeping cabin aboard the train and when he informs Joe of his engagement to Osgood are cinematic gems. The latter, a single page of script that manages to last two minutes on screen, was described by Lemmon as "the best single piece of comedy direction ever," not least for Billy Wilder's idea of separating each joke with "Daphne" shaking some maracas, thus allowing the audience enough time to laugh before hearing the next quip.

"I've never seen anything used so expertly to do the impossible, and that is to time laughs on film," said Lemmon. "A brilliant, brilliant idea, and I thought he was completely crazy when I walked on the set and he told me what to do! I had rehearsed the scene in a totally different way with [actress wife] Felicia the night before and I couldn't wait to do it, so when Billy told me his idea I was stunned. I went from there to make-up, and I was convinced he was ruining the best scene in the movie, but the more I thought about it the more I thought, 'Holy shit! Oh yes! What's the matter with me?' I didn't realize at first how great it was!"

While Jack Lemmon always Billy Wilder's first choice for the role, the Mirisch Company originally wanted bigger names such as Frank Sinatra or Danny Kaye. Tony Curtis had already been signed, and Mitzi Gaynor was being considered for the part of Sugar , but when Marilyn came aboard the financiers decided the project now had enough star power to enable the casting of Jack Lemmon. The fact that Sinatra hadn't shown up for a lunch meeting with Billy Wilder made that decision even easier.

Marilyn was, in fact, attracted to the *Some Like It Hot* project by the possibility of working again with Wilder, who, she asserted prior to the start of filming, was "the best

◄◄ *Tired of always ending up with "the fuzzy end of the lollipop," Sugar satisfies her yen for sax players and men who wear glasses in the form of a penniless musician posing as an oil magnate.*

An outraged "Daphne" interrupts the conversation between "Junior" and Sugar Kane, on the beach in front of the Hotel del Coronado. While filming here, Marilyn resided in the hotel's "Vista Mar" cottage.

director in Hollywood." This was apparently borne out by her superlative performance as Sugar, which combined immense charm and superb timing to once again confirm her unique qualities as a screen comedienne. Likewise, her renditions of the songs "Running Wild" and "I Wanna Be Loved By You" have become part of the Monroe legend.

If *Some Like It Hot* helped reaffirm Billy Wilder's status as a great director, then his activities behind the scenes on this project also earned him stripes as both a nursemaid and a psychologist. For while he had already encountered Marilyn's unpredictable behavior during production of *The Seven Year Itch,* nothing could have prepared him for the problems he now had to deal with, in the form of a troubled star whose deteriorating mental condition was exacerbated by her steady intake of drugs and alcohol.

One of Marilyn's most successful movies, *Some Like It Hot* marked a career high-point for many who participated in its making, and it is a testament to the skill and patience of those coworkers that the off-screen difficulties in no way detracted from the finished product. Initially aggravated at having to accept yet another dumb blonde role (partly to help pay for the legal costs arising from Arthur Miller's investigation by the HUAC), Marilyn was also irked by the fact that, contrary to the clause in her Fox contract, the United Artists picture was to be shot in black and white.

"At that time I was against color," Billy Wilder told me in 1994, citing the brilliant but artificial tones of processes such as Technicolor. "I also had the feeling that since it was a period picture we should do it in black and white, but when Marilyn saw the rushes she was very unhappy. So my wife and I had to tell her that she looked very beautiful, and that black and white is much more interesting and more difficult to use than color film. After all, any cameraman will tell you that with grey, black, and white shades the effects have to be much subtler, whereas with Technicolor almost anybody is a very good cameraman. Then I also told her that the two actors who were playing female musicians, you would be able to see through the makeup where they had shaved their faces. Now, I don't know if that was true or not, but it satisfied her."

So, no doubt, did a retort that Marilyn delivered to the film's costume designer before shooting began. "Orry-Kelly spent a lot of time taking all of our measurements," Tony Curtis recalled. "About four days after he'd taken my measurements he took Marilyn's, and while he was measuring her ass he looked up at her and said, 'Do you know Tony has a better-looking ass than yours?' to which she replied, 'Well, he doesn't have tits like these!'"

Nevertheless, while Marilyn may have been proud of her feminine attributes, she

While the crew sets up the next shot, Tony Curtis talks to Marilyn, who is seated in front of her black-garbed drama coach, Paula Strasberg.

was more than a little concerned that the cameras were focusing less on these than on the comedic efforts of her two costars. "I'm not going back into that fucking film until Wilder reshoots my opening," she reportedly threatened after viewing the early rushes. "When Marilyn Monroe comes into a room nobody's going to be looking at Tony Curtis playing Joan Crawford. They're going to be looking at Marilyn Monroe."

The result was that Wilder and Diamond expanded the sequence in which the musicians board the Florida-bound train by inserting a scene in which MM wobbles across the platform in high heels and then, as she is leered at by her two "female" admirers, skips past a puff of steam that blasts across her rear end. Nearly 25 minutes pass before Marilyn makes an on-screen entrance that echoes the subway breeze blasting up her skirt in *The Seven Year Itch*.

Still, despite such efforts, Marilyn was generally difficult, unreliable and uncharacteristically abusive throughout production. On one occasion, while reading Thomas Paine's *The Rights of Man* in her dressing room, she responded to an assistant director's call by telling him to "Go fuck yourself." On another, she refused to kiss Tony Curtis while rehearsing the segment in which Sugar and "Junior" smooch aboard a yacht. She would only comply when the cameras started rolling, and it may have been this attitude that prompted Curtis to stand up after watching rushes of the scene and announce that the experience was "like kissing Hitler."

When I spoke with Tony Curtis in 1995, he denied having said this, while asserting that Marilyn was "unique and interesting . . . a sweet and lovely woman." However, others who were present at the screening, including Jack Lemmon, insisted otherwise. Still, this wasn't the only time that the Nazi dictator's name came into use, for during production Marilyn herself was referring to Billy Wilder ("the best director in Hollywood") as a "little Hitler" who had no concern for her. Wilder, who was suffering from a very painful back complaint brought on by stress, no doubt saw things differently.

Newly pregnant and unable to sleep at night, Marilyn was absent due to illness for

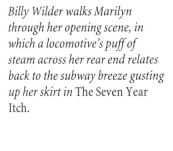

Billy Wilder walks Marilyn through her opening scene, in which a locomotive's puff of steam across her rear end relates back to the subway breeze gusting up her skirt in The Seven Year Itch.

nearly two weeks of the *Some Like It Hot* shoot, and almost another week was lost because of her chronic lateness on the set. Meanwhile, her male costars were left sweating under the studio lights in heavy clothes and makeup. "It used to be you'd call her at 9.00 A.M. and she'd show at noon," Billy Wilder observed at the time. "Now, you call in May and she shows up in October."

If and when Marilyn did arrive, everyone would be driven to distraction by her nervous, Method-induced habit of flailing her hands from side to side before each take, her inability to remember dialogue, and her insistence on reshooting time and again. Both Curtis and Lemmon would invariably be fresher in the earlier takes, while Marilyn often required time (and lots of it) to either find the right inspiration or just say her lines. In such cases, the perfect take was defined by Marilyn's best performance, not that of her costars, and this caused the two men, especially Curtis, to feel justifiably short-changed.

One of the more notorious examples took place aboard the yacht, where Marilyn was simply required to point up at a fish mounted on an archway and ask, "What is it?" to which "Junior" would reply, "It's a member of the herring family," and pop a champagne cork. Many, many corks were popped while Marilyn floundered in confusion. Finally she asked Tony Curtis to remind her of her line. "What is it?" he replied. "What is it?" she asked. "It's a member of the herring family," responded Curtis. Now Marilyn looked completely baffled. "What is it!" repeated Curtis. "That's your line: 'What is it!'"

For another scene, Marilyn was supposed to knock on a door and say, "It's me, Sugar," yet this took around 47 takes to perfect. "After take 30 I had the line put on a blackboard," Billy Wilder later recalled. "She would say things like, 'It's Sugar, me.'" However, the true record-breaker came in the form of the segment where a depressed Sugar enters the bedroom of "Josephine" and "Daphne," rummages through some drawers, and asks, "Where's that bourbon?" After about 40 takes of Marilyn saying things like "Where's the whiskey?" "Where's the bonbon?" or "Where's the bottle?" Wilder pasted the correct line in one of the drawers. Next, he pasted it in every drawer because she became confused as to where he had put it, and when the director then took her aside and told her not to worry, Marilyn just looked at him and said, "Worry about what?"

According to Wilder's varying recollections, anywhere from 59 to 83 takes were needed to complete that specific shot, yet one also has to question whether at this point he was indulging in a battle of wills —when Marilyn delivers the line her back is to the camera, so why not just film her looking through the drawers and then dub the dialogue during post-production?

"She only knew one way to work," asserted Jack Lemmon, "and so when it didn't feel right to her she would stop the scene and say, 'I'm sorry, it's not right,' and you'd swear she was doing the exact same thing take after take after take! Then she'd go all the way through it, doing the same damned thing, and say, 'That's it!' and you'd think, 'I don't know what the hell she is talking about!' But, whatever it was, it worked for her!"

And while others such as Laurence Olivier may have barred Paula Strasberg from the set, Billy Wilder told me that he regarded Marilyn's coach as a positive influence. "When Marilyn started muffing lines, Paula Strasberg would be there with a handkerchief to wipe the tears away," he said. "She was very helpful."

On the other hand, Tony Curtis recalled that, as early as Marilyn's first scene on the train platform, Wilder became exasperated by her habit of looking towards her drama coach at the end of each take. "How was that for you, Paula?" the director asked following the scene's completion. Strasberg didn't reply.

Confusion was the general order of the day. After all, while Marilyn could have trouble remembering just three words, she was letter-perfect almost immediately when

filming much longer, mentally demanding scenes such as that in the train berth with Jack Lemmon that was completed in one take, and another with Tony Curtis on the beach in front of the Hotel del Coronado, known in the movie as the "Seminole-Ritz"in Miami (note the high cliffs, nowhere to be found in Florida). Filming there was relatively trouble-free compared with that which took place at the Goldwyn Studios.

"There was an air base and every ten minutes a jet flew over the beach, so I thought it would take about four days to shoot that scene," said Wilder. "I tried to film between take-offs, but then on the second take everything was there; every sentence of two pages. Not one letter, not one comma was left out. We were finished in less than 20 minutes."

No one, least of all the beleaguered director, had a clue as to which kind of Marilyn they would have to deal with from one day to the next, and after the three-month project was completed on November 6, 1958, a relieved Wilder felt moved to say, "I am eating better. I have been able to sleep for the first time in months. I can look at my wife without wanting to hit her because she's a woman."

Comments such as these incensed Marilyn, resulting in a flurry of irate telegrams traveling back and forth between Arthur Miller and Billy Wilder. These culminated in Miller's assertion that his wife was "the salt of the earth," to which Wilder replied that "the salt of the earth told an assistant director to go fuck himself."

Billy Wilder would later sum up the entire *Some Like It Hot* ordeal by saying, "I knew we were in mid-flight, and there was a nut on the plane," but he was also prepared to admit that he would have jumped at the chance of working with Marilyn once again, for in the final analysis she was actually worth all the aggravation.

"I have an aunt in Vienna, also an actress," he said just prior to the film's release. "Her name, I think, is Mildred Lachenfarber. She always comes to the set on time. She knows her lines perfectly. She never gives anyone the slightest trouble. At the box office she is worth fourteen cents. Do you get my point?"

Certainly, one only has to glimpse the Monroe magic in *Some Like It Hot* to do so. For, as Wilder later stated, "I had a hunch when Marilyn did a good take, but then on the screen she looked even better. That's the kind of quality which God either does or doesn't give you."

The Critics' Views

"To get down to cases, Marilyn does herself proud, giving a performance of such intrinsic quality that you begin to believe she's only being herself and it is herself who fits into that distant period and this picture so well."

The New York Post

"As the band's somewhat simple singer-ukulele player, Miss Monroe, whose figure simply cannot be overlooked, contributes more assets than the obvious ones to this madcap romp . . . and also proves to be the epitome of a dumb blonde and a talented comedienne."

The New York Times

"To coin a phrase, Marilyn has never looked better. Her performance as 'Sugar,' the fuzzy blonde who likes saxophone players and men with glasses, has a deliciously naive quality. She's a comedienne with that combination of sex appeal and timing that just can't be beat."

Variety

Public Reaction

A December 1958 sneak preview of *Some Like It Hot*, held at the Bay Theatre in Pacific Palisades, California, was, in the words of Jack Lemmon, "as bad a preview as any I have ever been to," for instead of laughter there was merely the sound of people walking out at the sight of two men running around in drag. Perhaps the audience was confused, because for some reason the film comprised the second half of a "preview double-bill" that also featured the melodramatic *Suddenly Last Summer*.

Producers Walter and Harold Mirisch told Billy Wilder that a two-hour farce was too long, and that at least 15 minutes would have to be cut. The director, however, held his nerve and excised what he considered to be just one scene too many on the train: Lying with his back to Sugar in his sleeping berth, "Daphne" confesses that he is a boy. Yet, when he turns around, he discovers that, instead of Sugar, it is a highly aggrieved Joe to whom he has been talking .

A week after its first, disastrous preview, *Some Like It Hot* was shown to another audience in Westwood Village. This time, inexplicably, the reaction was the complete reverse. "You could not hear anything going on from one minute into that film," Jack Lemmon recalled. "All the kids, their parents, whoever, were screaming with laughter. It was an absolute smash, and it was the same film!"

Due to delays causing the production schedule to be extended by more than three weeks, *Some Like It Hot* ran about $500,000 over budget and ended up costing a total of $2.8 million. This, however, was countered by its runaway success at the box office, grossing around $7 million to come in third behind *Auntie Mame* and *The Shaggy Dog* as one of the biggest films of 1959.

Let's Make Love

The Plot

French-American billionaire Jean-Marc Clement is informed by his PR manager Alexander Coffman and lawyer John Wales that he is going to be spoofed in an off-Broadway show. Told by Wales that he should take action against this invasion of privacy, Coffman nevertheless feels that closing the show would create bad publicity, so he persuades Clement to attend a rehearsal and hopefully dissuade the producer from satirizing him. After they arrive, however, the wealthy playboy is mistaken for someone auditioning to play Clement, and he immediately lands the part, while also falling for the show's sexy costar, Amanda Dell.

Assuming the name of Alexander Dumas, the undercover billionaire is taken by the fact that Amanda, who criticizes the superficial lifestyle of the "real-life" Clement, is not particularly impressed by money. The only problem is, she does appear to be attracted to the show's male lead, Tony Danton, and so while "Alex" is determined to see if Amanda could love him for himself rather than his money, he has to utilize some of it in order to swing things in his favor.

"The Best Entertainment Offer You've Had in Years!" asserted the Fox publicists. Moviegoers didn't agree.

To that end, John Wales poses as a wealthy benefactor and purchases a 51 percent controlling interest in the cash-strapped production. Clement, meanwhile, hires the combined talents of Bing Crosby, Gene Kelly, and Milton Berle to teach him how to sing, dance, and tell jokes, and with these skills and his lawyer's support, "Alex Dumas" deprives Tony Danton of his lead role and takes Amanda out to dinner.

She subsequently confesses that she only accepted this invitation to give Tony a chance to impress the producers with his own abilities, yet realizing that this is due to feelings of sympathy rather than love, "Alex" proposes to Amanda and reveals that he is the real Jean-Marc Clement. Amanda thinks that "Alex" has taken leave of his senses, and she tries to assure him that he doesn't need money to entice her. However, when he persists with his claim, Amanda gets angry, so Clement then has to show her concrete proof of his true identity.

After John Wales announces that Jean-Marc Clement is taking out an injunction to stop the show, "Alex" suggests that Amanda visit the super-rich bachelor at his company headquarters and try to change his mind. Once there, however, it is her mind that is changed when staff members confirm that "Alex" is their boss. Finally convinced that it is Jean-Marc Clement who wants to marry her, and furious at the way that she has been led on, Amanda nevertheless admits that she is madly in love with him.

Behind-the-Scenes Facts & Opinions

Talk about going from the sublime to the ridiculous! After Marilyn had staked out a new career path for herself with superlative performances in *Bus Stop, The Prince and the Showgirl,* and *Some Like it Hot,* trust Twentieth Century-Fox to set things back by casting her in the kind of lamebrained nonsense that she had fought so hard to distance herself from.

With such weak material, Marilyn actually fares quite well as a sexy entertainer who knits and goes to evening classes in her spare time (!). She also sparkles during some of the musical numbers, most notably a sensuous and snappily choreographed rendition of Cole Porter's "My Heart Belongs to Daddy." Yet, despite the contributions of director George Cukor, support players Tony Randall and Wilfred Hyde-White, songwriters Sammy Cahn and Jimmy Van Heusen, and special guests Milton Berle, Bing Crosby and Gene Kelly, the proceedings are bogged down by substandard efforts on both sides of the camera, namely, the writing of Norman Krasna, Hal Kanter, and Arthur Miller behind it, and the performances of Frankie Vaughan and Yves Montand in front of it.

Billed with considerable overstatement in the film's publicity trailer as "the singing idol of England," Vaughan delivered a performance that ensured his adulation wouldn't spread across the Atlantic. His voice is fine, but the hip-jazz manner in which he sings—full of head swaggering and smarmy smiles—is pretty nauseating, while his attempts at dramatic acting put him in a class with Johnnie Ray.

Yves Montand, meanwhile, was announced in the same publicity trailer as "the greatest gift France has sent us since the Statue of Liberty." Be that as it may, Montand looks decidedly uncomfortable in the role of a roving-eyed billionaire, and so it's hardly surprising that he wasn't producer Jerry Wald's first choice for the part. Then again, he wasn't his second, third, fourth, fifth, sixth, or seventh choice, either.

Back in November of 1958, Fox production chief Buddy Adler announced that the studio had purchased the rights to Norman Krasna's screenplay *The Billionaire.* Allotted a budget approaching $3 million, the film would feature locales in New York, Europe, and the West Indies, as well as the same kind of all-star cast that had been

LET'S MAKE LOVE

★★½

A Twentieth Century-Fox Release
Produced by Jerry Wald
Directed by George Cukor
Screenplay by Norman Krasna
Additional Material by Hal Kanter
and Arthur Miller (uncredited)
Cinematography by Daniel L. Fapp
Sound by W.D. Flick and Warren B. Delaplain
Art Direction by Lyle Wheeler and Gene Allen
Music by Lionel Newman
Choreography by Jack Cole
Costume Design by Dorothy Jeakins
Edited by David Bretherton
Released: August 24, 1960
Running Time: 118 minutes
CinemaScope and DeLuxe Color

CAST

Amanda Dell	Marilyn Monroe
Jean-Marc Clement	Yves Montand
Alexander Coffman	Tony Randall
Tony Danton	Frankie Vaughan
John Wales	Wilfred Hyde-White
Oliver Burton	David Burns
Dave Kerry	Michael David
Lili Nyles	Mara Lynn
Abe Miller	Dennis King, Jr.
Lamont	Joe Besser

Uncredited:

Chauffeur	Oscar Beregi, Jr.
(Himself)	Milton Berle
Minister	Harry Cheshire
Comstock	John Craven
(Himself)	Bing Crosby
Jimmy	Ray Foster
Van Cliburn impersonator	Richard Fowler
Elvis Presley impersonator	John Gatti
(Himself)	Gene Kelly
Miss Manners	Madge Kennedy
Maria Callas impersonator	Marian Manners
Yale	Mike Mason
(Bit Part)	Larry Thor
Miss Hansen	Geraldine Wall

MM'S SONGS

"My Heart Belongs To Daddy" by Cole Porter

"Specialization" (with Frankie Vaughan) by Sammy Cahn and James Van Heusen

"Let's Make Love" (with chorus and with Frankie Vaughan) by Sammy Cahn and James Van Heusen

"Incurably Romantic" (with Yves Montand) by Sammy Cahn and James Van Heusen

employed in *Around the World in 80 Days*. According to producer Wald, there would be as many as 20 cameo appearances by the likes of Jack Benny, Juliette Greco, Danny Thomas, Dinah Shore, Groucho Marx, Jimmy Durante, and Gwen Verdon.

Norman Krasna submitted his First Draft Screenplay in February of 1959, and shortly thereafter Gregory Peck was cast in the central role of Mark Clemens. Next, Jerry Wald approached Marilyn about playing the part of Amanda. She approved his choice of Billy Wilder as director, but Wilder—who stated that he would have been happy to take the assignment—was already at work on his next movie, *The Apartment*, so Wald suggested George Cukor and Marilyn agreed. What she didn't like, however, was the script, which provided Gregory Peck with a bigger role than her own, and so after Marilyn signed to do the picture on September 30, the screenplay was revised by both Hal Kanter and—although he would remain uncredited—Arthur Miller.

Now the central character's name was Mark Bruester, but after taking one look at the revised script, Peck realized that he had been right to suspect that Marilyn's husband would rewrite the story in her favor. Worse still, much of the humor had been diminished, so after telling Miller that he thought the screenplay was "now about as funny as pushing Grandma down the stairs in a wheelchair," Peck walked off the picture. Jerry Wald and George Cukor then settled on Rock Hudson, but Universal refused to release him.

In mid-November, with Norman Krasna taking care of another rewrite, the male lead's name reverted to Mark Clemens while the film's title was changed to *Let's Make Love*. By then, Cary Grant had wisely turned down the role—although what a combination he and Marilyn would have made—and he was quickly followed by Charlton Heston, William Holden, James Stewart, and Yul Brynner. Then up cropped the name of accomplished French dramatic actor and singer Yves Montand, who had appeared in a 1957 French film version of Arthur Miller's play *The Crucible*, as well as in a successful one-man show on Broadway.

For Montand, a film costarring Marilyn Monroe appeared to be the ideal vehicle with which to introduce himself to a much wider audience, and so with him on board Norman Krasna—aided by Hal Kanter—spent December of 1959 introducing a French angle into his screenplay, while changing the central character's name to Charles Clement, then Jean-Pierre Clement, and finally Jean-Marc Clement. The only problem was, Montand would have to learn to speak better English, although for help he could always turn to his more fluent wife, actress Simone Signoret, who was staying with him in a bungalow at the Beverly Hills Hotel, as well as the Millers, who were residing next door. During the lengthy production, Montand's diction would improve so much that certain earlier scenes would have to be redubbed.

Let's Make Love commenced filming on January 18, 1960, and at first things didn't go too badly. However, no one, least of all Marilyn, was in any doubt as to how poor the script was, and so it was continually being revised up until the Writers Guild went on strike in early March over payment for film work being broadcast on TV. At that point, Arthur Miller, who was amending his *Misfits* screenplay at John Huston's home in Ireland, answered a call from Jerry Wald and returned to Hollywood. In return for a healthy payment, he secretly defied the strike and worked on the script to *Let's Make Love*, yet for Marilyn this was a hypocritical betrayal of her husband's own liberal ideals.

Thereafter, tensions resurfaced in the Monroe-Miller relationship. Marilyn would sometimes leave the studio without telling her colleagues, for as her insecurities heightened along with her intake of sleeping pills, so her performance in front of the cameras began to suffer.

▶▶ *Following the film's release, some critics would make disparaging remarks about Marilyn's weight gain, yet she still looked incredibly sexy in some pretty revealing outfits.*

"How did I get myself into this?" Marilyn's 28th film saw her returning to the kind of light froth that she had worked so hard to get away from.

"When they were shooting the scene in the restaurant, Marilyn's lines were written into the menu," recalled art director Gene Allen, who worked with George Cukor on a number of his movies. "Cukor would film it all in short pieces, and try to get her to concentrate and work on the lines, and she did pretty well. Of course, at that time Marilyn was driving Cukor mad with her acting coach, because whenever she did a scene she'd look past him towards Paula Strasberg and get a 'yes' or a 'no.' So, that sort of nonsense was going on, but Cukor took it very well."

Indeed, according to Allen, the canny director would do whatever it took to appease Marilyn, as was evidenced when a theater scene was being filmed on March 7, the day that the Screen Actors Guild was due to begin a strike paralleling that of the Writers Guild. "Arthur Miller was on the set, and we were going to film the scene and then quit because of the strike," Allen told me in 1995. "However, Marilyn kept saying, 'Just one more, George. I think I can do it better,' and finally he told the cameraman to not bother putting any film in, and he went ahead and let her do the scene so that Arthur Miller wouldn't be embarrassed. Well, Arthur Miller was embarrassed, and Marilyn kept drinking champagne in between takes, but again Cukor did everything he could to appease her and make her feel wanted, because he really saw a lot in her, as other great directors did. She had a certain spark that most people don't have."

"Yves, tell her; audiences are gonna love it!"—George Cukor gives directions to MM and Yves Montand on the theater set of Let's Make Love.

Gene Kelly's cameo role in the movie required him to appear with Yves Montand rather than Marilyn, but here all three spend some off-camera time together.

Evidently, Yves Montand managed to ignite that spark when he popped into Marilyn's bungalow one evening in late April, while Simone Signoret was filming in Italy and Arthur Miller was working in Ireland. Until the end of filming in mid-June, the costars of *Let's Make Love* would be acting out the title of their movie while reports of the affair would fill newspaper and magazine columns. Then, in true European fashion, Montand would reunite with his forgiving wife, and in true American fashion the Millers' marriage would head for the rocks. "The affair with Yves Montand added a spark to the filming," recalled Gene Allen. "The only problem we had was Marilyn putting on weight and the costumes having to be altered."

Clearly this was the case for the idiotic "Specialization" production number—featuring supposedly "funny" impersonations of Maria Callas, Elvis Presley, and Van Cliburn, while 'Jean-Marc-Clement shouts "cock-a-doodle-doo!"—which was filmed over the course of four days at the end of May and start of June. Wearing a tight full-length dress, Marilyn looks the heaviest of her entire career. Still, for choreographer Jack Cole, this was the least of his concerns, for he bore the brunt of MM's ongoing demands to do "just one more take' of seemingly perfect routines."

"Marilyn is not a great dancer and she knows it," Cole told *Life* magazine shortly after the end of filming. "The motivation is a terrible fear of failure. She is a great star without the background or experience. She is afraid and insecure. That's why she is late. That's why she stalls. She is always looking for more time—a hem out of line, a mussed hair, a scene to discuss, anything to stall facing the specter, the terrible thing of doing something for which she feels inadequate."

Meanwhile, as if Jack Cole's job wasn't complicated enough, the censor then decided to add his two cents' worth with regard to the *Let's Make Love* dance sequence that he had watched being rehearsed on June 10. "The action involved a man and a woman on couches attached to a swivel, one above the other," stated a report filed four days later. "Their actions, in conjunction with the lyrics titled 'Let's Make Love,' were deemed completely unacceptable by reason of offensive sex suggestiveness."

The studio's reponse appears to have been, "Oh dear, what a shame, never mind." The sequence as described made it into the film.

When production wrapped in mid-June of 1960, the project was, due to the strikes and MM's insistence on retakes, 28 days over schedule. Yet, not everybody involved in the film's making was unhappy with this turn of events. "Thank you my dear," Wilfred Hyde-White reportedly told Marilyn as he gave her a kiss on the last day of shooting, "for the longest and most remunerative contract I've ever had."

The Critics' Views

"The old Monroe dynamism is lacking in the things she is given to do by the cliché-clogged script of Norman Krasna and by George Cukor, who directed the film. It doesn't seem very important that she is finally brought together with Mr. Montand."

NEW YORK TIMES

"In the acting department, Miss Monroe is not impressive as in comedy-type roles. She plays a straight part here and does little that is effective. Visually? Marilyn offers her famous curves, not a little on the fleshy side. Diet, anyone?"

HOLLYWOOD CITIZEN NEWS

Public Reaction

Thanks to all the delays, *Let's Make Love* (puzzlingly titled *The Millionaire* in France) ran more than half a million dollars over budget, clocking in at $3,585,000. All things considered, this really wasn't bad, but unfortunately the same couldn't be said for the box office returns.

"The Best Entertainment Offer You've Had in Years!" trumpeted the film's publicity trailer. "Forget it!" responded the great American public, who contributed a lousy $1.8 million to the Fox coffers.

The Misfits

THE MISFITS

★★★½

A United Artists Release
A Seven Arts Productions Presentation of a
John Huston Production
Produced by Frank E. Taylor
Directed by John Huston
Screenplay by Arthur Miller
Cinematography by Russell Metty
Sound by Philip Mitchell
and Charles Grenzbach
Art Direction by Stephen Grimes
and William Newberry
Music by Alex North
Miss Monroe's Wardrobe by Jean Louis
Edited by George Tomasini
Released: February 1, 1961
Running Time: 125 minutes
Black & White

CAST

Gay Langland	Clark Gable
Roslyn Taber	Marilyn Monroe
Perce Howland	Montgomery Clift
Isabelle Steers	Thelma Ritter
Guido	Eli Wallach
Old Man in Bar	James Barton
Raymond Taber	Kevin McCarthy
Church Lady	Estelle Winwood
Young Boy in Bar	Dennis Shaw
Charles Steers	Philip Mitchell
Old Groom	Walter Ramage
Fresh Cowboy in Bar	J. Lewis Smith
Susan	Marietta Tree
Bartender	Bobby LaSalle
Man in Bar	Ryall Bowker
Ambulance Attendant	Ralph Roberts
Young Bride	Peggy Barton

Uncredited:

(Bit Part)	Rex Bell

The Plot

After Roslyn Taber divorces her husband in Reno, she and her landlady, fellow divorcée Isabelle Steers, are introduced by auto mechanic Guido to Gay Langland. Also divorced, Gay is a free-spirited, middle-aged cowboy who earns money as he goes, and he quickly sells Roslyn on the idea of living a simple country existence. He has no place of his own, she is not ready to return East to the big city, and so when Guido invites them to stay in the vacant, partially completed ranch house where his own wife died, they gladly take him up on the offer.

While the lonely Guido has his eyes set on Roslyn, she and Gay fall in love. The sensitive, insecure young woman quickly takes to life amid Nevada's desert terrain, yet not to the manner in which Gay and his hard-drinking buddies sacrifice animals to their own needs and desires. When Gay, Guido, and alcoholic rodeo rider Perce Howland decide to round up some wild horses, Roslyn is distressed to learn that this will result in the animals' slaughter and conversion to dog food. She tries to dissuade Gay, but he insists that this is how he makes a living, and when all the men manage to round up are a stallion, four mares, and a colt, this turns into a point of principle.

While a stallion is being roped, Roslyn pleads with Gay to let it go, but he throws her off. Guido's offer to abort the operation if Roslyn will give herself to him simply provokes her disgust, and when the men discuss how they will share the spoils after roping a mare and her colt, Roslyn vents her anger and accuses them of being murderers. Only Perce appears to have moral principles, and after jumping in the truck with Roslyn he sets all the horses free. Gay proceeds to recapture the stallion, but then, after winning the battle, and in the face of bitter objections from Guido, he concedes the war and sets the horse free. Having always prided himself on not "working for wages," Gay resolves to change his lifestyle, and he and Roslyn make plans for having a family together.

Behind-the-Scenes Facts & Opinions

The Misfits is an interesting movie, yet it by no means lives up to producer Frank Taylor's expressed intention to make "the ultimate motion picture." The talent on both sides of the camera is, of course, second to none, and the actors all deliver the goods, most notably Clark Gable, who in his last film gives one of his finest performances. Yet, Arthur Miller's story about an emotionally scarred and fragile woman's moral conflict with a bunch of hard-drinking loners has more pretensions than substance.

Despite alluding to outdated values and personal isolation by way of self-consciously "deep and meaningful" lines of dialogue, nothing much happens beyond Roslyn hooking up with Gay and persuading him and Perce to be kinder to animals. Each of the characters' personal problems are neatly packaged: Roslyn has never experienced true love and affection; Gay's kids are not interested in knowing him; Guido's pregnant wife died when a flat tire prevented him from rushing her to the hospital; Isabelle's former husband married her best friend; and Perce has a better relationship with the bottle than with his remarried mother. Still, we never get to know these people, and it is difficult to empathize with them even though their inherent sadness pervades the movie.

▶▶ *Three screen greats—Montgomery Clift, Marilyn Monroe, and Clark Gable, July 1960.*

Marilyn was in an emotionally fraught state throughout the making of *The Misfits*, and this time around—unlike the well-disguised results of comedy films *The Prince and the Showgirl* and *Some Like It Hot*—her extreme fragility and sense of despair come right through the screen. This has to be her most real performance, yet it is sometimes difficult to judge where the self-analysis stops and the acting begins. Indeed, it is not always easy to watch and hear Marilyn speaking lines that are clear references to her own troubled past, while the other actors mouth husband Arthur Miller's opinions about her.

"She's crazy," Guido says about Roslyn towards the end of the movie. "Thay're all crazy. You try not to believe that because you need them. She's crazy! You struggle, you build, you try, you turn yourself inside out for them. But it's never enough. So they put the spurs to you. I know, I've got the marks. I know this racket, I just forgot what I knew for a little while."

Roslyn, meanwhile, expresses her uncertainty about having a child, and talks about a husband who took no interest in her, as well as a father who disappeared early on. When Isabelle points out that she did have a mother, Roslyn asks, "How do you have somebody who disappears all the time?" For much of Marilyn's life, her own mother had been in and out of mental institutions.

The Millers' shattered relationship was now characterized by mutual antipathy. However, the writer's decision to publicize their personal problems and have his brittle wife touch on some extremely sensitive topics is highly questionable. As for why Marilyn would agree to perform the role, well, when her husband started working on the *Misfits* screenplay back in 1957, it was intended to be, as she described it, his "valentine" to her, depicting MM's sensitivity to people, animals, and the environment. At that time he was still in love, yet over the course of the next three years and numerous rewrites, Miller fashioned the script to reflect his evolving—and diminishing—feelings towards her. "He could have written me anything, and he comes up with this," Marilyn would say. "If that's what he thinks of me, well, then I'm not for him and he's not for me."

The short story that had originally been published in *Esquire* magazine in 1957 was based on Arthur Miller's observations of real-life horse wranglers while he was staying in Reno to divorce his previous wife. It was photographer friend Sam Shaw who suggested expanding it into a full-length screenplay and fleshing out the character of Roslyn especially for Marilyn, and after Miller acted upon this he brought friend and former editor Frank Taylor on board as producer.

On July 14, 1959, Miller wrote to John Huston, offering him the original screenplay that he had written. "I have been holding it for months, not knowing what to do with it," Miller explained. "I'd only add that Marilyn is advisable for the girl."

On September 18, Marilyn received clearance from Fox to work on *The Misfits,* at which time Robert Mitchum was being considered for one of the lead roles. "Not since 'Salesman' have I felt such eagerness to see something of mine performed," Miller wrote to Huston on October 5. "Marilyn asks to be remembered to you, as always; she is slowly getting onto tiptoe for the great day."

Big-hearted Roslyn is about to give her paddle-ball earnings to the church—On location in Reno with (l–r) Estelle Winwood (holding mug), Eli Wallach, Monty Clift, and Clark Gable.

According to John Huston's files, Marilyn made an up-front request for "three to four weeks of complete rest and privacy before she starts 'The Misfits.'" Accordingly, because of the late finish on *Let's Make Love,* location shooting was pushed back to July 21 of 1960, when daytime temperatures in the Nevada Desert were averaging 110° Fahrenheit.

"We had about five wigs made for her to wear out there because of the sweatiness of the desert," Marilyn's makeup artist, Whitey Snyder, recalled in 1994. "Instead of having to stop and have the stylist straighten her hair, curl it, or whatever, we'd just take the wig off and put another one on."

Unfortunately, within a very short time everyone else's hair was starting to curl, and not just because of the desert heat. In front of cast and crew, Marilyn and Arthur Miller waged open warfare, as they did back in their suite at the Mapes Hotel, where night after night the actress was handed newly written lines of dialogue to memorize. Consequently unable to sleep, the actress was often in no fit state to work by day, even though the call time had been specially changed from 9:00 A.M. to 10:00 A.M. prior to the start of production.

"All her life as an actress, when Marilyn finished work and went home, if she couldn't sleep she'd take a sleeping pill," Whitey Snyder explained. "Often she'd do this at seven or eight o'clock and go to bed early, and then if she couldn't sleep she'd take another one at nine or ten, and then maybe again at midnight or one in the morning. Well, by six in the morning the pills would all start to work and she'd be drugged up, and when this happened on *The Misfits* I would just let her lay there in bed while I did her makeup.

"Sometimes she would say, 'Oh, I'm so tired, I don't want to do this,' especially in Reno when it got bad. I'd go over to her hotel room and she'd lay there and lay there, and Harriet her maid would wait for 20 minutes and then wake her, and she'd say, 'No, no, I don't feel like it.' So, I'd talk to her for a few minutes and we'd have coffee, and I'd say, 'Marilyn, let me know if you're not going out on the set, because then I'll call the production manager.' They had to go 60 or 80 miles out into the desert and so I would tell her, 'It will cost them a lot of money to run the company out there and set everything up if you're not going to show up.' She'd lay back and say, 'Well, let's do the makeup and see how I feel,' so I would do that and then she'd say, 'Okay, let's do it, let's go on out.' Time and time again that happened. Very seldom did I end up having to call the production guy."

In a June 11, 1961 interview with Vincent Doyle of the *The Sunday Press,* John Huston would point out that "The real trouble with Monroe is that she is over-dedicated. And that's why she kept on turning up late for rehearsals. She read and re-read her lines in order to appear word perfect on the set. If she felt she didn't know her lines that was just your hard luck. You just had to wait, but you knew you were waiting for the best."

"John Huston was a master diplomat, tactician and guide," said Eli Wallach, who portrayed Guido in the film. "There were many difficult undercurrents which all impinged on the outcome. Marilyn's marriage to Miller was breaking up, and Clift—who had studied very hard for the role by going to rodeos throughout the Southwest—arrived with a bashed nose as a result of falling off a horse. However, Huston was the man at the tiller, and he steered that ship. He knew what he wanted and how to do it, and he and Miller got along very well."

Indeed they did. In early August, as rumors circulated about an affair between Arthur Miller and set photographer Inge Morath—whom he would later marry—Marilyn moved out of their suite and into that of drama coach Paula Strasberg. By that

The screen goddess and the King of Hollywood—as a child Marilyn would fantasize that Gable was her long-lost father. Following his death less than two weeks after the end of shooting, she would say, "He never got angry with me once for blowing a line or being late or anything. He was a gentleman. The best."

time, Huston was firmly on Miller's side, and towards the end of the month, with Marilyn reporting for work increasingly late and noticeably dazed from her massive intake of barbiturates, the director had her checked into L.A.'s Westside Hospital for what her physician, Dr. Hyman Engelberg, described as "acute exhaustion." Not everyone, however, went along with this diagnosis.

During the making of her last completed movie Marilyn Monroe was a troubled woman, and for the first time her face began to show signs of the strain.

Reportedly, Huston, whose lifestyle made that of rugged cowboy Gay Langland look tame by comparison, had dropped more than $50,000 at the craps tables of Harrah's and the Mapes Hotel casino. When the debts were called in, he had to utilize production money to pay them off, and with *The Misfits* now clean out of cash he was forced to shut down production until United Artists approved more funding. Marilyn took advantage of this by returning to Los Angeles for a much-needed rest, and, so the story goes, she was then persuaded to check into the hospital at the expense of UA's insurance company, thus serving as the scapegoat for Huston's folly.

"We had the Errol Flynn of directors," asserted Marilyn's stand-in, Evelyn Moriarty. "He had dames being imported from Europe, and when they weren't available there'd be the hookers from Reno. Big John was a playboy, and he was also into the gambling tables. He used to sleep on the way to the set, and sleep on the way home."

Eli Wallach, nevertheless, had great respect for Huston's directorial skills: "He allowed the actor a lot of leeway in the development of a character, and he was never threatened by Marilyn's guru, Paula Strasberg. I mean, if Marilyn didn't like a scene or it didn't feel right, she'd turn and look at Paula, and if she shook her head Marilyn would say, 'Can we do it again?' Well, Huston never fought or said, 'Oh no, I know what's going on here!' He was a wonderful psychologist, and he'd say, 'Of course, do it again. Sure. You'll feel better.' Because he had control of the cutting. You see, what people don't understand is that what's on the screen is not decided by the actor."

Intriguingly, on August 29, the day after Marilyn had checked into the hospital, Frank Taylor sent Clark Gable a letter on *Misfits* stationery stating that he was putting in writing his intention to replace her on the picture. This implies that Gable had already been informed about such a plan, yet regardless of its genesis it never came to fruition, and on September 4 production resumed when Marilyn returned to the set and filmed a four-and-a-half minute sequence with Montgomery Clift.

For his troubles, Clift—described by Marilyn as "the only person I know who's in worse shape than I am"—was also accorded the Arthur Miller truth-in-script treatment: A chronic alcoholic whose emotional instability stemmed in part from a love-hate relationship with his mother, Clift had his handsome face virtually reconstructed after a horrific 1957 car accident. Now here he was, portraying alcoholic rodeo rider Perce Howland, who in his opening scene tells his mother on the phone, "My face is fine. It's all healed up. It's just as good as new. You would too recognize me."

Like Marilyn, Monty Clift had attended the Actor's Studio in New York, as had Eli Wallach, and their varied Method acting techniques flew in the face of the more conventional old-school approach employed by Clark Gable. Nevertheless, according to Wallach, this was not among the sources of tension on the set.

"The first time he and I had a scene was in a truck, and I kept staring at him and he kept staring at me," Wallach recalled more than three decades later. "Finally, Huston

said, 'What's the matter with you two? You're like the boa constrictor and the rabbit; you keep staring at one another. For Chrissakes, just say your lines!' And both of us smiled, because I was wary of the King of the Movies and he was wary of this man from New York with this mysterious Method. However, I had great respect for Gable. He was an instinctive actor and a talented man."

While Gable objected to his stand-in being subjected to multiple takes and a hoof in the face for the scene in which Gay single-handedly tries to rope a steed, tame horses were utilized for the segments in which some horses are wrestled to the ground. "The wild horses would die fighting before you'd ever get them down," Eli Wallach explained.

During the location shoot there were bit parts for sound recordist Philip Mitchell, whose Actor's Equity card came in handy when script rewrites called for a brief appearance by Isabelle Steers' ex-husband, Charles; and Marilyn's masseur, Ralph Roberts, in a small role as an ambulance attendant. Roberts had acted sporadically in films since he was 13 before switching professions in the mid-1950s.

On October 4, filming relocated to Paramount Studios in Hollywood for the interiors and process shots. After viewing some of the rushes, Paramount execs asked for retakes of several of the Nevada scenes, but Clark Gable had a script approval clause in his contract and he vetoed the idea. Still, he had to endure more late showings by Marilyn.

"Gable was a true pro," Eli Wallach recalled. "He knew his lines and he always got there on time. Anyway, when we returned to California, the film was over schedule,

The Unfinished Project: Something's Got to Give

SOMETHING'S GOT TO GIVE

Twentieth Century-Fox
Produced by Henry T. Weinstein
Directed by George Cukor
Screenplay by Arnold Schulman, Gene Allen,
Nunnally Johnson, and Walter Bernstein
Based on the screenplay *My Favorite Wife*
by Samuel and Bella Spewack
From a Story by Samuel and Bella Spewack,
and Leo McCarey
Cinematography by Franz Planer,
Charles Lang Jr,
William Daniels, and Leo Tover
Art Direction by Gene Allen
Costume Design by Jean Louis
Editing by David Bretherton
Filmed April 23–June 4, 1962
CinemaScope and DeLuxe Color
Unreleased

CAST

Ellen Wagstaff Arden	Marilyn Monroe
Nick Arden	Dean Martin
Bianca Russell Arden	Cyd Charisse
Stephen Burkett	Tom Tryon
Shoe Clerk	Wally Cox
Johnson,	Phil Silvers
Insurance Man	
Dr. Herman Schlick	Steve Allen
Tim Arden	Robert
	Christopher Morley
Lita Arden	Alexandra Heilweil
Mrs. Duncan,	
Housekeeper	Madge Kennedy
Judge Walter Bryson	John McGiver
Court Clerk	Grady Sutton
Miss Worth, Nick's	Elouise Hardt
Secretary	

▶▶ *Having shed about 20 pounds since the filming of* Let's Make Love *less than two years before, Marilyn looked to be in peak physical shape.*

The Plot

Five years after Ellen Arden, the official photographer in a trans-pacific yacht race, was swept overboard by a wave and reported missing, an L.A. judge pronounces her officially dead. Seconds later, Ellen's lawyer husband, Nick, asks the same judge to marry him and his new love, Bianca, yet what none of them know is that following five years on a desert island, Ellen has been rescued by a U.S. submarine.

Arriving in Honolulu, the former castaway immediately calls home and speaks to her young children, Timmy and Lita, only to learn that their father has gone away with their "new Mommy." Ellen is rocked by this news, but while trying to check into a hotel where she and Nick used to stay, she spots her husband and his new bride arriving for their honeymoon. The happy couple get into an elevator to go up to their suite, and as the doors start to close, a stunned Nick sees Ellen staring at him from the lobby. Charging everything to his account, she buys some chic new clothes and checks into another suite, where Nick tracks her down after telling Bianca that he needs to get a shave in the hotel barber shop.

Ellen describes her desert island ordeal, and within seconds she and Nick are in each other's arms, restating their love for one another. Yet when Nick wants to go all the way, Ellen refuses, insisting that he must first resolve the situation with the new Mrs. Arden. Nick agrees, but he doesn't have the nerve or the know-how, and the result is that he and a confused Bianca spend their honeymoon night in separate suites, while an exasperated Ellen leaves Hawaii for Los Angeles.

Returning home to kids who don't recognize her, Ellen poses as a Swedish nanny named Miss Ingrid Tic when the newlyweds arrive a short time later. Bianca is determined to get her marriage back on track, Ellen is determined to derail it, and Nick is caught in the middle while paying his first wife more attention than the second. Already neurotic and increasingly angry, Bianca seeks advice from her analyst, Dr. Herman Schlick, while Nick's problems are compounded when an agent for the company that paid Ellen's life insurance investigates a report that a woman fitting her description has been rescued. Worse still, the agent mentions that a young man named Stephen Burkett was also discovered on the island, and that when he and his cohabitant were aboard the submarine, a sailor overheard them addressing each other as Adam and Eve.

After Nick confronts Ellen about this, she convinces a mousy shoestore clerk to pose as Burkett and state that his only activity for five years was to research the island's flora and fauna. Nick, however, has already located the real Burkett, a handsome, muscle-bound hunk, who arrives at the Arden residence just as the weedy impostor is leaving. He has been invited over to trap Ellen, but instead "Adam" announces that he'd like to marry "Eve," Ellen refuses to tell Nick what took place on the island, and threatens to accept Burkett's offer if Nick won't deal with Bianca.

Just when it appears that things couldn't get any more complicated, two men from the DA's office arrest Nick for bigamy, and before long he is standing before the same judge who made Ellen's death official and Bianca his new wife. The latter is now seek-

A tantalizing glimpse of what might have been—Marilyn films a hair test for Something's Got to Give, *April 10, 1962.*

ing an annulment, while the former, declared officially alive, wants a divorce because Nick doesn't love her unconditionally. In an ante room, "Adam" proposes to "Eve" so that she and the children can return with him to the desert island. However, Ellen wants to patch things up with Nick, and Burkett agrees to help her in this regard.

After Bianca storms out of the courtroom on the arm of her analyst, Nick hears "Adam" and "Eve" openly talk about marriage, as well as a return to the island along with the Arden kids. Stirred into action, he patches things up with his favorite wife, while Bianca finds love with Dr. Schlick.

Something's Got to Give *would have been Marilyn's 30th film, and the third of four which she was obligated to appear in under the terms of her current Fox contract.*

June 1, 1962—on her 36th birthday, Marilyn goes before the movie cameras for the last time, filming the scenes in which Ellen introduces "Adam" to her husband Nick.

Behind-the-Scenes Facts & Opinions

A remake of the 1940 hit comedy *My Favorite Wife,* starring Cary Grant, Irene Dunne and Gail Patrick, *Something's Got to Give* was intended as another in the cycle of glossy bedroom farces that had commenced with the 1959 box office smash *Pillow Talk,* starring Doris Day and Rock Hudson. However, while Marilyn would have undoubtedly introduced far more sensuality to the genre than Doris, the footage that was shot for *Give* indicates that, if completed without extensive retakes, it would have been a pretty feeble picture. As such, it may well have laid an egg, whereas the controversy surrounding its making and the melodramatic allure of its tag as "the film that Marilyn Monroe never lived to complete" have ensured a much longer-term interest.

For several decades following her firing from the project in June of 1962 and her death just eight weeks later, it was reported that Marilyn only featured in seven usable minutes. Furthermore, it was alleged that most of these showed her acting, according to screenwriter Walter Bernstein, "in a kind of slow motion that was hypnotic," while art director/associate producer Gene Allen alluded to "a kind of vague expression on her face when I watched the dailies. . . . For the purposes of the story that was being told, she really wasn't playing the scenes the way Cukor wanted her to."

This is somewhat true, but it hardly tells the whole story. A 35-minute version of the unfinished film that has been patched together from over 500 minutes of digitally restored footage features about 14 on-screen minutes of Marilyn. Only half of this is adequate in terms of her acting—the awkwardly contrived poolside scene with the children being one example—while the remainder is undeniably substandard, but it has to be said that Marilyn's often-expressionless performance simply matches the efforts of the other actors. The characteristically laid-back Dean Martin practically sleepwalks through his role, while Cyd Charisse and Steve Allen display thespian talents that are clearly outweighed by their respective abilities as a dancer and talk show host.

For the most part, bedroom comedies elicited smiles rather than belly laughs, yet the script in this case is particularly dire. Worse still, it is poorly interpreted by George Cukor who, given his track record of films such as *Dinner at Eight, The Philadelphia Story, Adam's Rib,* and *Born Yesterday,* directs with surprisingly little humor while extracting practically nothing out of his cast. After all, it's one thing to criticize Marilyn's performance, but she was hardly responsible for the similar inadequacies of the scenes in which she didn't appear.

At the same time, the unedited footage reveals that when she was on the set Marilyn was in good spirits, laughing and joking with her colleagues while working hard at her performance. Cukor can consistently be heard approving her efforts at the end of a take, and it is doubtful that these were just words of encouragement, because he doesn't sound nearly as enthused when demanding countless retakes from a couple of kids whose wooden, stumbling performances are often painful to watch.

So, where did things go wrong? And why, given Marilyn's well-known propensity for causing production delays, did she take so much heat this time around? Well, to answer that question we should take a look at the entire *Something's Got to Give* project, which was troubled virtually from day one.

Initially, former Fox story editor and executive vice president David Brown was scheduled to make his debut as a producer on the film. In early 1961 he hired staff writer Arnold Schulman to adapt a screenplay from that written by Sam and Bella Spewack for *My Favorite Wife,* itself based on Alfred Lord Tennyson's poem *Enoch Arden.* Frank Tashlin was then installed as the director, and the costars were to be Marilyn—fulfilling the third installment of her four-picture obligation to Twentieth Century-Fox—and actor/director Vittorio De Sica.

Marilyn, however, had director and script approval, and neither in this case met her demands; Tashlin was not on her list of preferred directors, and she understandably wanted the screenplay to be more favorable in its attitudes towards her character—in Arnold Schulman's story line, Ellen Arden is seduced by her husband's boss. Fearful of the consequences, she heads for the Far East, but misses a connecting flight from Hawaii that ends tragically when the plane goes down in the Pacific. Reported dead, Ellen remains in Honolulu for the next five years, and only returns home when another affair goes sour. . . Not exactly the kind of behavior that would endear audiences. Therefore, while George Cukor was recruited in place of Frank Tashlin, art director/associate producer Gene Allen was asked to revamp the *Give* screenplay along with story editor Ted Strauss. (Allen had recently become a member of the Writers Guild when helping out on the script of Cukor's *The Chapman Report.*)

"Cukor wanted the story to be closer to *My Favorite Wife,* so all I did was try to put together something that was similar," Gene Allen explained in 1995, while plainly admitting, "I'm not a writer. Marilyn, on the other hand, was having sort of secret meetings with Nunnally Johnson. I don't even know if Cukor was aware of this at the time. There was a lot of intrigue."

So much intrigue, in fact, that by January 10, 1962, after Honolulu locales had already been scouted for ten days' shooting of the hotel scenes, and while negotiations were underway for James Garner to costar instead of Vittorio De Sica, David Brown was off the project. This was due to what *Daily Variety* described as a "disagreement with studio over concept of story treatment." Filming had been scheduled to start five days earlier. Now Henry Weinstein, a friend of Marilyn's psychiatrist Dr. Ralph Greenson, took over as producer. He didn't realize what he was in for.

Greenson, the latest in a long line of Svengali figures who had attached themselves to Marilyn Monroe, took it upon himself to assure the studio that his manic-depressive client would be able to function in a professional capacity. To that end, Weinstein would serve as his on-site helper, and this caused immediate friction with George Cukor, who resented not being consulted about either David Brown's firing or Nunnally Johnson's script.

In February of 1962, while Johnson was doing rewrites in London, James Garner turned down the role of Nick Arden. He had demanded $200,000 for the work, Fox had offered $50,000 less. The following month, Dean Martin was signed for $300,000, and his company, Claude Productions, would now coproduce the picture, budgeted at $3,254,000. Marilyn, as per the terms of her 1956 contract, was earning $100,000, the

May 25, 1962—filming of the scene in which Nick and Bianca return home from their abbreviated honeymoon to be greeted by Ellen posing as a Swedish nanny named "Ingrid Tic."

same as it was costing the studio to build a replica of George Cukor's Beverly Hills house. Shooting was scheduled to start on April 16.

"It was my idea to base the set on his home," stated Gene Allen. "We didn't have a great deal of time to prepare, and his house was so nice that we thought it would be great to recreate it. So, I sent my assistants there, we measured the place, photographed it, and built it. We recreated the various levels, the little side entrance off Cordell Drive, and all of the interesting features. Even the pool was in the same place. Cukor was going to pose for his Christmas card that year standing in front of his duplicate house, but that would have been in bad taste after all of the problems that occurred."

Indeed. On March 30, Nunnally Johnson arrived from the Mexican state of Baja California Norte with the finished script, and Marilyn duly approved it. George Cukor, however, wasn't nearly so keen, and he therefore brought in friend Walter Bernstein to tune up the drab and unfunny dialogue. Initially, Marilyn went along with this, having script conferences with Bernstein and telling him, "Remember, you've got Marilyn Monroe. You've got to use her."

And use her he certainly did, adding a sequence where Ellen greets Nick in her hotel suite attired in a negligée; another where she swims naked in the Arden family pool; and yet another where, after falling fully clothed into the pool, she removes her wet garments under a bedsheet while her husband and former island companion look on. The only problem was, Walter Bernstein continued to revise the script on a daily basis not just before but also throughout production, meaning that Marilyn and her colleagues would have to spend each night memorizing new lines for the following day's shoot. "That's where the trouble began," recalled Marilyn's stand-in, Evelyn Moriarty. "They were giving her rewrites, and rewrites of the rewrites, and she'd been ready in January to do that picture."

In an ill-conceived and poorly executed production Marilyn gave a disjointed performance, yet she imbued her role with a combination of sexuality and vulnerability that couldn't be emulated by any other Hollywood actress.

As it was, Marilyn, having shed more than 20 pounds since working on *The Misfits*, looked terrific when she showed up at Fox to film costume and makeup tests on April 10. The next morning, young producer Henry Weinstein naively called on Marilyn at six in the morning, and after discovering her in what he described as a "barbiturate coma," he panicked and immediately suggested that the picture be shelved. His superiors, familiar with the hammer-blow effect that Nembutal had on the star, didn't listen. They were banking on Marilyn's earning potential, and besides, should anything happen to her in midproduction, they could always collect on the insurance.

In mid-April, Marilyn flew to New York to rehearse her role with drama coaches Lee and Paula Strasberg. Then, when she returned to Hollywood in time for the start of filming on Monday, April 23, she was suffering from acute sinusitis, and so for the first week the other principals shot around Marilyn while she recuperated at home. She didn't even show up when the Shah and Empress of Iran visited the *Give* set on the 24th—having converted to Judaism before marrying Arthur Miller, Marilyn told Henry Weinstein that she didn't want to meet the Shah because he was "anti-Israel."

Whatever. On April 30, she did at last report for work to film the segments where Ellen Arden returns home and first sets eyes on her children playing in the pool. Still suffering from a sore throat and a 101° temperature, Marilyn expertly conveyed her character's conflicting feelings of joy, hesitation, pride, concern, and insecurity. However, by 4 P.M., having run through six different setups and a total of 27 takes, she was exhausted, and the following day her doctor again pronounced her ill with a severe sinus infection.

For the next week, Marilyn continued to receive the nightly script updates at home while the rest of the cast shot scenes that didn't require her. Then, on Monday, May 7, she reported for work at 7A.M. but, suffering from a fever, she nearly passed out under a hairdryer, and was sent home after half an hour. Again, the company shot around her, even switching location to the Balboa Bay Club for an outdoor scene featuring Tom Tryon and a bevy of bikini-clad extras, but by May 10, 14 days into production and five and a half days behind schedule, work shut down. The following Monday, May 14, Marilyn was back on the set, and for the next three days she was filmed around the pool with the children, as well as with Tippy the dog, named after one that she had owned as a child.

The cocker spaniel's inability to hit his marks or bark on cue clearly amused Marilyn— "He's getting good!" she laughs at the end of yet another take, as the dog wanders away and the trainer manically shouts commands off-camera. Yet, just after 5 P.M. on May 16, the company was again forced to stop shooting when Marilyn fell ill. The next morning, she was on the set at 9:20, but there was no filming planned for either that or the next day. The reason? At around 11:30 A.M., actor Peter Lawford arrived in a helicopter on the Fox lot and whisked Marilyn and her press agent Pat Newcomb to Los Angeles International Airport, from where they flew to New York for President Kennedy's birthday gala at Madison Square Garden.

Marilyn, due to sing at the all-star bash, had obtained the studio's permission to attend prior to the start of production on *Something's Got to Give* (note: although the JFK event was captured by TV cameras, it was never broadcast as a show). Now, however, George Cukor and the Fox execs didn't want her to go, for what was taking place behind the scenes amounted to an utter fiasco that was definitely not of Marilyn Monroe's making.

In short, Twentieth Century-Fox was on the verge of bankruptcy thanks to one film, *Cleopatra*, which had gone before the cameras in 1960 as a $6 million, London-based epic starring Elizabeth Taylor, Peter Finch and Stephen Boyd, and by 1962 was a $30 million-plus, Rome-based money-guzzler starring Liz, Rex Harrison, and Richard Burton. To stay afloat, the studio laid off nearly two-thirds of its employees, closed down its commissary and talent school, and stopped watering its lawns. The previous year it had collected $43 million by selling its 260-acre West L.A. lot to real estate developers, who then leased 75 acres back to Fox before converting the rest into Century City.

Amid this wreckage, *Something's Got to Give* had been rushed into production as a quick money earner. Now it had difficulties its own, and sensing that their heads were about to be served up on a plate to the stockholders, the Fox execs had to find a scapegoat. The most obvious candidate would have been Liz Taylor, whose numerous bouts of meningitis, pneumonia, and lovesickness for Richard Burton had caused some of the horrendous delays on *Cleopatra*. However, that film was still in production and the studio needed her to help recoup at least some of the costs. Marilyn Monroe, on the other hand, although earning only a tenth of Liz's $1 million salary, was more easily expendable, and so it was her head that went on the block when she left for New York.

May 14, 1962—while Marilyn had a long-standing reputation for requiring multiple takes, a cocker spaniel gave her a taste of her own medicine on Something's Got to Give. *Perhaps identifying with the dog's work methods, she displayed good humor and great patience throughout.*

▲ *May 21, 1962—frolicking with a pair of screen children who didn't exactly match up to the talents of a Mickey Rooney or a Shirley Temple.*

Something's Got to Give was only seven and a half days behind schedule, but the script still didn't have an ending. Walter Bernstein's rewrites extended to the courtroom scene where Ellen Arden and Stephen Burkett try to stir Nick into action by talking about marriage and a return to the desert island. Yet, how this would be resolved hadn't been decided. Accountable to the Fox front office, George Cukor and Henry Weinstein were in a bind, and they therefore begged Marilyn to stay in Hollywood and help get the project back up to speed. Furthermore, on May 11, production boss Peter Levathes had sent her a letter, stating that in light of the production delays her permission to leave for New York was being rescinded.

Thus, when Marilyn flew away from the lot, it was perceived as a declaration of open war between two parties who had virtually no respect for one another, and within an hour the studio filed a breach of contract notice, making it clear that it wouldn't take much more for Marilyn to be fired. Exhausted from her trip and unable to shoot close-ups, she returned to work the following Monday and was accorded a cool reception by the producer, director, and assistant director. Hereafter, according to Evelyn Moriarty, this is how things would continue.

"I would stand in for Marilyn while they were setting up, and I never left the set until she walked on," Moriarty recalled. "However, when they called for her they weren't always ready, and she'd be waiting around while they changed the lighting or whatever because the assistant director, Buck Hall, never told her that she could leave. Most other people would have walked away, but not her. You could feel the tension on the set. They treated her like a piece of meat. On the other hand, the crew—the technicians, the electricians, the grips, the extras—all adored her. It was the production office that hated her."

"Marilyn wasn't awkward when she was on the set," agreed Gene Allen. "She had a sense of humor and she didn't take herself seriously around the crew. I mean, she wasn't any prima donna, and she was full of fun, but she was also looking for that escape. To me, that whole picture was a series of her thinking, 'I'm gonna do it, I'm not gonna do it.'"

When Dean Martin turned up with a cold on Tuesday, May 22, Marilyn refused to work with him on the grounds of her own susceptibility and the advice of her doctor, and she went home after a couple of hours. Dino was persona non grata for the next couple of days, but the time was used well—on the Wednesday, dispensing with a flesh-colored body suit, Marilyn filmed the nude pool scene that, as captured by on-set photographers Jimmy Mitchell, Lawrence Schiller, and William Woodfield, would subsequently appear on magazine covers in no fewer than 32 countries during the coming months. This was the first nude scene by a major American movie star. It helped that MM looked more stunning than ever.

Dean Martin returned to work on May 25, and Marilyn, although suffering from an ear infection, did an excellent turn as a phony Swedish nanny. Then, over the weekend, the infection worsened and she was unable to report to the studio on the Monday. On the Tuesday, Marilyn and Dean shot the poolside scene in which Nick confronts Ellen about her desert island companion. Wednesday was Memorial Day, Thursday was spent filming a shoe store scene with MM and Wally Cox, and then on Friday, June 1, her 36th birthday, Marilyn went before the movie cameras for what would turn out to be the very last time.

This was for the scene in which Ellen introduces Nick to the fake "Adam" in the back yard of the Arden home, and the shoe clerk proceeds to describe their supposed existence on the island. Out of sequence, the final segment that Marilyn ever filmed was that in which Ellen calls down to Nick from a landing and asks if he wishes to meet "Adam." Afterwards, with a full day's work on celluloid, George Cukor allowed Evelyn Moriarty to wheel out a birthday cake that she had bought earlier that morning, yet the atmosphere was tense, the pleasantries were false, and within half an hour most of the "revelers" had left. "There was a pall over it," Henry Weinstein would later confirm. "We had gone through so much."

"As Marilyn was leaving I was with Bunny Gardel [body makeup] and Agnes Flanagan [hairstylist]," Evelyn Moriarty recalled, "and I said, 'She's not going to be here Monday, because of the way that Buck Hall and the others just treated her on the set.' Still, I didn't know she was never going to be in again."

Indeed, upset and angry, Marilyn was reluctant to work in a hostile environment where she felt as if she was being set up for a fall. On Monday, June 4, while the call sheet stated "Marilyn Monroe unable to report for work due to illness," the rest of the

On the set with close friend and personal makeup artist, Allan "Whitey" Snyder, and behind them, Marilyn's longtime wardrobe supervisor, Marjorie Plecher. Whitey and Marge would subsequently marry.

cast continued to film, but by now even easygoing Dean Martin was fed up. At 4 P.M. he walked off the set, basically rendering the company inactive, and following word from drama coach Paula Strasberg that Marilyn wouldn't be returning until she'd spoken with her advisers, Fox went on the attack.

On the evening of June 5, the studio threatened legal action if Marilyn didn't report for work immediately, and at a meeting the next day George Cukor urged the Fox executives to get rid of her. Afterwards, Cukor informed gossip columnist Hedda Hopper that this was being done, and on June 7 the studio leaked word to the press that Marilyn had been fired from *Something's Got to Give,* and that Kim Novak "and every other actress in and out of town" were being contacted to replace her.

"The studio does not want her anymore," Henry Weinstein told columnist Sheilah Graham. "She's not ill. I have had no official notification of illness. All I get from her is she will not be reporting. Out of 33 days of shooting Marilyn has come to the set only 12 times and will only do one page a day, which adds to a total of four days of work only. Everytime she says she is ill and we have to close down the picture, 104 persons lose a day's pay. I'm convinced she is in willful breach of contract."

At least, he hoped she was, for that very day Fox filed a suit against Marilyn in the amount of $500,000. "The star system has got way out of hand," asserted Peter Levathes. "We've let the lunatics run the asylum and they've practically destroyed it."

At 10 P.M. on June 8, after Marilyn's psychiatrist, Ralph Greenson, had made a vain attempt to reassure the studio that he could get his patient to comply with their demands, a Western Union Telegram was sent to George Cukor: "Dear George, please believe me it was not my doing. I had so looked forward to working with you. Warmly, Marilyn."

Earlier that day Lee Remick had been named as the new Ellen Arden. (Kim Novak and Shirley MacLaine had already turned down the role.) However, when Dean Martin exercised his costar approval by refusing to work with anyone other than Marilyn, Fox sued him for $500,000. On June 11, the cast and crew were officially put on suspension, and Cyd Charisse then sued Dino for $14,000 in lost earnings due to his causing the film to be shelved. At the same time Fox upped the ante against Marilyn by raising its lawsuit to $750,000, and on June 19, with seemingly no other way to recoup all of the production costs, the studio decided to sue Dean Martin for $3,339,000, prompting him to countersue for $6,885,000. (Both parties would drop the litigation a year later.) And to think, they had all been so cordial to one another just a short time before.

Towards the end of June, Spyros Skouras (after receiving a sharp push from shareholder Darryl Zanuck), retired as Fox's chairman of the board, and the studio searched around for an outside company to take over production of *Something's Got to Give*. First up was United Artists, which offered to pay $1 million and turn the movie over to Filmways Productions, but the deal collapsed when Fox demanded a huge completion bond. Then Filmways offered to put up a $500,000 bond in return for 5 percent of the gross, but again Fox declined, and the same happened in the first week of July when Filmways offered to finance the entire production in return for the company's president, Martin Ransohoff, receiving a producer's fee and bonus.

Marilyn, now making her own efforts to resuscitate both the project and her endangered career, was involved in the conversations with Filmways, and considering that Fox was at least a couple of million dollars in the hole with nowhere to go, it wasn't surprising that there was soon talk of reinstating her on the *Give* project, along with a new director and—you've guessed it—a revised script. George Cukor's 26-week, $225,000 deal had ended on May 26, since which time he had worked and been paid on a week-by-week basis. Now he was off the picture for good, and Hal Kanter was hired to do the rewrite.

On July 25, armed with Kanter's revised screenplay, and bypassing the out-of-favor Henry Weinstein, Peter Levathes visited Marilyn at her home in Brentwood. There, in an air of reconciliation, he listened to her script suggestions, promised to drop the lawsuit, and agreed to reemploy her for *Something's Got to Give*. On August 1, she signed a $1 million, two-picture deal—$250,000 for this picture and $750,000 for the next, about which the studio would subsequently keep very quiet—and on Marilyn's recommendation Jean Negulesco was hired to direct. In return, she agreed to keep the disruptive Paula Strasberg away from the set. Filming would resume towards the end of October.

Unfortunately, neither Peter Levathes nor Marilyn herself would be around to enjoy the fruits of that new deal. In a desperate—and ultimately successful— attempt to salvage Fox, Darryl Zanuck had returned as president, and he appointed his son Richard to take over from Peter Levathes as vice president in charge of production. Days later, Marilyn was dead and *Something's Got to Give* was laid to rest. The following year, however, Hal Kanter's script would be revised by Jack Sher, renamed *Move Over Darling*, and filmed with an entirely new cast and crew, including Doris Day and James Garner in the lead roles.

Back on June 13, Marilyn had sent a telegram to Mr. and Mrs. Robert Kennedy, declining their invitation to a party in honor of Peter and Pat Lawford. "Unfortunately," she wrote, "I am involved in a freedom ride protesting the loss of minority rights belonging to the few remaining earthbound stars. All we demanded was our right to twinkle."

Fade-Out: Immortal Images

NEVER HAVING TO SUFFER the infirmities of old age, the loss of physical beauty, or the ignominy of a slipping career, Marilyn the icon passed into immortality; forever young, forever sensuous, forever a symbol of the downtrodden individual who battled her way through a troubled childhood and oppressive, chauvinistic studio system to realize her ambition of becoming a star.

And what a star she became; a true superstar, one of only a handful of people whose names and faces are known the world over, no matter the culture or the generation. For what Marilyn achieved in this regard goes far beyond the conceivable hopes of an aspiring actress or the most far-flung expectations of an established luminary. To still be perceived, four decades after her death, as the apotheosis of sexuality and stardom, admired by feminists, and desired by males who fantasize how they could have saved her—this is almost mythic.

> *"Fame will go by and—so long, fame, I've had you! I've always known it was fickle. It was something I experienced, but it's not where I live."*
>
> MARILYN MONROE, 1962

While Marilyn's demise was a personal tragedy, it turned out to be a great career move, circumventing hypotheses of what might have been by projecting her celebrity into another stratosphere. Yet, amid the wealth of Marilyn memorabilia, MM impersonators, lurid disclosures of her private life, and conflicting theories over the manner of her death, where does her film work really fit in? After all, practically everyone knows who Marilyn Monroe was, but how many people—including a good many of her fans—are actually familiar with her cinematic achievements?

This book summarizes the performances and documents the details, but nothing can supplant the experience of seeing Marilyn on-screen (and preferably on the big screen); of watching her as Rose Loomis in *Niagara*, Lorelei Lee in *Gentlemen Prefer Blondes*, The Girl in *The Seven Year Itch*, Cherie in *Bus Stop*, Elsie Marina in *The Prince and the Showgirl*, and Sugar Kane in *Some Like It Hot*; of sampling her incomparable renditions of songs such as "Kiss," "Diamonds Are A Girl's Best Friend," "Heat Wave," "Running Wild," and "I Wanna Be Loved By You"; or even of seeing her steal the show in an early supporting role, as she does in the low budget surroundings of a *Home Town Story*, and among seasoned veterans like Cary Grant and Ginger Rogers in *Monkey Business*.

It is in such instances that Marilyn accomplishes her oft-expressed desire to simply "be wonderful." For while just about every other facet of her life may be open to conjecture, her on-screen appearances are eternal, irrefutable, and, insofar as her professional efforts and popular appeal are concerned, the real thing. Nothing else comes close.

"If I am a star, the people made me a star," Marilyn once said. "No studio, no person, but the people did." Again, this can be debated, yet what is undeniable is that Marilyn Monroe was—and still is—a star of the first magnitude, and that her wide-ranging film career, although curtailed, captures many of that star's most riveting moments.

Viva Marilyn!

Index of Names and Movie Titles

Adams, Casey, 125
All About Eve, 18, 56–62, 63, 64, 65, 67, 69, 74, 79
Allan, Richard, 125
Allen, Fred, 108–109, *117*, 118
Allen, Gene, 227, 228, 244, 245, 247, 251
Allen, Steve, 245
Allyson, June, 67
Anderson, Daphne, 109, *207*, 211
Andes, Keith, 95–96, *97*, *98*, 99
The Asphalt Jungle, 18, 48–52, 55, 64, 65, 67, 119, 194
As Young As You Feel, 18, 73, 74, 76–79, 85
Autry, Gene, 36

Bacall, Lauren, 11, *148*, *150*, 151, 152–153, *153*, 155, *155*
Baker, Roy Ward, 101, 104
Bancroft, Anne, 104
Barnett, Cliff, 71
Bates, Barbara, 62, 87
Baxter, Anne, 42, *56*, *58*, 59–60, 62, *117*
Beckett, Scotty, 26–27
Begley, Bert, 55
Benny, Jack, 146–147, *147*
Berle, Milton, 223
Berlin, Irving, 171
Bernstein, Walter, 244, 247
Blakeley, James, 140, 182
Born Yesterday, 35
Brand, Harry, 16
Breen, Joseph I., 163–164, 209–210, 229
Brennan, Walter, 110
Brooks, Rand, 33, *34*
The Brothers Karamazov, 74
Brown, Barbara, 71
Brown, James, 55
Brown, Joe E., 212, 215
Bus Stop, 9, 10, 189, 190, 195–203, 223, 255

Calhern, Louis, 51, 52, *52*, 78
Calhoun, Rory, *153*, 163, *164*
Cardiff, Jack, 9–10, 208, 209, 210
Carey, Macdonald, 85, 87, 88, *89*
Chakiris, George, 140–141, 142–143, *142*, 173, 174
Charisse, Cyd, 245, 253
Clash By Night, 75, 92–99, 104
Clift, Montgomery, 11, 190, 230, *231*, *232*, 233, 234, 236, 238, 239
Coburn, Charles, 113, 137, 140
Cohn, Harry, 33
Colbert, Claudette, 85, 87, 88
Cold Shoulder, 18, 63–64, 69
Cole, Jack, 228–229
Collins, Russell, 125
Conte, Richard, 63–64, *63*
Cook, Elisha, Jr., 78, *104*
Cotten, Joseph, 11, *75*, *120*, 123, 125, 126
Cox, Wally, *244*, *247*, 252
Crain, Jeanne, *117*
Crawford, Joan, 131
Crisp, Donald, 69
Crosby, Bing, 223
Cukor, George, 11, 35, 190, 223, 224, 227, *227*, 229, 244, 245, 246, 247, 250, 252, 253
Curtis, Donald, 26
Curtis, Tony, 11, *213*, *214*, 215, *216*, 217, *217*, 218, 219, 220, *220*

Dailey, Dan, 42, *166*, 170, 171, *172*, 173, 175
Dangerous Years, 7, 16, 24, 25–27, 69
D'Arcy, Alex, 151
Davis, Bette, 11, *56*, 59, 62
Dekker, Albert, *78*, 79
DiMaggio, Joe, 75, 126, 132, 133–134, 162, 171, 173, 184, 185
Don't Bother to Knock, 74, 91, 100–105
Dougherty, Jim, 13
Douglas, Paul, 95, 96
Dumke, Ralph, 55

Emerson, Hope, 110
Ewell, Tom, *134*, *176*, *177*, *181*, 182, 184, 185

Fay, Frank, 80, 82, *82*, 83
Feldman, Charles, 152
Field, Betty, 10
The Fireball, 18, 53–55, 63, 65, 67, 69
Fisher, Eddie, 61
Fury, Ed, 143

Gable, Clark, 11, 190, 230, *231*, *232*, 233, *235*, 236, 237–238, 239
Gabor, Zsa Zsa, 109
Garnett, Tay, 55
Gaynor, Mitzi, *166*, 170, 171, *172*, 173, 174, 175
Gentlemen Prefer Blondes, 9, 17, 35, 42, 75, 131, 132, 136–145, 146, 154, 173, 255
Gilchrist, Connie, 43, 45, *47*
Grable, Betty, 11, 131, *148*, 149, 151, 153, *153*, 155, *155*
Granger, Farley, *117*
Grant, Cary, 11, *112*, 113, *115*, 255
Gray, Dolores, 174
Greene, Amy, 193, 194, 206
Greene, Milton, 135, 187, 189, 190, 193, 194, 202, 206, 209, 210, 211
Guest appearance, TV, 146–147

Hale, Alan, Jr., 69, 71
Hathaway, Henry, 122, 123, 125, 127, 128, 129
Haver, June, *12*, 13, 22, 80, 82, *82*
Hawks, Howard, 11, 52, 113, 139, 141, 143, 145
Hayden, Sterling, *48*, 51
Heckart, Eileen, 10, *195*, 199, 200, *201*, 202, 203
Holm, Celeste, *58*, 59, 60–62
Holmes, Taylor, 143
Home Town Story, 18, 68–71, 255
Homolka, Oscar, 185
Hopper, Hedda, 33
Hornblow, Arthur, Jr., 18
How to Be Very, Very Popular, 187, 189
How to Marry a Millionaire, 132, 146, 148–155
Huston, John, 11, 18, 48, 51, 52, *52*, 190, 194, 199, 233, 234, 236–237, 238, *238*, 239
Hyde-White, Wilfred, 223, 229

Jack Benny Show, 146–147
Jaffe, Sam, 51
Jergens, Adele, *32*, 33, *92*
Jones, Harmon, 76, 79
Joy, Leatrice, 80, *82*, 83

Kanin, Garson, 35
Karlson, Phil, 33
Kelley, Tom, 17, 75, 96
Kelly, Gene, 223
Kennedy, John F., 250
Kennedy, Robert, 253
King, Henry, 90

Ladies of the Chorus, 30–34, 92
Lang, Fritz, 11, 95, 96
Lang, Walter, 20, 171, 174
Lange, Hope, 10, 197, 202
Laughton, Charles, 11, *117*, 118, *118*, 119
Lemmon, Jack, 9, 10, 11, 212, *213*, 215, *216*, 218, 219, 220, *220*, 221
Let's Make It Legal, 74, 79, 84, 85–89
Let's Make Love, 190, 222–229, 234, 240
Levant, Oscar, *117*, 118
Levathes, Peter, 252
Logan, Joshua, 11, 189, 199, 200, 201, 202, 203, 207–208
Loos, Mary, 16, 42–43, 45, 87, 188
Love Happy, 7, 17, 37–41
Love Nest, 74, 80–83, 85

Lundigan, William, 80, 82, *82*
Lynn, Jeffrey, 68, 69, *69*, 71
Lytess, Natasha, 17, 91

MacHarg, Judy, 16–17, 30, 33
Mackenzie, Joyce, 43, *44*, 45, 47
Mandaville, Molly, 79, 81, 103, 165
Mankiewicz, Joseph L., 11, 59, 60–61, *60*, 62
Marilyn, 154
Marlowe, Hugh, 59, 62
Marshall, Marion, 43, *44*, 45, *46*
Martin, Dean, 190, 192, *244*, 245, 246, 251, 252, 253
Marvin, Lee, 109
Marx, Chico, 38, 40
Marx, Groucho, 11, 17, 38, *39*, 40, *41*
Marx, Harpo, 38, 40
Marx Brothers, 17, 38, 40
Massey, Ilona, 40
Mature, Victor, 63, 64
Merman, Ethel, 11, *166*, 170, 171, *172*, 173, 174, 175
Merrill, Gary, 58
Meryman, Richard, 11
Miller, Arthur, 189, 190, 206, 207, 210, 217, 220, 223, 224, 227, 228, 230, 233, 234, 236, 238, *238*, 239
The Misfits, 190, 230–239, 251
Mitchell, Cameron, 92, *153*
Mitchell, Philip, 237
Mitchum, Robert, 11, *156*, 160, *160*, 161, 162, 163, 165
Monkey Business, 111–115, 255
Montalban, Ricardo, 67
Montand, Yves, 190, 223, 224, *227*, 228, *228*, 229
Moore, Roger, 79
Moore, Victor, 185
Moriarty, Evelyn, 192, 236, 247, 251, 252
Murray, Don, 10, 11, *196*, 197, *197*, *198*, 199–202, 203
Murrow, Edward R., 192–194

Negulesco, Jean, 11, 151, 152, *154*, 164, 165, 253
Newman, Joseph, 81
Niagara, 9, 74, 75, 120–129, 153, 189, 255
Night Without Sleep, 91
Noonan, Tommy, 137
Nyman, Ron, 141, 143, 174

O'Brien, Pat, 55, 92
O'Connell, Arthur, *195*, 199
O'Connor, Donald, 10, 11, *166*, 170, *170*, 171, *172*, 173, 174
O'Dea, Denis, 125
O. Henry's Full House, 116–119
Okinawa, 34, 92
Olivier, Laurence, 9, 11, 189, *189*, 190, *204*, 205, 206, 207–210, *210*, 211, 219

Paar, Jack, 82, *82*
Parsons, Louella O., 64
Peck, Gregory, 224
Person to Person, 192–194
Peters, Jean, 14, 24, 74, 77, 78, 79, 90, *117*, 118, 123, 125, 126, 151–152, 154
Pierson, Arthur, 25, 27, 69
Pink Tights, 132–133, 171, 192
Plowman, Melinda, 71
Powell, Dick, 67, 67
Preminger, Otto, 11, 161–162, 163, 165
The Prince and the Showgirl, 9, 189–190, 204–211, 223, 233, 255

Randall, Tony, 223
Ratoff, Gregory, *58*, 61, *117*
Rattigan, Terence, 209–210
Ray, Johnnie, *166*, 170, 171, *172*, 173
Rettig, Tommy, *160*, 161
Riders of the Whistling Pines, 36
Right Cross, 18, 65, 66–67
Ritter, Thelma, 62, 78

River of No Return, 17, 132, 133, 134, 156–165
Roberts, Ralph, 237
Robertson, Dale, *117*
Rogers, Ginger, 11, 108–109, *112*, 113, 114, 255
Rooney, Mickey, 11, *53*, *54*, 55
Royal Triton Gasoline, 65
Rubin, Stanley, 161–162, 163, 165
Russell, Jane, 11, *136*, 137, *138*, 139, 140, 142, 143, 145
Ryan, Robert, *93*, 95, 96

Sale, Richard, 42, 45, 84, 87
Sanders, George, 11, *56*, *58*, 59, 60, 61, 62
Sarris, Bill, 113, 140, 143, 174, 183–184
Scott, Zachary, 85, 87
Screen Test #1, 20–21, 174
Screen Test #2: *Born Yesterday*), 35
Screen Test #3: *Cold Shoulder*, 18, 63–64, 69
Screen Test #4: *Let's Make It Legal*, 84
Screen Test #5: *Wait 'Til the Sun Shines, Nellie*, 90, 91
Screen Test #6: *Night Without Sleep*, 91
Scudda Hoo! Scudda Hay!, 16, 22–24, 26, 87, 194
The Seven Year Itch, 9, 14, 17, 133, *134*, 135, 137, 171, 175, 176–185, 187, 194, 197, 216, 218, 255
Shamroy, Leon, 20
Showalter, Max, 9, 10, 74, 123, 125, 126–127, 189
Skolsky, Sidney, 82, 135
Skouras, Spyros, 74
Smith, Barbara, 43, *44*, 45, 47
Snyder, Allan "Whitey," 20, 202, 209, 234
Some Like It Hot, 9, 137, 190, 212–221, 223, 233, 255
Something's Got to Give, 190–192, 240–253
Stanwyck, Barbara, 11, 95, 96
Stone, Milburn, 55
Strasberg, Lee, 192
Strasberg, Paula, 203, 209
Strauss, Robert, 180
Sturges, John, 67

Tamblyn, Rusty (Russ), 79
Television advertisement, 65
Television interview, 193–194
There's No Business Like Show Business, 20, 133–134, 135, 166–175, 190
Thorndike, Sybil, 209
A Ticket to Tomahawk, 18, 42–47, 119, 194
Townsend, Colleen, *12*, 13, 14, 16, 23–24, *23*
Tryon, Tom, 250
Tyler, Beverly, 55

Vaughan, Frankie, 223

Wagner, Robert, 84, *84*, 87
Wait 'Til the Sun Shines, Nellie, 90, 91
Wallach, Eli, 11, 190, *232*, 233, 234, 236–238
Wayne, David, 10, 74–75, 78–79, 90, 106, *107*, *108*, 110, *117*, 118, 119, 151, *153*, 154, 187
Weinstein, Henry, 247, 252
We're Not Married, 104, 106–110
Widmark, Richard, 11, *100*, 104, *117*, 118
Wilder, Billy, 10, 11, 73, 135, 179, 180, 182, *183*, 184–185, 190, 194, 212, 215–216, 217, 218, *218*, 219, 220–221, 224
Williams, Rhys, 92
Winwood, Estelle, *232*, 233
Wood, Natalie, 22
Woodbury, Judy, *32*, 33, *92*
Woolley, Monty, 77, *78*, 79
Woulfe, Michael, 96
Wurtzel, Paul, 125, 163, 182–183

Zanuck, Darryl F., 79, 81, 87, 102, 103, 123, 132, 139, 163, 164–165, 170, 171